First
BIBLE

Stories

BACK**PACK**BOOKS
NEW YORK

© 2001 by Parragon Books Ltd

This 2002 edition published by Backpack Books, by arrangement with Parragon.

Adapted by Jillian Harker and Michael Phipps

ISBN-13: 978-0-7607-3452-0
ISBN-10: 0-7607-3452-6

Printed and bound in China

9 11 13 15 14 12 10

First
BIBLE
Stories

Illustrated by John Dillow

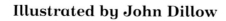

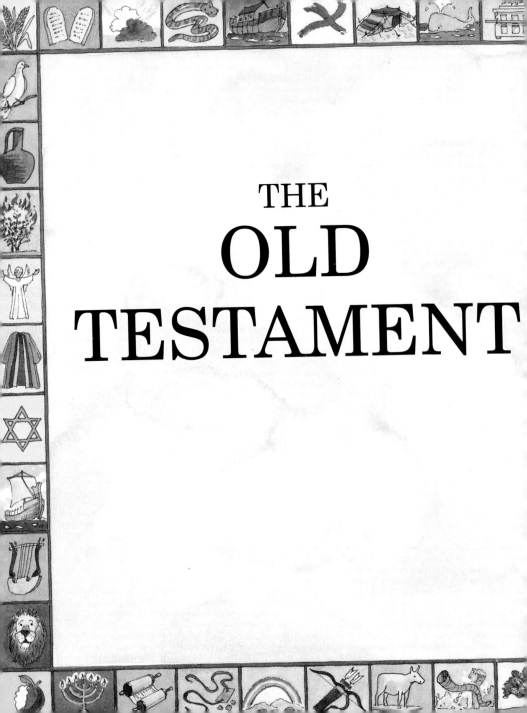

THE
OLD
TESTAMENT

And so the world began   10
GENESIS: 1-2

No longer perfect   16
GENESIS: 2-3

Two sons, Cain and Abel   24
GENESIS: 4

A fresh start   28
GENESIS: 6-9

The tallest tower   38
GENESIS: 11

Father of a great nation   42
GENESIS: 12-13, 15, 18, 21

The right wife for Isaac   48
GENESIS: 24

The children of Israel   56
GENESIS: 25, 27-29, 32-33

Sold for twenty silver pieces   68
GENESIS: 37

Thrown into prison   74
GENESIS: 39-41

Reunited   82
GENESIS: 42-47

You have been chosen   90
EXODUS: 1-4

Let my people go   98
EXODUS: 5-14

God looked after His people   108
EXODUS: 16-17

God's ten laws   114
EXODUS: 19-20, 24-27, 32, 34-40

In the desert for forty years   122
NUMBERS: 13-14, 17, 21

Down crashed the walls   128
JOSHUA: 1-6

The secret of his strength   138
JUDGES: 13-16

Your God will be my God   146
RUTH: 1-4

We want a king   152
1 SAMUEL: 1, 8-10, 15-16

The champion of Israel   160
1 SAMUEL: 16-17

A great leader   168
2 SAMUEL: 1-6, 11-19; 1 KINGS: 1

The wisest of men   174
1 KINGS: 1-4, 10

A wonderful temple for God   180
1 KINGS: 5-8

Israel will be taken   186
1 KINGS: 11

The true God   188
1 KINGS: 12, 16-19

The prophet Isaiah   196
ISAIAH: 9, 11

Thrown to the lions   198
DANIEL: 1, 6

An enormous fish   206
JONAH: 1-4

The King of Peace   214
MICAH: 5

THE
NEW
TESTAMENT

The angel messenger   218
LUKE: 1

Chosen   222
MATTHEW: 1

The little town of Bethlehem   224
LUKE: 2

The shepherds   228
LUKE: 2

The three wise men   232
MATTHEW: 2

My Father's house   238
LUKE: 2

God's King is coming   242
MATTHEW: 3; MARK: 1; LUKE: 3; JOHN 1

Changed into wine   246
MARK: 1; JOHN: 2

Chosen twelve   250
MATTHEW: 4, 10; MARK: 1, 3; LUKE: 5-6

The paralyzed man   258
MATTHEW: 9; MARK: 2; LUKE: 5

Our Father in heaven   264
MATTHEW: 5-7; LUKE: 6

Good, solid foundations   272
MATTHEW: 7

A Roman officer   274
MATTHEW: 8; LUKE: 7

A fierce storm   278
MATTHEW: 8; MARK: 4; LUKE: 8

Only believe   282
MATTHEW: 9; MARK: 5; LUKE: 8

The Good Shepherd   288
MATTHEW: 18; LUKE: 15; JOHN: 10

The seeds that fall in good soil   292
MATTHEW: 13; MARK: 4; LUKE: 8

"I am the farmer… "   296
MATTHEW: 13

Five thousand people   300
MATTHEW: 14; MARK: 6; LUKE: 9; JOHN 6

Moses and the prophet Elijah   304
MATTHEW: 17; MARK: 9; LUKE: 9

My son was lost   308
LUKE: 15

The good Samaritan   316
LUKE: 10

The raising of Lazarus   322
LUKE: 10; JOHN: 11

Have mercy on us   332
LUKE: 17

Zacchaeus, the chief tax collector   334
LUKE: 19

Entering Jerusalem   336
MATTHEW: 21; MARK: 11; LUKE: 19; JOHN: 12

Thirty pieces of silver   340
MATTHEW: 26; MARK: 14; LUKE: 22

The last meal   342
MATTHEW: 26; MARK: 14; LUKE: 22; JOHN: 13

A garden called Gethsemane   348
MATTHEW: 26; MARK: 14; LUKE: 22

I do not know him   354
MATTHEW: 26; MARK: 14; LUKE: 22-23; JOHN: 18

Father, forgive them   360
MATTHEW: 27; MARK: 15; LUKE: 23; JOHN: 18

The Son of God   366
MATTHEW: 27; MARK: 15; LUKE: 23; JOHN: 19

The tomb   370
MATTHEW: 27-28; MARK: 15-16; LUKE: 23-24; JOHN: 19-20

Risen from the dead   376
MATTHEW: 28; MARK: 16; LUKE: 24; JOHN: 20-21

The Holy Spirit   380
ACTS: 1-2

THE
OLD
TESTAMENT

And so the world began

GENESIS: 1-2

Long, long ago, before time began, there were
no rivers or mountains, no streams or hills.
There was nothing to see at all, nothing but
darkness. But God was there and, into this
darkness, God commanded light. So, the very
first day began.

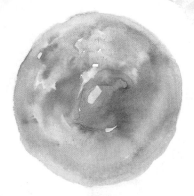

Then God started to make the seas...

and, in between the seas, He made dry land,
covering it with all kinds of trees and plants.

Over all this, God placed a dazzling sun to shine by day...

and a shimmering moon to shine by night. He studded the sky with billions of twinkling stars...

and so the world began.

Then God filled the seas with fish of many colors. He added creeping crabs, sly sharks and huge, wallowing whales.

Above the land, He made birds soar and swoop, dip and loop. Beautiful butterflies, busy bees and bustling bats filled the air.

All over the land, God made animals of every kind. He made them to gallop and trot, lope and hop.

Then God created the very first man and woman, Adam and Eve, trusting them to care for all the creatures.

Everything was happy and contented. It had taken six days to complete this new world. So, on the seventh day, God decided to set it apart as a day of rest, the Sabbath.

No longer perfect

GENESIS: 2-3

In one special place, God laid out a garden for Adam and Eve to live in. It was full of lovely, lush plants and fantastic flowers. Sparkling streams bubbled up from the ground and every tree was covered with delicious fruit for Adam and Eve to eat.

So many different types of animals lived in the garden, that it took Adam many hours to give each one a name… gecko, gibbon, giraffe, gorilla, hare, hippo, horse, hyena…

Adam and Eve lived happily in the Garden of Eden, caring for it and the creatures that lived there. They had everything they needed.

In the center of the garden grew a special tree. It was called the Tree of Knowledge. God made it very clear that this tree was different to all the other trees.

"You must not eat the fruit of this tree," God warned Adam and Eve. "You can eat fruit from all the others, but if you eat fruit from this one, bad things will happen."

And for a time, Adam and Eve did as they were told.

But there was a cunning snake living in the Garden of Eden, who wanted to play a trick on Eve.

One day, the snake saw Eve standing by the Tree of Knowledge. It slithered up to her, whispering softly, "Look at the lovely fruit."

"I mustn't touch it," said Eve.

"S-Smell how s-s-sweet it is," the snake hissed.

"God told us to leave it alone," Eve protested.

"Ha!" laughed the snake. "God doesn't want you to know the things He does, the things that are good and the things that are evil!"

Eve looked at the delicious fruit, wondering what it would be like to know all that God knew. Reaching out, she picked a juicy looking fruit and took a bite.

Then she passed it to Adam, for him to try. From that moment on, things started to go wrong.

When God spoke to Adam and Eve that night, He knew what they had done. He was angry and told them to leave the garden at once.

As Adam and Eve left, God sent an angel to stop them from returning.

When they had lived in the Garden of Eden, Adam and Eve had had everything they needed and they would never have grown old there. Now all that had changed. They had to work hard and knew that one day, they would die.

God's world was no longer perfect.

Two sons,
Cain and Abel

GENESIS: 4

After they left the Garden of Eden, Adam and
Eve had two sons, Cain and Abel. As they grew
older, Cain worked on the land, growing food,
while Abel took care of the sheep.

One day, the two brothers decided to offer some gifts to God. Cain gave food from his harvest, while Abel gave a lamb.

But God was only pleased with Abel's gift. He had looked into the hearts of both brothers, and saw that Abel was good and honest, while Cain was evil and angry.

Cain was furious and, jealous of his brother, decided to kill him.

So, one day, Cain suggested to Abel that they should go walking. While they were out, Cain killed his brother. He thought no one had seen him, but God had.

When God asked Cain where Abel was, he lied and said, "I don't know."

"You have done a terrible thing," said God. "You cannot stay any more in this land."

"This punishment is too much," cried Cain. "You are driving me from my land and your presence. People will want to kill me for what I have done."

"No," said God, "I won't allow that to happen. I will make sure no one harms you."

Cain left his home, never to return and went to live in a land called "Wandering" for the rest of his life.

A fresh start

GENESIS: 6-9

As the years passed, God's people grew more
and more evil. He looked at the world and saw
that it was not as He wanted it to be. So, God
decided to put an end to it all. The world needed
a fresh start.

God would send a huge flood to wash every bad thing away. But He intended to save Noah, who was a good, kind man and his family.

So, God gave Noah very careful instructions, and told him to prepare for the flood.

He told Noah to build an enormous boat, called an ark. Everyone laughed at Noah, because there was no open water for miles. But Noah ignored them.

For months, he went on building, until he had made an ark so huge, that it was as high as the tallest house.

31

When the boat was finished, Noah filled it
with enough food to last a very long time.
Then, he gathered together two of every kind
of animal in the world and led them into the
ark. On and on stretched the line, with
creatures slithering and sliding, crawling and
creeping, plodding and prancing, until, at last,
they were all on board.

When Noah, his wife and the rest of Noah's family had joined them, God shut the door – tight and safe behind them.

33

Then it began to rain. Soft drizzle fell at first. Then, it began to fall faster and harder, beating down on the earth like an enormous drum! Streams turned into rivers and rivers flowed into seas. And then the seas all joined together as one. The water spread and rose across God's earth, until there was not a single mountain top to be seen. All the people and animals drowned beneath the waves.

For forty days and forty nights, it rained and
it rained and with nothing to see but water,
the world felt a very sad and lonely place.

At last, the rain stopped
and the water began to go
down. Noah opened a
window and sent out
a raven. But water still
covered everything, and
the raven didn't return.

Noah waited a while, then released a dove.
But, it soon came back, because the water
was still too high.

When Noah tried again, the dove returned,
carrying a bright, new olive leaf in its beak.
Noah knew that the water was going down and
that plants and trees must be growing again.

When Noah sent the dove out once more, it
didn't come back. The flood had completely gone.

He opened the doors of the ark and the animals poured out onto the dry land.

"Never again will I destroy all living things by a flood," God promised Noah. "Whenever you see a rainbow in the sky, think of my promise and be sure that I will keep it."

The tallest tower

GENESIS: 11

In the years after the great flood, Noah's family grew bigger and bigger and bigger. There were grandchildren, great grandchildren and great, great grandchildren. They began to fill all the corners of the world, as God had wanted them to do. The language that they all spoke, however, remained the same, so that everyone could still talk with one another.

One group made their home in a place called Babylonia. Slowly, they learned new skills, like how to make bricks. They used tar to stick the bricks together and built their homes with them.

One day, someone suggested that they should build the tallest tower that anyone had ever seen. This would make them famous all over the earth. So, work soon began.

God watched the walls of this tower grow higher and higher and He was very sad. He knew that this now meant that people only wanted to make themselves important and grand. They would think they were just as great as God. They would get bigger and bigger ideas and become as wicked as people were before the great flood.

God didn't waste any time. The people needed to be able to talk to each other in order to finish this tower. If they spoke in different languages and couldn't explain their ideas to one another, building would have to stop.

So, God made all his people speak in many languages and sent them to live in other countries around the world.

41

Father of a great nation

GENESIS: 12-13, 15, 18, 21

So it came about, that one of Noah's descendants, Abraham, settled in a place called Haran. Abraham was a good man, who still believed in God. He and his wife, Sarah, were both quite old and had no children of their own.

One day, God told Abraham to leave the land that he thought of as home and move to a country called Canaan. "If you place your trust in me," God said, "I will make you the father of a great nation."

Abraham did trust God. So he packed up everything he owned and set off with Sarah, his servants and shepherds and his nephew, Lot, for an unknown land.

It was a difficult journey and it was many years before Abraham and his people finally settled in Canaan.

Things went well for a while, until one day, Abraham realized that there was not enough food and water for everyone. He agreed that Lot and his family should move to the lush lands below, while he and Sarah stayed where the ground was poorer.

When Lot had gone, God spoke to Abraham. "I will give you all the land you can see and it will be yours for ever," said God. "You will have as many children, grandchildren and great grandchildren, as there are stars in the sky. And you will be the father of a great nation, that will last through the ages."

One day, a few years later, Abraham saw three men approaching him. Abraham offered them freshly baked bread, roasted meat, milk and cream.

After the meal, the men told Abraham and Sarah, "You will have a baby son in nine months." Sarah laughed – surely she was too old to have a child!

But, nine months went by and God's promise
came true. Sarah and Abraham had a son, Isaac.
When he was born, Abraham recalled that God
had told him that his children would form the
beginning of a great nation. Abraham knew
that one day, this would be true.

The right wife for Isaac

GENESIS: 24

Time passed and Isaac grew up into a fine young man. After Sarah died, Abraham decided that Isaac should marry. He sent for his most trusted servant.

"You must go to my home country," said Abraham. "Find Isaac a wife. She must be someone from my own people."

"What if the girl doesn't want to come back here?" asked the servant. "Shall I take Isaac with me to your homeland?"

"No!" Abraham told him, firmly. "This land is part of God's plan for my people. If the girl won't come, return without her."

So, camels were loaded and the servant set out on the long journey.

49

At last, the servant arrived at the place where Abraham's brother, Nahor, lived. It was late in the afternoon and the camels were very tired. The servant settled the weary camels down to rest at the town well and began to pray.

"Please, God, help me to do what Abraham asked. Soon, the women will come to fetch water from the well. I shall ask one of them to give me a drink. If she is thoughtful enough to bring water for the camels, too, she will be the right wife for Isaac." Suddenly, the servant looked up and saw a beautiful girl, carrying a water jar.

The servant watched the girl fill her jar with water and then asked her for a drink. She gave him the jar and ran to fetch some water for his camels.

"Would it be possible," he asked, "for me to stay the night at your father's house?"

"I'm sure it would be," she replied, saying that she was Nahor's granddaughter, Rebecca. The servant thanked God for leading him straight to Abraham's family.

Rebecca ran home to tell everyone what had happened.

Her brother, Laban, welcomed the stranger and prepared food for him.

Then, the servant explained the reason for his journey and Rebecca's family understood that God intended Rebecca to be Isaac's wife.

Next morning, Abraham's servant was eager to set off for home. Although it meant leaving her family and going to live far away, Rebecca agreed to go with him. She said goodbye to everyone and then the two of them began the long journey back to Canaan.

It was evening time when Isaac first saw the train of camels approaching his home.

Isaac tried to listen to the old servant telling the story of his journey, but he hardly heard. He was too busy staring at the beautiful girl, who had travelled so far to be his wife.

They were married soon after and Isaac loved Rebecca very much.

The children
of Israel

GENESIS: 25, 27-29, 32-33

Some time after Isaac and Rebecca were
married, Rebecca gave birth to twin boys.
They grew up very different to each other.
Esau, the elder, who was Isaac's favorite,
loved the outdoor life. He liked to hunt and
often brought meat home from his hunting
trips, which Isaac enjoyed eating very
much in tasty stews.

Jacob, the younger son and Rebecca's favorite, was much quieter. He preferred to stay at home.

Esau and Jacob even looked different. Jacob didn't have Esau's red hair or his brother's hairy skin.

As Isaac grew old, he went blind. He thought he might die soon. At that time, it was important that a dying father bless the oldest son, as the new head of the family. So, one day, Isaac sent Esau out hunting, so that they could share a meal of Isaac's favorite meat before the blessing.

Rebecca wanted Jacob to have the blessing. Isaac would never know if Jacob pretended to be his brother.

So, she made Isaac's favorite stew and dressed Jacob in Esau's clothes. She covered his arms with goatskin, to make them seem hairy like his brother's. Then, she sent him to Isaac with the food.

At first, all went well. Isaac smelled the delicious food. He reached out to his son and the feel of the hairy goatskin made him think it was Esau's arm that he was touching. But the voice sounded wrong.

"Are you really Esau?" he asked his son.

"Yes, I am Esau," Jacob lied to his father.

So, Isaac prayed to God to bless Jacob, thinking that he was his older son.

When Esau returned and took food into his father, he learned the truth. He became so angry that Rebecca was afraid. She managed to persuade Isaac that it would be a good time for Jacob to seek a wife from their own people.

And so, it was decided to send Jacob to stay with Rebecca's brother, Laban, until Esau had calmed down.

Jacob set off, feeling lonely and frightened. At sunset, he made camp in a valley and settled down to sleep. During the night, he had a dream. He saw a staircase reaching up to heaven, with angels moving up and down it. Then God spoke to Jacob, "I will give you and your children the land on which you lie. I will watch over you and look after you wherever you go."

When Jacob woke up, he was very afraid. A long journey to a strange land lay ahead of him. "If you protect me and bring me safely back home as you have said," Jacob prayed, "you will always be my God." Then, filled with renewed strength, he continued on the journey to his mother's country.

63

When Jacob finally arrived, he was made
very welcome. He fell in love with Rachel,
the youngest daughter of Laban. However,
it was the custom for the oldest daughter to
be married first, so Jacob took Leah, Rachel's
sister, as his first wife. After some time, he
also married Rachel.

Many years later, Jacob decided to return home to Canaan with his wives and family. But, on the way, he suddenly became afraid. How would Esau treat him? Would he be forgiven? So, Jacob sent messengers ahead, who returned with worrying news. Esau was on his way, with four hundred men.

Jacob chose various animals as presents for Esau, to be sent ahead with his servants. Alone in the camp, Jacob was worried about his reunion with his brother and preyed to God for help. Suddenly, a stranger appeared and the two men began to wrestle. This stranger was God and had come to reassure Jacob that he was doing the right thing. When the stranger left, Jacob knew that he had been blessed and from that time on, he would be known as Israel.

When Jacob saw Esau approaching with his men, the trouble that he expected did not happen. Esau greeted his brother with open arms and all the old quarrels were forgotten.

"Seeing your welcoming face was like looking into the face of God," Jacob said, full of joy.

Many years later, Jacob's family came to be known as the children of Israel. God's promise had been fulfilled.

Sold for twenty silver pieces

GENESIS: 37

Jacob had twelve sons, ten with Leah and two—
Joseph and Benjamin—with Rachel. Jacob's
favorite was Joseph and he spoiled him.
Because of this, the other brothers disliked
Joseph. When their father gave Joseph a
special coat, the brothers were very jealous.

Joseph made matters worse, because he insisted on telling everyone about his dreams, in which he was always the most important person.

In one dream, Joseph said that his brothers' sheaves of corn bowed down before his sheaf. "Do you think you are going to be king and rule over all of us?" asked his brothers. Joseph didn't answer.

One day, Jacob sent Joseph to see his brothers, who were looking after the sheep.

When the brothers saw Joseph approaching, they laid a plan to kill him. They would then throw his body into a deep, dry well and pretend that a wild animal had eaten him. They had had enough of Joseph and his dreams.

When Joseph arrived, the brothers seized him, but the oldest one, Reuben, persuaded them to think again. "Let us lower him into the well and leave him there to die," he said, planning to secretly rescue Joseph later.

Joseph could do nothing against so many of
his brothers, as they ripped his coat from him
and threw him into the deep, dark well.

A little later, as the brothers sat eating, some spice merchants passed by, on their way to Egypt. Seeing them, Judah had an idea.

"We won't gain anything if Joseph dies," he said. "Why don't we sell him as a slave?"

And so it was agreed. The terrified Joseph was dragged from the well and sold for twenty silver pieces to the next group of merchants who came along.

Then, the brothers killed
a goat and smeared its blood
on Joseph's coat.

When Jacob saw the
torn coat, he was convinced
that Joseph had been
killed by a wild animal.
He was heartbroken.

Meanwhile, in Egypt, the
merchants had sold Joseph to
Potiphar, the Captain of the Guard
at the Pharaoh's court.

Thrown into prison

GENESIS: 39-41

Over the years, Joseph served Potiphar well. In time, he was put in charge of Potiphar's house and, later, all of his lands. But trouble was brewing.

Potiphar's wife was displeased with Joseph and told her husband lies, pretending that Joseph had attacked her. Potiphar had Joseph thrown into prison.

It just so happened that Pharaoh's butler and baker were also in the same jail. Joseph was given the job of serving these men.

One night, both of them had worrying dreams. "God can show us what dreams mean," said Joseph. "Tell me what you saw."

The butler told Joseph of a grapevine with three branches. He had squeezed the grape juice into Pharaoh's cup and given it to him to drink.

"The meaning is clear," said Joseph. "In three days, you will be free and back at work. Please, put in a good word for me."

Joseph turned to the baker. "You say that in your dream, you were carrying three baskets full of bread and pastries on your head and birds flew down and pecked at them."

Joseph shook his head, sadly. "This dream is not good," he said. "In three days, Pharaoh will kill you."

Joseph was right. Three days later, the butler was back at work in Pharaoh's palace and the baker was dead.

As soon as the butler was released, he forgot about the promise he had made and so Joseph remained in prison.

Two years later, Pharaoh's sleep was disturbed by strange dreams. In one dream, he was standing in a field by the River Nile, when seven plump, well-fed cows came out of the water and began to feed on the grass. These were followed by seven thin, bony cows, who ate up the first cows.

All the wisest men in Egypt couldn't help Pharaoh to understand what his dream meant. Then the butler remembered Joseph and mentioned him to Pharaoh. Joseph was instantly brought to the palace.

"There will be seven years of good harvests," explained Joseph. "After that, seven years of bad harvests will follow. You must store food in the good years, to help you through the bad."

Pharaoh could see that Joseph was a man of God. He was so impressed with him that he made Joseph his chief minister and gave him his own gold ring, a gold chain and fine clothes, as a mark of his new role.

Once again, everything happened just as
Joseph predicted.

After Pharaoh, he was the most powerful man
in Egypt and, because he had planned well,
there was still plenty to eat when the years of
famine came.

Reunited

GENESIS: 42-47

In Canaan, times were hard for Jacob and his family. He decided to send his sons, all except for Benjamin, to Egypt where corn was for sale.

So, Joseph's brothers stood before him and, not recognising him, asked if they might buy some corn. Joseph knew them at once and decided to see if they were still as cruel as they used to be.

Pretending to think they were spies, he had them thrown into prison.

Three days later, he told them to return home and bring back their youngest brother. Joseph loved Benjamin and very much wanted to see him again. Joseph kept one brother behind, to make sure that the others would return.

Joseph ordered his servants to fill his brothers' bags with corn, before they set off for home.

Back in Canaan, the brothers told Jacob everything, but he refused to let Benjamin go. He was terrified of losing another son.

Eventually, the corn ran out. Judah begged his father to let them return to Egypt, promising to look after Benjamin. Finally, Jacob agreed. And so the brothers came once again to Joseph, who had to fight back tears when he saw Benjamin.

"Is your father well?" he asked them. As they replied, they bowed low to him, just like the corn sheaves had bowed in Joseph's dream so many years before.

Joseph ordered food to be brought in and told the servants that Benjamin was to be given more than anyone else.

Then. the brothers' sacks were filled with food. This time, Joseph had his own silver cup hidden in Benjamin's bag. The brothers set off, but Joseph sent his guards after them, to look for the missing cup.

Horrified at the discovery of the cup, the brothers went back to Joseph and threw themselves at his feet.

"The man in whose sack my cup was found, must stay here as my servant. The rest of you can go!" Joseph commanded.

"Let me stay instead," begged Judah. "Father will die of grief if Benjamin doesn't return."

Now Joseph was sure that his brothers had changed. He sent the servants out of the room, burst into tears and announced, "I am Joseph!" His brothers stood, shocked and terrified.

"It was God's plan that I was sent here to Egypt," Joseph told them, "so that I would be in a position to look after you when difficult times came. There are still five more years of famine to come. You must go home, and bring the rest of the family here to live near me."

Joseph hugged Benjamin, then the rest of his brothers, as tears of joy streamed down his face.

So, Jacob and all of his family, the children of Israel, left Canaan and came to live in Egypt. There, Jacob was reunited with his much-loved son, Joseph.

Jacob settled comfortably in Goshen, the best part of Egypt and lived to be a great age.

You have been chosen

EXODUS: 1-4

While Joseph was alive, his people lived happily in Egypt, but after his death, things changed.

A new Pharaoh came to power, who did not know how Joseph had helped Egypt during the famine. The new Pharaoh watched the Israelites grow in number. He became afraid that they would outnumber the Egyptians and be much more powerful.

So, he set them to work for him, making bricks and building new cities. Gradually, he turned them into the slaves of cruel Egyptian masters. Life became very difficult, but still the Israelite numbers grew. Finally, Pharaoh gave orders that any baby boy born to an Israelite family was to be killed.

At this time, an Israelite woman had a baby boy. While he was tiny and slept a lot, she managed to keep him hidden. But, after three months, this became difficult. He was beginning to make lots of noise!

So, the woman made a basket from reeds and waterproofed it by covering it with tar. Then, she placed her baby in it and with great care, hid it in the tall grasses at the edge of the river.

Her daughter, Miriam, stayed close by to watch. Soon, Pharaoh's daughter came to the river to bathe. She saw the basket and, as she opened it, the baby began to cry. She realized that this was an Israelite boy and felt sorry for him.

Quickly, Miriam stepped forward. "Would you like me to find someone to look after the child for you?" she asked. Pharaoh's daughter agreed and, of course, Miriam ran to fetch her mother.

So, the mother looked after the baby until he was old enough to live in Pharaoh's palace.

Pharaoh's daughter gave the boy the name of Moses. He was well cared for but, as he grew older, Moses never forgot that he was an Israelite. It greatly saddened him to see his people being treated so badly.

One day, Moses saw an Egyptian master kill an Israelite worker.

He leapt at the Egyptian and killed him. Moses knew that Pharaoh would hear of what he had done and fled to the safety of the desert.

Moses went to live in a land called Midian, where he stayed for a long time, working as a shepherd.

One day, as he was watching over his flock, he noticed that a bush was on fire. Strangely, the bush remained whole. As he got nearer, Moses heard a voice, saying, "I am the God of Abraham and your ancestors. I have seen how the people of Israel are suffering. You are to go to Pharaoh and free my people."

"Please choose someone else," pleaded Moses. "No one will listen to me."

"You have been chosen," replied God. "Return to Egypt, find Aaron, your brother, and go with him to ask Pharaoh to set my people free."

Let my
people go

EXODUS: 5-14

So, Moses and Aaron went to Pharaoh and said,
"The God of Israel says that you should let *His*
people go."

But Pharaoh didn't believe in God and became very angry. As a punishment, he made Moses' people work harder than ever.

"Give the Israelite slaves no more straw to make their bricks," he ordered. "Let them find their own. But they must make just as many bricks as before."

Moses went to tell God. "I will force Pharaoh to let my people go," said God. "Go and tell him that if he refuses again, dreadful things will happen."

Moses and Aaron returned to Pharaoh, determined to make him free the Israelites.

To show Pharaoh that they had been sent by God, Aaron threw his walking stick on the ground. Miraculously, it turned into a snake.

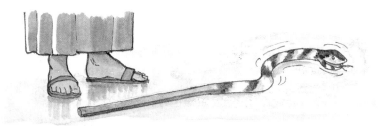

But Pharaoh's magicians could do the same and Pharaoh was not convinced. He refused to listen to Moses. So, God turned the waters of the River Nile into blood.

Then, frogs swamped the entire country.
This was followed by swarms of gnats and flies.
Only Goshen, the place where the Israelites
lived, remained free of these things. But still,
Pharaoh would not let the Israelites leave Egypt.

So, one by one, the Egyptian animals began to die, all except the ones in Goshen.

Even when the Egyptians became covered in boils, Pharaoh would not believe in God or set the Israelites free.

Then, God sent hail. It hailed like no one had ever seen before. Thundering hail, that beat down the crops and killed all of the remaining cattle.

Plagues of locusts followed, great humming swarms that ate every last green shoot, even the tiniest new leaf. At last, complete and total darkness covered the land and it remained that way for three whole days.

Pharaoh tried reasoning with Moses. But Moses insisted that all the Israelites, men, women, children and cattle, were freed – Pharaoh refused.

Then, late one night, God killed the eldest son of every Egyptian family, including Pharaoh's own son.

The Israelite families remained safe. God had told each family to kill a lamb or a goat and to splash a little of its blood on the doors to their homes. Then, they were to roast the meat and eat it with bread made without yeast.

The blood was a sign that Israelites lived in that house and so the angel of death 'passed over' any house marked in this way.

God said that the Israelites should always celebrate that day as a special festival. Every year afterwards, they ate a 'Passover' meal, to remember how God had saved them.

Pharaoh had finally had enough. He sent for Moses and Aaron and said, "Take your people and leave at once!"

The Egyptians gave the Israelites gold and silver to try to hurry them on their way.

But after Moses and his people had left, Pharaoh changed his mind and sent his soldiers after them. They caught up with the Israelites at the Red Sea.

Moses stretched out his arm and God sent a wind to blow back the water.

The Israelites hurried across the pathway of dry land.

When the Egyptian soldiers followed, the water rushed over them and killed every one. Moses' people were free! That night, the Israelites celebrated with music and songs.

God looked after His people

EXODUS: 16-17

It didn't take long for the Israelites to start grumbling. They complained that they had very little to eat. They remembered all the fish and wonderful vegetables they had had in Egypt. They forgot about their cruel masters and turned on Moses and Aaron.

"We would rather have died in Egypt, than starve to death in the desert," they moaned.

God heard their complaints. "You will have meat to eat each night and bread every day except on the Sabbath, my day of rest," God promised.

And that night, a huge flock of birds called quail flew down and landed where the Israelites were camped. Now, there was plenty of meat for everyone.

Next morning, the ground all around the camp was covered with dew. As the dew dried, something white and flaky, as delicate as frost, was left behind.

"This is special food that God has sent for you," said Moses. "Gather as much as you need."

The Israelites collected it quickly. It tasted just like honey. It appeared each morning. And every sixth day, they collected twice as much as usual, to last them through the Sabbath, or God's day of rest. They called the food manna.

111

But Moses' problems did not end there. The hot sun beat down on the desert, the people's throats grew dry and they became thirstier and thirstier. There was very little water, so the grumbling began all over again.

Moses turned to God for help. "Go ahead of the people," said God, "and when you reach a rock at Mount Sinai, strike it with your stick."

Moses did as he was told. Lots of water came, gushing and gurgling out from the rock, cool and refreshing – everyone had plenty to drink.

In this way, God looked after His people, as they wandered through the desert on their long journey to the land of Canaan.

God's ten laws

EXODUS: 19-20, 24-27, 32, 34-40

At the foot of Mount Sinai, Moses and his people set up camp.

"I have brought you here to be my chosen people," said God. "Will you obey me?" The Israelites agreed that they would. Then, God said that He would give them ten laws, His commandments, to show them how to serve Him well and to help them understand how to behave towards one another.

Two days later, thunder roared and lightning flashed at the top of the mountain. Moses and Aaron went up alone, and there, God gave them His laws.

These are God's ten laws.

"Honor and serve Me alone, for I am the only God.

Do not make or worship any idols.

Treat My name with respect.

Keep every Sabbath as a day of rest.

Respect your father and mother.

Do not kill another human being.

Husbands and wives must keep their love only for one another.

Do not steal.

Do not tell lies.

Do not be greedy about things that other people have."

Because Moses was His special prophet,
God explained to him how the laws worked.
Moses explained them to the people and
everyone agreed to obey the laws.

But, when Moses went back up the mountain to talk with God, he was gone so long that the people grew restless. They spoke to Aaron.

"Where has Moses gone?" they asked. "Make a new god to lead us."

So, Aaron collected all the gold, melted it down and made it into a golden bull calf. The people worshipped this bull.

When they saw how quickly the people had forgotten their promises, God and Moses were really angry. Moses threw the stone tablets, on to which God had carved his laws, on to the ground and they smashed to pieces.

Moses was absolutely furious, but he loved his people and asked God to give them another chance. God made new stone tablets and, once more, the people kept their agreement, their 'covenant', with God.

To show that He was always near them, God asked for a special tent to be made, in which a wooden box, covered with gold, was to be kept. This box contained the stone tablets.

Everyone happily gave the things that were needed to make the tent, or tabernacle, and the finest craftsmen worked on it. It was beautiful and was lined with richly colored linens.

Around the tent was a courtyard, where people could offer a lamb or a kid, in payment for things they had done wrong. God wanted to remind His people that He loved them. Although they were not perfect, they could always come to say they were sorry and give thanks.

121

In the desert for forty years

NUMBERS: 13-14, 17, 21

From Mount Sinai, the Israelites moved towards Canaan. At the border, they chose twelve men to spy out the land.

After forty days, the spies returned carrying bunches of grapes, figs and pomegranates. "Canaan is a very fertile land," they said, "but the cities are defended like fortresses. If we try to take over the land, we will be crushed!"

The people were devastated. "We should go back to Egypt," they cried.

Joshua and Caleb, two of the spies, protested. "No! We must trust in God. He will protect us and give us this land." But no one would listen.

God was angry. "Because you will not trust me," He told them, "you will wander in the desert for forty years. Only Joshua and Caleb will enter Canaan."

The Israelites didn't like this idea and decided to fight the Canaanites, but they were very heavily defeated.

The people were angry, so they turned on Moses. "What gives you and Aaron the right to be our leaders?" they asked.

Moses replied, "Let each of our twelve tribes choose a leader and carve his name on an almond branch. Tonight, the branches will be left in God's tent. God will choose one man to lead His people."

Next morning, only Aaron's branch had burst into flower and produced almonds. He had been chosen.

Things calmed down, but when, years later, Aaron died, the complaints started again.

"Why did we leave Egypt? There's no proper food or water here. We're tired of eating manna," they moaned.

This time, God sent poisonous snakes to punish the rebels. They spread into the camp, killing people with their bites.

The Israelites pleaded with Moses. "We realize we've been wrong to speak against God. Please ask Him to take these snakes away."

So Moses prayed to God.

"Make a brass snake and fix it to a pole," said God. "Anyone who is bitten by a snake, need only look at this pole to be healed."

In this way, those who trusted God were made well again.

Down crashed the walls

JOSHUA: 1-6

Eventually, the forty years in the desert came to an end. When Moses died, God chose Joshua as the new leader.

From their camp on the far side of the River Jordan, Joshua sent two spies to Jericho.

In a house on the city wall, lived a woman called Rahab. She offered the men shelter for the night. But the king of Jericho heard of this and sent his soldiers to capture them.

Rahab hid the spies on her roof and, when questioned, told the soldiers that they had left.

Rahab knew that God intended to give Canaan to the Israelites. "We are all afraid," she said. "Promise me that you will look after my family and keep us safe when you take this city."

"We give you our word, if you promise to tell no one what we have been doing here," said the men. "When we invade, tie a red cord to the window, so we can recognize your house again. Then, gather all of your family together and we will make sure they remain safe."

And so, Rahab promised.
Then, she let the men down
from her window on a rope
and they made their way
back to Joshua.

Not long afterwards, the people of Israel prepared to cross the River Jordan to take Jericho. The water in the river was very high. The priests went ahead, carrying the box with God's laws in it. As they stepped into the river, the banks collapsed upstream, damming the water. At Jericho, the people were able to cross the river bed easily.

Then, the Israelites took twelve stones from the middle of the river bed. They piled them up on to the bank, as a sign of God's help in bringing them into Canaan. Then, the river flooded through again.

The Israelites set up camp outside the walls of Jericho and celebrated Passover.

The walls of Jericho were high and thick and the gates were shut tight against the Israelites. No one could get in or out. Then, God spoke to Joshua, "Each day, for six days, you are to march round the city walls. Place seven priests at the front. The men with my box of laws must go next. The priests should have trumpets made of rams' horns and they are to blow on the horns as you march. Everyone else must be silent.

"On the seventh day, march round the city seven times. Then, the priests are to play one long note on their trumpets and all the people are to shout loudly. The walls of Jericho will fall, the city will be yours."

So each day, the Israelites went out and marched around the walls of Jericho and, each night, they returned to their camp.

On the seventh day, they marched round the city seven times. The last time, when the priests sounded the trumpets, Joshua gave the order and a great shout went up.

Down crashed the walls and the people of Israel took the city. Only Rahab and her family were saved.

The city was set on fire and burnt to the ground. This was the first of Joshua's victories in Canaan. With him as their leader, the Israelites slowly conquered the 'promised land'.

137

The secret of his strength

JUDGES: 13-16

Many, many years passed. But after Joshua's death, the Israelites began to forget God again. As a punishment, God let the Philistines rule over His people for forty years.

One day, God sent an angel to a man called Manoah—he was told that he and his wife would have a son, who would help protect the Israelites from their enemies.

138

When the boy was born, he was called Samson. As a sign that Samson belonged to God, his parents never cut his hair.

Samson grew up very strong. Once, he even killed a lion with his bare hands...

From that point, Samson realized that God
had given him a special strength to use
against the Philistines. And over the years,
Samson did... he destroyed their crops
and, once, killed a thousand of them,
using only a donkey's jawbone
as a weapon.

When they tried to trap
him, he always escaped.

The Philistines were
determined to have their revenge.

Their chance came when Samson fell in love with a beautiful Philistine girl, called Delilah. The five Philistine kings went to her. "We will each give you eleven hundred silver coins, if you can make Samson tell you the secret of his strength," they said. Delilah agreed.

But, each time Delilah asked Samson to tell her the secret of his strength, he told a different story. "If you tie me up with new bowstrings, I'll be as weak as anybody else," he said and then, "use brand new rope to tie me up... weave my hair into a loom... "

Delilah tried all these but, Samson remained strong. "If you won't tell me, you don't really love me," Delilah nagged.

Eventually, Samson gave in. "My hair is a sign that I belong to God. If it were cut, I would lose all my strength," he told her.

So, that night, when Samson was fast asleep, Delilah called a man to cut off his hair. Then, the Philistines came and took him prisoner.

Samson was blinded, chained and taken to a prison in Gaza and made to work very hard.

But slowly, Samson's hair grew back...

One day, the Philistines held a feast in honor of their god, Dagon. They had Samson brought from the prison to the temple. The place was crowded with thousands of people, who jeered and laughed at him.

Samson prayed to God, to give him strength. He reached out and pushed with all his might, against the two pillars that supported the building. The temple collapsed and all inside were killed. It was Samson's final act against the enemies of Israel. He had been leader for twenty years.

Your God will be my God

RUTH: 1-4

Many years later, there was a famine in Israel. One man from Bethlehem took his wife, Naomi, and his two sons to live in Moab.

Sadly, it wasn't long before the father died. The sons grew up and married but, ten years later, both men also died.

Naomi, feeling all alone, decided it was time to return to her homeland. Her daughters-in-law, Orpah and Ruth, set out with her. "You must go back to your people," Naomi told them.

Unhappily, Orpah agreed, but Ruth said, "I'm coming with you. Your people will be my people, your God will be my God."

147

Eventually, Naomi and Ruth reached the town of Bethlehem at harvest time. They were very poor so, every day, Ruth walked behind the workers in the fields, collecting any corn that had been dropped. She then exchanged the corn for a small amount of money. The hours were long and it was very hard work.

Unknown to her, she had chosen the field of one of Naomi's relatives, a rich man called Boaz. When he came to check the work, he noticed Ruth and asked about her. Hearing that she was a relative of Naomi's, he told her that she was always welcome to work in his field.

Naomi was delighted when Ruth told her. She wanted to find a husband for Ruth and she knew that Boaz was a good man. In Israel at that time, the nearest relative would take care of a man's family if he died. Naomi wanted to claim this right, so she sent Ruth to find out if he would marry her.

Boaz agreed, which made Naomi very happy and, eventually, Ruth and he had a son.

So it was, that Ruth, who had put her trust in the God of Israel and had helped and loved her mother-in-law, was to become the great-grandmother of Israel's greatest king – David.

We want
a king

1 SAMUEL: 1, 8-10, 15-16

Near Jerusalem, there lived a woman called
Hannah. She had no children and this made
her very sad. One day, when Hannah was
praying silently to God, she didn't realize she
was mouthing the words to her prayer.

Eli, the priest, watched her and, seeing her lips move without the words being spoken, he believed she was drunk. When Hannah explained, Eli said, "May God give you the son you long for."

In time, God did give Hannah a son—Samuel. When he was old enough, Hannah took the boy back to Eli. "This is the son God gave me," she said. "Now I am giving him back to God."

So Samuel grew up loving and obeying God.

In time, God chose Samuel to lead the Israelites. Samuel was a good and gentle man, who loved God and the simple, honest way of life of his people. His two sons, however, were not like him. They were only interested in money. The Israelites did not want either of them to lead when Samuel died, so they asked Samuel for a king to rule over them, as in other nations.

Samuel was worried. God was the only true leader, so he prayed for guidance.

God told Samuel to tell the people what a king would be like. "He will make your sons fight in his armies," said Samuel. "He will force you to work the land for him and he will take the best crops. You will become his slaves."

But the people insisted.

When Samuel told God that his words hadn't changed the Israelites' minds, God replied, "Do as they wish. Give them their king."

One day, Samuel met a tall, handsome man - Saul. God had told Samuel where and when he would meet Israel's future king and so was not surprised when he heard God say, "This is the man, who is to rule."

At dawn the next day, following tradition, Samuel poured oil onto Saul's head, as a sign that he was the chosen one.

At first, Saul was a good and popular king. Under his leadership, his people won many battles, but soon, he became proud. He began to think more of himself than he did of God. So, God told Samuel that it was time to find a new king.

157

God told Samuel to go to Bethlehem, as He had chosen one of Jesse's sons to succeed Saul.

When Samuel arrived, he invited Jesse and his sons to witness an offering for God. He spoke to all of the sons in turn. Each time, he thought, "This fine-looking, young man must be the chosen one." But each time, God said, "No."

"What's important is not what a person looks like," God said, "but what he is like inside."

After Samuel had rejected seven of Jesse's sons, he asked if there were any more. Jesse said that the youngest, David, was out looking after the sheep. Samuel asked Jesse to send for him.

As David walked in, God spoke to Samuel, saying, "This is the one!"

So, Samuel anointed David and from that time on, David always felt that God was with him.

The champion of Israel

1 SAMUEL: 16-17

David continued looking after his father's sheep.
Each day, he grew in wisdom and strength.
He had to be skillful and strong to fight off
the wild animals, that often attacked the flock.
David began to use a sling shot, to scare off
the bears and lions and soon became an expert
with it.

To pass the time, David also practiced playing his harp and he quickly became very good at this, too. News of his skills spread far across the land.

Meanwhile, Samuel no longer visited Saul at his palace and the king felt distant from God. He had terrible moods and was tormented by an evil spirit.

One of Saul's attendants suggested that harp music might soothe the king.

David was sent for and indeed, whenever David played, the music calmed Saul. Once the king felt better, David would return home.

Then, news came that the Philistines had set up camp on one side of the Valley of Elah. Only a small stream separated them from the Israelite army, who were on the other side.

The Philistines had a mighty champion in their army – Goliath – nearly ten feet tall and stronger than an ox. He paraded up and down, day after day, jeering at the Israelites.

"Where's the champion of Israel?" he would shout. "Send him to fight me! If he kills me, we will be your slaves. If I kill him, you will be ours." But no one would face Goliath. They were all too terrified.

David had three brothers in Saul's army.
One day, when he was bringing food to them,
he heard Goliath's taunts across the valley.

"Who is he, to challenge the army of the living
God?" David said. "Let me go and fight him."

The soldiers looked at the boy and laughed. But,
when Saul heard about this, he sent for David.

"I've fought lions and bears to protect my father's sheep," David told him. "God protected me then and he will do so now."

Saul eventually agreed. He gave David his own armor and his sword. But because the armor was so heavy and large, David couldn't move with it on. So, he took it all off and picked up his sling. He chose five smooth stones from the stream and went out to meet the giant.

When Goliath saw him coming, he roared with laughter. "Is this your champion?" he sneered at the Israelites.

"I come in the name of the God of Israel," said David, calmly. "He will put you in my power."

He took a stone from his bag, placed it into his sling and took aim. The stone hurtled towards Goliath and struck him on the forehead with such force, that it broke his skull. The giant man fell face down on the ground.

When the Philistines saw that their hero was dead, they ran into the hills. The joyful Israelites gave chase — victory and the land of the Philistines was theirs!

A great leader

2 SAMUEL: 1-6, 11-19; 1 KINGS: 1

Years later, after Saul's death, David became King of Israel, but there were difficult times ahead for him. Supporters of Saul fought against David and the Philistines were always waiting for a chance to return to the country. David longed to conquer the city of Jerusalem, so that he could bring the sacred box of God's laws there.

What a celebration they had when, at last, David attacked and captured the city! There was music and dancing, feasts were held and gifts were offered – David had made Jerusalem the city of God.

David was a great leader, loved by all his people and faithful to God. But he was not perfect. He fell in love with Bathsheba, even though she was already married. David made sure that her soldier husband was killed in a battle. God saw what David had done and let him know through Nathan, the prophet. David prayed to God to forgive him and God saw that he was truly sorry.

"You will remain King," God said to David, "but the task of building my temple, I will give to your son, Solomon."

Alone and upset, King David began to draw up plans for the temple and wrote music, that would be used there to praise God.

Later, David married Bathsheba and his kingdom remained strong, although trouble was rarely far away.

Absalom, one of David's sons, was handsome and popular – and he wanted to be king. So, he plotted to take his father's throne and marched on Jerusalem.

At first, King David took flight, but then he rallied his army and went into battle against his son. David's army defeated Absalom, who tried to flee, but was captured by some of David's soldiers. They ignored the King's orders to spare Absalom's life and killed him.

The king was overcome with grief.

"Oh, my son, my son," he cried, "I wish that I had died in your place!"

As Absalom was dead, David's next son, Adonijah, decided that he would claim the throne for himself. But King David said that Solomon would succeed him.

David told Zadok the priest, Nathan the prophet and Benaiah to take Solomon to Gihon, to anoint him as king.

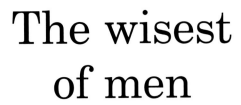

The wisest of men

1 KINGS: 1-4, 10

There was great celebration when Solomon became king.

Before he died, King David spoke to Solomon. "Be a strong king. Trust in God and follow His commands. Then God will keep His promise that my descendants will rule this nation."

So, immediately King Solomon expelled his father's old enemies and set out new districts throughout his kingdom.

Then, Solomon ruled over
the kingdom of Israel for
many years and loved God.
He was to become one of Israel's
most famous kings. And the people
of God lived together in a time of peace.

175

One night, God appeared
before Solomon in a dream.
"What would you like
me to give you?"
God asked.

"I am very young to rule over so many people,"
Solomon replied. "Please give me the wisdom
I need to make the right and true decisions."

God was very pleased, because Solomon had
not asked for things for himself.

"I'll give you more wisdom and understanding,"
said God, "than anyone has ever had before."

God kept his promise and Solomon became
the wisest of men. But Solomon always
remembered that his wisdom came from God.

One day, Solomon had to judge who was the real mother of a baby. Solomon thought and then suggested that they cut the baby in half. The false mother agreed. But the real mother said, "No!" The wise king knew at once who the real mother was.

Such tales of Solomon's wisdom spread far and wide across the world. Eventually, they reached the land of Sheba.

When the queen of that land heard about Solomon, she decided to see him for herself.

She thought up a list of very difficult questions and then, taking jewels, gold and spices with her, set out for Jerusalem. She made quite an impression, when she entered the city!

The queen asked Solomon all her questions, and he was able to answer them all very easily. "I can see," she said, "that God has given His people a wise king, because he loves them so much."

Then, the queen returned to Sheba.

A wonderful temple for God

1 KINGS: 5-8

In the fourth year of Solomon's reign, he began to build a wonderful temple for God.

For the foundations and walls, fine large stones were used, as well as quality woods, such as cedar.

Because lots of cedar wood was needed and the best cedars grew in Tyre, Solomon made a treaty with Hiram, the king of that country.

Once cut, the wood was tied together in rafts and floated down the coast, to where Solomon was building the temple. In return, Solomon supplied Tyre with loads of wheat and olive oil.

The temple was going to be a wonderful place where God's special box, containing the laws, would be kept.

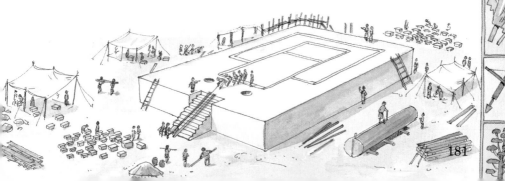

When the temple was finished, it was amazing. At the rear, was a windowless square, with floors and walls covered in gold. The room would hold the box containing God's laws. It was decorated with carved figures of winged creatures, palm trees and flowers, also covered in gold.

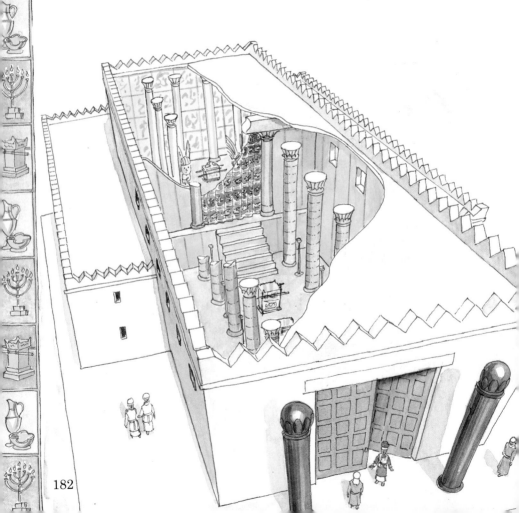

The outer room had a gold altar and ten gold lamp stands. The other furnishings in the temple were made of gold, including the tables, cups, bowls and even the pans that were used to carry coal to the fires. It was as beautiful as King Solomon could make it and contained the very best of everything.

Outside were courtyards, where people could offer their gifts to God.

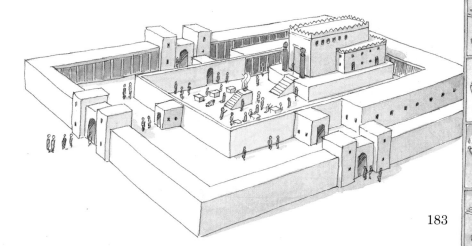

183

Thousands of men had worked on the temple and it had taken seven years to complete.

So, Solomon decided to hold a very special ceremony. The priests made offerings and the box containing God's laws was carried inside. It was then that the temple was completely filled with a dazzling light – the presence of God. King Solomon prayed, "Lord, God of Israel, hear the prayers of your people. Listen to them in your home in heaven and help them always."

Then, Solomon spoke to his people, "Be true to God and obey his commands."

After the ceremony, a great feast was held and the celebrations lasted for a week.

185

Israel will be taken

1 KINGS: 11

During Solomon's reign, Israel flourished. Beautiful buildings and great cities were built. But, to pay for the buildings, people had to pay taxes. Men had to work for the king, and not on their own farms.

Solomon also married many foreign princesses, who worshipped their own gods. It helped to keep peace between the lands and it was good for trade, but it also brought many problems.

Over many years, Solomon was persuaded by his wives to worship these foreign gods. He did not remain faithful to God, as his father had.

So, God said to him, "The kingdom of Israel will be taken from your son, since you have not followed my commands."

Eventually, this came to pass.

The true God

1 KINGS: 12, 16-19

After Solomon's death, Israel was divided in two. The southern part, Judah, followed Solomon's son – Rehoboam. In the north, the people followed Jeroboam, son of Nebat.

None of the kings, who succeeded Jeroboam, were faithful to God. One king, Ahab, married a woman called Jezebel and began to worship her god, Baal. Queen Jezebel had many of the prophets, who remained loyal to God, killed. But one prophet, Elijah, spoke out for the Lord.

One day, Elijah brought a message to King Ahab – there would be no rain in Israel until God said so.

189

After Elijah had delivered the message, God told him to go to a place on the other side of the River Jordan, where he would be safe.

For three years, Elijah stayed away and God watched over him, sending ravens to bring him food, and telling Elijah where to find people who would look after him.

And in all that time, it did not rain once.

One day, God told Elijah to return to Ahab.

"Why have you come back, troublemaker?" asked the King.

"You have disobeyed God," replied Elijah. "Send your people and the prophets of Baal to meet me on Mount Carmel."

Ahab did as Elijah had asked and when everyone was gathered together, Elijah said, "It is time to see who is the true God."

Then, Elijah challenged the prophets of Baal.

"Offer a bull to Baal and I will offer one to God. The true God will be the one who sends fire from the sky and sets light to the altar."

So, the priests of Baal made their altar and laid a bull on it. They called out to their god all day long, but there was silence and nothing happened.

Then, Elijah built his altar with a ditch surrounding it, which he filled with water. He placed his bull on the wood and poured water over everything. Then, Elijah began to pray. God sent fire down and, even though the wood was soaked, it burst into flames.

The people cried, "The Lord is the true God."

193

Then, Elijah asked God for rain. The skies grew dark and a strong wind blew and the rain fell once more. It was a wonderful day for Elijah. But Queen Jezebel swore to kill the prophet, in revenge for what he had done.

Elijah heard about the queen's plan and fled.

He travelled a great distance and arrived, at last, at Mount Sinai. Suddenly, he heard God's voice, asking why he was there.

"The people of Israel have killed all your prophets. I am the only one left," Elijah explained. "Now they want to kill me."

"You must go back," God replied. "There is lots more work to be done."

The prophet Isaiah

ISAIAH: 9, 11

More than a hundred years after Elijah's death, the northern part of Israel fell to the Assyrians and the people were taken into exile.

The southern kingdom of Judah was also under threat from Assyria, but God sent the prophet Isaiah to help King Hezekiah to save Jerusalem. The city was safe for a time, but Isaiah warned the King, "You must remember, Jerusalem will not fall, if you obey God's laws."

Isaiah also gave the people a lasting message of hope. "For unto us a child is born, a son is given and government will be on his shoulders," said Isaiah. "He will be called the Mighty God, Everlasting Father, Prince of Peace. There will be no end to his rule and peace."

Everything Isaiah said came true.

197

Thrown to the lions

DANIEL: 1, 6

Over many, many years, God's people continued to disobey Him. So, the Lord allowed the king of Babylon, Nebuchadnezzar, to gain control of Judah.

The king took many people as prisoners, including a group of young boys from Jerusalem, one of whom was Daniel.

Then, the king ordered his chief official to pick men from noble families, who could be trained to serve in the royal court. Daniel and his friends were some of the chosen men.

As they grew up, they studied the great writings and learnt to speak Babylonian. As the years passed, Daniel became very wise.

Then, one year, the Persians captured Babylon and their leader, Darius, became king.

Darius made Daniel one of his chief advisors and Daniel served him loyally. But the king's other advisors grew jealous of Daniel and the attention he received and plotted against him.

When they discovered that he prayed to God everyday, they said, "If we want to get Daniel into trouble, it will have to be something to do with his religion."

The advisors persuaded the king to make a new law, saying that for thirty days, no one was to ask for anything from any god or any human being, except from the king himself. Anyone who broke the law was to be thrown to the lions.

Daniel heard about the law, but continued to pray three times a day. He made no secret of it. His enemies were delighted – their plan had worked and they rushed to tell the king.

What could the king do? Daniel had broken the law. The king was very upset. He liked Daniel, but could not find a way to save him.

So, at sunset, Daniel was thrown into a deep pit, filled with hungry lions.

That night, the king couldn't eat.

He didn't want music.

He couldn't sleep.

He paced up and down.

As soon as dawn broke, Darius hurried off to the lion pit.

The king didn't expect to find Daniel alive and called down to the pit, "Was your God able to save you from the lions?"

Darius expected silence. But, instead, he heard Daniel's reply, "Yes, your majesty. God knew that I was innocent and He has kept me safe. I have done you no wrong."

Darius was amazed. He gave orders to have Daniel set free and for the men who accused him to be thrown to the lions instead.

Then, the king made a new law. "Let everyone in my kingdom fear and respect the God of Daniel, for He is the one true, living God."

An enormous fish

JONAH: 1-4

Being God's messenger was often a dangerous and unpopular job and not all of the prophets were willing to say "Yes" to God's call to them. One reluctant prophet was Jonah.

One day, God told Jonah that he was to go to the city of Nineveh, the capital of Assyria. The Assyrians were the enemies of God's people.

"Tell the Assyrians, in forty days, Nineveh will be destroyed," said God. "I know about the wicked things they are doing – they must stop!"

"I am going to look stupid," Jonah thought to himself. "God is loving and forgives people. He will not destroy Nineveh."

So, Jonah went to Joppa instead and boarded a boat that was bound for Spain.

God was angry with Jonah for not doing what He had asked. No sooner had the boat set sail, than God created a huge storm. Everyone feared that the boat would be ripped apart.

"Pray to your gods," the crew shouted.

Meanwhile, Jonah was fast asleep below deck. When the captain woke him and told him to pray like everyone else, Jonah wouldn't.

The storm worsened and, as the boat was tossed about, Jonah told the crew, "It's my fault that you are caught in this violent storm. Throw me into the sea and it will calm down."

The captain refused but, as the storm got worse, he had no choice and reluctantly threw Jonah overboard. The sea instantly calmed.

Jonah was convinced that he would drown and, as he sank down into the ocean, he called out for help.

God heard his cries and sent an enormous fish, that swallowed him alive.

For three days, Jonah was inside the dark belly of the huge fish. He was truly sorry for disobeying God and told Him in his prayers.

God listened to Jonah and, when He was sure that Jonah was truly sorry, He made the fish throw Jonah up onto a beach.

Once again, God told Jonah to take his message to Nineveh. Jonah rushed off at once.

The people of Nineveh listened to Jonah and immediately changed how they lived. God saw that they had given up their wicked ways and did not destroy the city.

"This is exactly what I said you would do!" Jonah complained to God. "So now, let me die." He sat outside the city, in the scorching sun.

But, God made a plant grow up, to shade Jonah and he began to feel less miserable.

Next day, the plant died and the sun beat down again.

"I'm sorry that the plant has gone. I was glad of it," said Jonah.

"You did not make that plant grow, but you are sorry for it," said God. "Just think how I feel about the people of Nineveh – the innocent children, the animals – I gave them all life."

At last, Jonah understood how much God still loved and cared for His world.

The King
of Peace

MICAH: 5

There were many times when the people of
Israel forgot God's laws and many times when
his prophets warned of the trouble this would
bring. Some prophets also spoke of the wonderful
things God planned for the future.

The prophet Micah spoke of God's promise of
a ruler for Israel, who would come from the tiny
town of Bethlehem.

"He will rule over his people with the majesty
of God," said Micah. "And it won't be in just
Israel that he is famous. All over the world,
people will recognize his greatness. He will be
the King of Peace."

Micah was speaking about Jesus, whose story
is told in The New Testament.

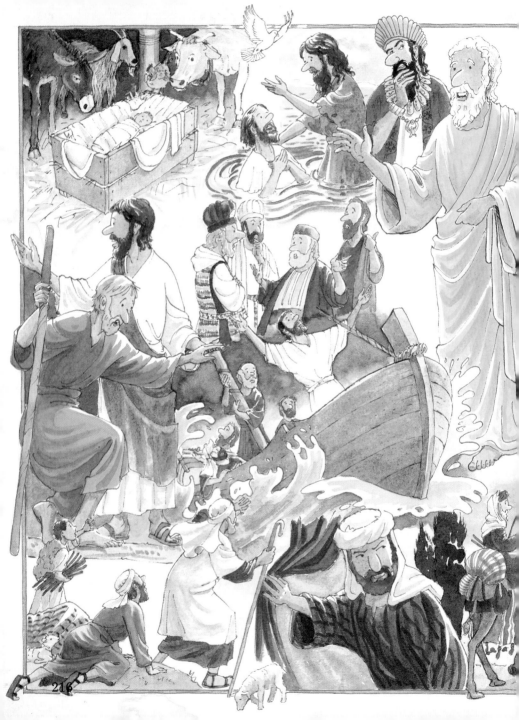

THE
NEW
TESTAMENT

The angel messenger

LUKE: 1

In Nazareth, a small town in Galilee, to the north of Israel, there lived a girl named Mary. She was engaged to Joseph, who was a descendant of King David. Joseph was the town carpenter.

One day, as Mary went about her daily tasks, she noticed a stranger watching her.

"I am Gabriel," the stranger told her. "Peace be with you, Mary. The Lord God has sent me with a special message for you. He has greatly blessed you."

Mary stared at the angel messenger.
She wondered what he could have to tell her.

Gabriel could see that Mary was frightened.

"Do not be afraid, Mary," he said. "God loves you very much. He has chosen you, above all others, to be the mother of his promised King. You will have a baby, God's own son. You will name him Jesus."

But Mary did not understand.

"How can this be?" she asked.

"The Holy Spirit will fall upon you and God's power will rest within you. He will take care of everything," Gabriel told Mary. "Remember your cousin, Elizabeth, who thought she could never have children. She is expecting a baby, too. God can do anything, if you trust Him."

Then, Mary knew that she did not need to ask any more questions. She just needed to trust in God.

"I am the Lord's servant," she said. "I will do whatever He wants."

Chosen

MATTHEW: 1

When Joseph found that Mary was expecting a baby, he was greatly troubled. Joseph was a good man and did not want to disgrace Mary in public. So, he decided to quietly break off their engagement.

Before he did so, Joseph had a dream, in which an angel of the Lord spoke to him. "Do not break your engagement to Mary," he told Joseph. "She has done nothing wrong. She has been chosen to be the mother of God's son and you will name the baby Jesus. He will grow up to save the world from its' sins."

When Joseph woke up, he knew what he must do. He would marry Mary and look after the baby, as the angel had told him to do.

223

The little town of Bethlehem

LUKE: 2

Not long afterwards, an order was sent out across the Roman Empire by the Emperor Augustus. He wanted to make sure that all the people were paying their taxes.

The only way to do this was by making everyone return to the town where their family came from, so that their names could be written down and recorded.

Because Joseph's family came from a town called Bethlehem, in Judea, he and Mary had no choice, but to return there. They set out on the long journey, with Mary sitting on their donkey.

Mary's baby was due to be born at any moment and she was exhausted. After travelling for many days and nights, they finally reached the little town of Bethlehem.

The town was noisy and overcrowded with all the people, who had come to register. Mary and Joseph searched for somewhere to stay.

But the inns were full and it seemed that there was no place for them. Mary looked so tired at one inn, that the innkeeper felt sorry for her and offered Joseph his stable.

The stable was full of animals and very smelly and dirty, but at least it was somewhere for Mary to rest.

Mary gave birth to her son that very night. She wrapped him warmly, in strips of cloth, and laid him gently in a manger, to sleep.

227

The shepherds

LUKE: 2

Out on the hills above Bethlehem, shepherds were looking after their flocks of sheep.

Suddenly, there was a dazzling blaze of light in the sky above them. The shepherds were terrified. They had to cover their eyes. Whatever could it be?

Then, the angel of the Lord appeared and spoke to the shepherds.

"Do not be afraid," said the angel. "I come with good news, which will bring great joy to all people. God's promised King, your Saviour, has been born in Bethlehem today. Go now and look for the baby. You will find him asleep, lying in a manger."

Then, a huge crowd of angels appeared in the sky, singing, "Praise be to God. Peace to everyone on earth."

The angels disappeared and the sky went dark again. The shepherds knew they had to hurry to Bethlehem, to see this new baby. They made their sheep safe and set off.

In Bethlehem, they found Mary and Joseph, with their baby. He was asleep in a manger, just as the angel had said.

The shepherds told Mary and Joseph all the things the angel had told them. Then, they set off for the fields again. As they made their way back to their sheep, they sang songs praising God. They would never forget this night.

The three wise men

MATTHEW: 2

Far away to the east, some wise men, who
studied the skies, had noticed a special star.
They knew it was an important sign and
decided to follow it, to see where it led.
They travelled many days and nights and
eventually arrived in Jerusalem.

"Where is the baby, who is born to be King of the Jews?" they asked. "We have seen his star and we have come to worship him."

When Herod, who already was the King of the Jews, heard about the wise men, he was furious.

He called together all of his chief priests and advisors and asked them where this new king could be found.

"In the town of Bethlehem in Judea," they replied. "That is what God's prophets wrote."

So, Herod arranged a secret meeting with the three wise men. He wanted to know the exact time that the star had appeared, so that he could work out how old the baby was. Then, he sent them on to Bethlehem to find the baby. He pretended that he, too, wanted to see the baby and pay his respects. But he had something much more evil in mind!

The wise men left Jerusalem
and were overjoyed to see ahead
of them, the star they had noticed
in the east.

When it stopped over one of the
houses in Bethlehem, they knew that
they had finally found their King.

Inside the house, where Mary and Joseph were now staying, the three wise men knelt before the baby Jesus and gave him the presents they had brought – gold, sweet-smelling frankincense and a spicy-smelling ointment, called myrrh.

Not long afterwards, in a dream, God warned the wise men not to go back to Herod, but to journey home by another road.

When they left, God sent a messenger to warn Joseph, too.

"Herod will be looking for the child, in order to kill him. You must take him and Mary to Egypt, at once. Stay there, until I tell you it is safe to leave."

So, Joseph and Mary gathered their things together and fled towards Egypt.

My Father's house

LUKE: 2

After Herod's death, God's messenger told Mary and Joseph to return to their home in Galilee. So, Jesus grew up in Nazareth and was a very eager student.

When he was twelve years old, his parents took him to Jerusalem to celebrate the Feast of the Passover.

On the way back home, Mary and Joseph thought Jesus was travelling somewhere in their large family group and did not worry that they had not seen him for a while.

They journeyed for a whole day, before they realised that Jesus was missing. They started to look for him amongst their family and friends, but no one had seen him.

That night, they lay awake, unable to sleep for fear and worry.

Early next morning, they returned to Jerusalem and searched the whole city for him.

On the third day, they found him in the temple. He was sitting with the men who taught God's Laws, carefully listening to everything they had to say, as well as asking questions himself. Everyone who heard him was amazed at how much of the teachings he understood.

"Why have you worried us like this?" Mary asked him. "You must have known, Jesus, how anxious we would be."

Jesus seemed surprised.

"Surely you knew that I would be here, in my Father's house?" he said.

Joseph and Mary did not understand what Jesus meant and Jesus did not explain further. Then, they all journeyed back to Nazareth.

God's King is coming

MATTHEW: 3; MARK: 1; LUKE: 3; JOHN: 1

Mary's cousin, Elizabeth, had given birth to a son, called John and his father, Zechariah, brought him up to follow God's Laws.

When he was older, John went to live alone in the desert of Judea. He wore clothes of camel hair and ate locusts and wild honey. John was God's messenger and people came from Judea, Jerusalem and far and wide to hear him speak.

"God's King is coming soon," he would tell them. "Say sorry to God. Change your ways and be baptized, then God will forgive you the things that you have done wrong."

John took all those who wanted God's forgiveness to the banks of the River Jordan. He led them in and dipped their heads below the water. This was called 'baptism'. It was a sign that God had forgiven them their sins and had washed them away.

John taught people that they should share what they had with those less fortunate than themselves. Some of them began to wonder if he could be the promised King.

But John said, "I am here to tell you that someone much greater than I will come soon and I am not worthy to carry his shoes."

At this time, Jesus arrived from Nazareth and came to the River Jordan to be baptized by John. They had never met before, but John knew at once, that this was God's promised King.

"You should be baptizing me, Lord," said John.

But Jesus persuaded him.

Then, as Jesus came up out of the water, God's spirit came down upon him in the form of a dove and a voice came from Heaven, saying, "This is my own blessed Son and I am pleased with him."

Changed into wine

MARK: 1; JOHN: 2

Soon afterwards, John was put into prison.
So, Jesus went about Galilee preaching the
same message, "The Kingdom of God is near.
Change your ways and believe the good news!"

Along the way, he met people who were to
become his followers, including Andrew and
his brother, Simon (who Jesus called Peter),
John and Nathaneal.

One day, as he travelled through the country, Jesus was invited to a wedding in Cana, along with his mother and his friends. During the wedding feast, the wine ran out and Mary told Jesus of this. Nervously, Jesus began to speak, "It is not yet my time... " But Mary had already turned away to the servants and said, "Do exactly what he tells you to do."

Nearby stood six large water-jars. Guests had used the water from them to wash with before the meal, according to Jewish law. Now, the water-jars stood empty.

"Fill these jars with water," said Jesus, to the servants. "Then, pour out a little of the water and take it to the man in charge of the meal."

The servants did as they were told and took the water to the man.

It had changed into wine!

The man in charge called to the bridegroom.

"Everyone else serves the best wine first and keeps the ordinary wine until last. But you have saved the best until now!"

This was the first of the miracles that Jesus performed and only the servants who had drawn the water, knew Jesus' secret.

249

Chosen twelve

MATTHEW: 4, 10; MARK: 1, 3; LUKE: 5, 6

News about Jesus and his teachings quickly spread. He spoke with such authority and power, that crowds of people came from all around to hear him speak.

One day, Jesus was preaching on the shores of Lake Gennesaret. The crowd got bigger and bigger and began to push closer and closer to the shore. Jesus noticed two fishing boats pulled up onto the beach. The fishermen were nearby, washing their nets. Jesus stepped into one of the boats and asked Simon, the fisherman, to take him a little way out onto the lake. And from there, sitting in the boat, he was able to continue teaching the people.

251

When he had finished, Jesus told Simon to row further out and drop his fishing nets into the lake.

"We have worked all night, without any luck," Simon said. "But, if you say so, we will try again."

Simon and his brother, Andrew, took the boat out further and let the nets down into the water. Immediately, they filled with such a huge number of fish, that the nets almost broke and the boat started to sink!

"Come, help us!" the two men shouted to James and John, who were in the other boat. The fishermen were astonished.

As the boats reached the shore again, loaded with their catch, Jesus said, "Do not be afraid. I want you all to follow me. From now on, you will be catchers of people, not fish."

So, the four men left their boats on the shore and became followers of Jesus.

One day, Jesus went to see a tax collector, called Levi and told him to leave everything behind and follow him. So, Levi got straight up and did just that!

Tax collectors were not popular with the Jewish people, as they collected taxes for the Romans. Many made extra money by over-charging the Jews. So, when Levi gave a feast for Jesus at his house, some of the more religious people were disgusted that Jesus went.

"Why do you eat and drink with such outcasts, Jesus?" they demanded, angrily.

"People who are well do not need a doctor," replied Jesus. "Like a doctor, I heal the sick. I do not need to help those who have already *found* God. I have come to help those, who are *far away* from God."

On some nights, when Jesus had finished teaching and the crowds had gone home, he often went up into the hills, where he could be quiet and pray. Sometimes, he prayed all night.

Once, Jesus called his followers together. He had chosen twelve of the most loyal to be his special friends or disciples. These twelve were: Simon (whom Jesus named Peter) and his brother Andrew, James and John, Philip and Bartholomew, Matthew, Thomas, James (son of Alphaeus), Simon, Judas (son of James) and Judas Iscariot.

Jesus explained to them why God had sent him to earth. The disciples became his closest friends and travelled with him wherever he went, witnessing the wonderful things that he did.

The paralyzed man

MATTHEW: 9; MARK: 2; LUKE: 5

News spread across the land that Jesus could cure people who were sick and diseased. Soon, crowds came from far and wide, just to be touched by him.

One day, Jesus was teaching at a house. So many people arrived to hear him, that the house quickly filled up. There was no room left anywhere. Even outside, people waited in crowds just to see and touch Jesus.

Then, four men arrived. They were carrying a friend on his bedmat. The poor man was paralyzed and the friends truly believed that Jesus would be able to cure him. But, try as they might, they could not find a way through the crowd and into the house, to see Jesus.

259

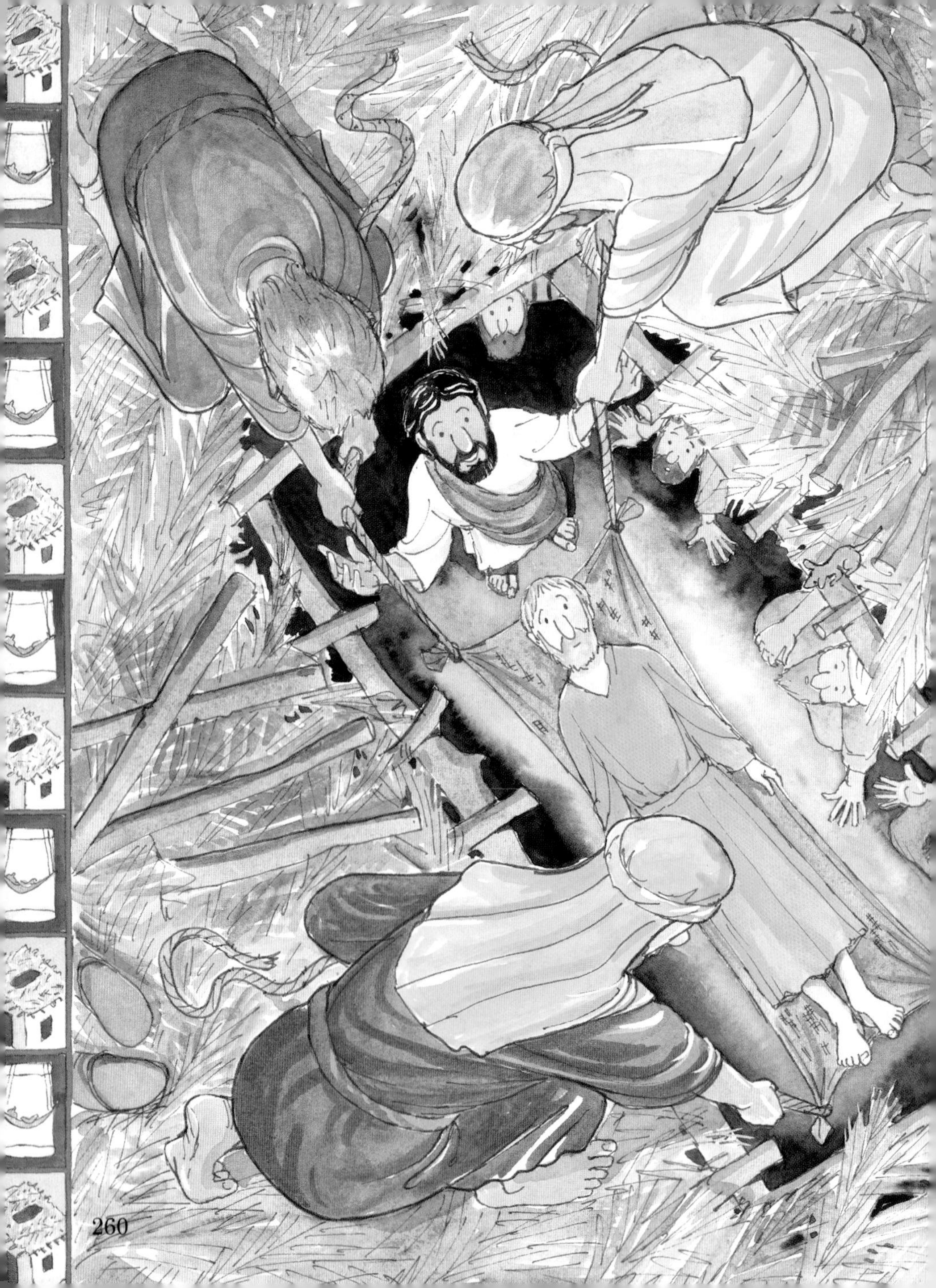

The men did not give up. Instead, they carried their friend up onto the flat roof, made a hole and lowered the paralyzed man down to where Jesus was speaking and teaching.

When Jesus saw what the men had done, he was moved by their faith. How caring they were, to do so much for their friend. Jesus turned to the man on the mat and said, "Your sins are forgiven."

There were also some teachers of the Law in the house and they were furious that Jesus would dare to say this.

"How can he talk like this?" they thought. "Only God, Himself can forgive sins."

Jesus knew exactly what
the teachers were thinking.

"Why do you feel like that?"
he asked. "Tell me, which do you think
it is easier to do – to say to this man, 'Your
sins are forgiven', or to make him get up and
walk again? I want you to understand that
God has given the Son of Man the power
to do both these things."

Then, Jesus spoke to the man on the mat. "Get up, pick up your mat and go home!"

As they watched, the man did as Jesus said. Everyone was amazed. and praised God, saying, "We have never seen anything like this before."

Our Father in heaven

MATTHEW: 5, 6, 7; LUKE: 6

Jesus often went up into the hills around Galilee. One day, a crowd gathered to hear him speak to them about blessings from God.

"Happy are the poor in spirit, for theirs is the Kingdom of heaven," said Jesus. "God will comfort everyone who mourns and reward those who are humble.

"Happy are they who want to do God's desire, for they shall be fulfilled. Show mercy to others and mercy will be shown to you. The pure in heart shall see God and those who work for peace will be called God's children. If you are ill-treated for doing what He asks, the Kingdom of heaven will belong to you. Be happy, for great is your reward in heaven."

Jesus used everyday pictures to help the people understand his teachings more easily.

"You are like the salt we put in our food to stop it rotting. You will keep God's world from going bad," he said.

"Your kind deeds will be like lamps shining out in the darkness, lighting up God's world. People will thank God for them.

"God has given you Laws and you must follow them in all ways. God says, 'You shall not murder anyone.' But it is also wrong to feel angry enough to *want* to murder someone. God wants us to love our enemies and to show kindness to those who do us wrong."

Then, Jesus spoke to them about prayer.

"Go somewhere quiet when you want to pray and speak to God. He knows exactly what you need. This is how you should pray to Him:

Our Father in heaven,
May Your holy name be honored;
May Your kingdom come;
May Your will be done on earth,
as it is in heaven.
Give us today, the food we need.
Forgive us the wrongs we have done,
As we forgive the wrongs that others
have done to us.
Do not bring us to the point of temptation,
But keep us safe from evil.

Ask and trust God," Jesus said, "and He will not let you down.

"Do not store up money or buy things here on earth that could be taken from you. Instead, store up your riches in heaven, where God will give you everything you need," said Jesus.

"Do not worry where your next meal will come from. Look around you, at the birds in the air...

"... they do not sow seeds or gather a harvest, but God takes care of them. You are far more important to Him than they are.

"Do not worry about what you are going to wear. Look at the way God has clothed the flowers in the fields. They do not work, but He takes care of them all the same. Put your trust in God and He will provide you with all these things."

Good, solid foundations

MATTHEW: 7

People loved to listen to Jesus telling them stories. "If you follow my teachings," he said, "you will be like a person, building a house on good, solid foundations, like in this story...

"Two men decided to build houses for themselves. The wise man built his house on rock. The rains came, the floods rose and the winds blew, but his house stood firm.

"But, if you ignore what I say, you are like the other man. He was foolish enough to build his house on sand. There were no foundations and, when the rains, floods and winds came, his house fell down!"

Everyone who listened to Jesus' stories was amazed at how simply they told the truth of God.

A Roman officer

MATTHEW: 8; LUKE: 7

Once, when Jesus had finished talking, he went to a town called Capernaum, where there lived a Roman officer.

Generally, the Jews hated the Roman soldiers, but this particular Roman was very different. He was kind to the local people.

One day, his servant fell ill. When the officer heard that Jesus was in town, he asked his Jewish friends if they would go to Jesus, to see if he would come and heal the man.

"Please come," the friends begged Jesus. "This Roman officer really deserves your help. He is a good man. He paid for a synagogue to be built for us."

So, Jesus agreed and set off towards the soldier's house with them.

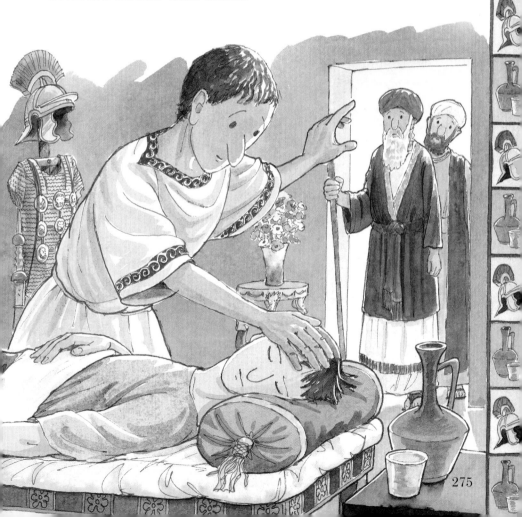

They had almost reached the house, when some more friends of the officer arrived.

The Roman had asked his friends to tell Jesus not to come into his house. He felt that he was not good enough for Jesus to enter, or good enough to bring the message to Jesus in person. He said that he knew his servant would get better if Jesus gave the order, like a soldier.

Jesus was amazed. He turned and spoke to the crowd that was following him.

"I have never seen faith like this," he said, "not even among the Jews." Then, he sent this message back to the officer, "As you have believed in me, it shall be done."

When the messengers returned to the officer's house, they found that the servant was well again, just as Jesus had promised.

A fierce storm

MATTHEW: 8; MARK: 4; LUKE: 8

One evening, when Jesus had finished his teachings, he suggested to his followers that they get into a boat and cross to the other side of the lake.

So, off they set and, with the gentle water lapping against the boat's side, it was not long before Jesus fell fast asleep. It had been a long day and he was very tired.

After a while, the wind suddenly changed. It grew much stronger and whipped the water up into huge waves. A fierce storm blew up. The waves grew bigger and bigger and washed over the sides of the little boat. But all the noise and commotion did not wake Jesus.

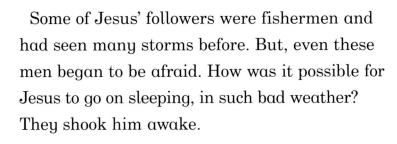

Some of Jesus' followers were fishermen and had seen many storms before. But, even these men began to be afraid. How was it possible for Jesus to go on sleeping, in such bad weather? They shook him awake.

"Master, wake up!" they shouted. "We are all going to die."

Jesus stood up. "Be still!" he commanded the waves and the wind.

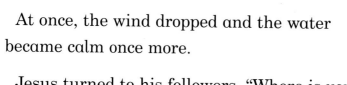

At once, the wind dropped and the water became calm once more.

Jesus turned to his followers. "Where is your faith?" he asked them. They did not reply. They stared in amazement and awe at this man, who looked just like them, but who gave orders that the wind and waves obeyed. Who could he be, to have such power?

Only believe

MATTHEW: 9; MARK: 5; LUKE: 8

When Jesus returned to the side of the lake,
a large crowd was waiting for him. Among them
was Jairus, a leader from the local synagogue.
He threw himself down in front of Jesus and
begged him to return home with him.

"My only daughter is very ill," he said. "She's
only twelve years old and is dying."

Jesus set off with the man at once. The crowd followed, jostling him as he went.

In the crowd was a woman, who had been ill for many years. She knew that Jesus had the power to cure her, so she came up behind him and touched his coat. She was instantly healed.

Even though there were many people, bumping against him, Jesus felt the woman's touch.

"Who touched my coat?" he asked.

"Who can say?" replied Peter. "There are so many people around you."

"Someone wanted to be healed," said Jesus, "and they touched me. Who was it?"

When the woman heard Jesus speak, she knew she had been found out. Nervously, she stepped forward and explained why she had touched his coat and how she had immediately been healed.

"Your faith has made you well again," Jesus said to her. "Go in peace."

As Jesus was speaking to the woman, a messenger arrived from Jairus' house.

"Your daughter has died," he said to Jairus. "Do not bother the Teacher any longer."

Hearing this, Jesus said to Jairus, "Do not be afraid. Only believe and she will live again."

They all hurried to the house, where they found everyone outside, weeping.

"Do not cry," Jesus told them. "The girl is not dead. She is just sleeping." He went into her room, took hold of her hand and said, "Get up, child." The girl sat up at once.

"Give her something to eat," said Jesus. The girl's parents were amazed. They could hardly believe what they had seen.

The Good Shepherd

MATTHEW: 18; LUKE: 15; JOHN: 10

All sorts of people came to Jesus and he never turned anyone away. But some of the teachers of the Law grumbled. Why was he mixing with people like tax collectors and wrong-doers? So, one day, to help to explain to them, Jesus told these teachers a story.

"If a shepherd has a hundred sheep," said Jesus, "and one of them gets lost, what would the shepherd do? He would leave the other ninety-nine sheep, safe in the field, and go off to look for the lost sheep. He would not give up looking until he found it.

"Then, the good shepherd would be happy," continued Jesus. "He would lift the sheep onto his shoulders and carry it home, calling to his friends and neighbors to come and celebrate with him for he had found his lost sheep.'

"It is like that in heaven," said Jesus. "I am the Good Shepherd. I have come to look for people, who have wandered away from God, to bring them home to Him. A good shepherd never leaves his flock, even when wolves attack. The shepherd knows every single one of his sheep. The people who follow me are my sheep. I lead them and I protect them. I am willing to give up my life for them."

291

The seeds that fall in good soil

MATTHEW: 13; MARK: 4; LUKE: 8

Jesus told many stories, or parables, to explain what God's kingdom was like.

"Once, there was a man," said Jesus, "who went out to sow corn. As he scattered it around, some of it fell onto the path. Birds flew down and ate it.

"Some seed fell onto rocky ground. It soon sprouted, but there was not enough soil for it to take root well. So, when the hot sun came out, the young plants dried up.

"Some of the seed fell among weeds, which choked the plants as they grew. And some of the seed fell onto good soil. The seeds grew into healthy plants and produced lots of corn."

Then Jesus explained what the parable meant.

"People who hear God's message, but do not understand it, are like the seeds on the path. They do not accept it. The seeds that fall on rocky ground are like people who are glad when they hear the message, but, as soon as trouble comes along, they give up. The seeds that fall among weeds are like people who let their love of money and other worries smother the message.

"The seeds that fall in good soil are like people who hear what God is saying. The way they live shows that they understand Him and are putting His message into practice."

"I am the farmer..."

MATTHEW: 13

Jesus told another parable to explain about God's Kingdom.

"A man sowed good seed in his field," said Jesus. But, he had an enemy and, one night, when everyone was asleep, the enemy came and sowed weeds among the newly planted seed.

"When the plants started to grow, the farm workers noticed the weeds and asked the farmer, 'Where have the weeds come from? You sowed good seed. Shall we pull them out?'

"The farmer said, 'No! Leave them. You might pull up some wheat as well. When harvest comes, we will get the harvest workers to pull out the weeds first and burn them. Then, we will easily see where the wheat is and be able to gather it and store it in my barn'."

Later, when the crowd had gone home and Jesus' friends were alone with him, they asked him what the story of the weeds meant.

"I am the farmer, sowing the good seed, spreading the message of God," said Jesus. "The field is the world. The good seed is the people who believe God's message. The weeds are those who belong to God's enemy, the Evil One. The harvest will come at the end of time. The harvest workers are God's angels and they will sort out God's people from those who have turned away from Him or done evil things!"

Five thousand people

MATTHEW: 14; MARK: 6; LUKE: 9; JOHN: 6

As time passed, the crowds, who came to listen
to Jesus, grew larger and larger. Jesus spoke
for long hours, but time passed quickly,
without people realising it. On one occasion,
Jesus was teaching by Lake Galilee. At sunset,
there was still a large crowd gathered round
him. It had been a long day and they were all
hungry.

"Send the people away, so that they can go to the farms and villages to find food," said the disciples.

"You, yourselves, should give them something to eat," replied Jesus.

"Where can we go and buy enough food to feed all of these people?" asked the disciples.

Then, the disciple, Andrew, spoke, "Here is a small boy, with five barley loaves and two small fish. But it certainly isn't enough to feed all these people."

"Tell the crowd to sit down on the grass," Jesus told his disciples. He took the bread and fish and thanked God for them.

Then, Jesus gave the food to the disciples who kept breaking them and giving them to the people. Everyone ate as much as they wanted to. And, when the leftovers were collected, they filled twelve whole baskets.

Five thousand people were fed that day.

Moses and the prophet Elijah

MATTHEW: 17; MARK: 9; LUKE: 9

Jesus knew that word of his teachings was
spreading fast. One day, he asked his disciples,
"Who do people say that I am?"

"It is said that you are John the Baptist or
one of the prophets come back to life," they
told him.

"And you?" Jesus asked them. "Who do you
think I am?"

304

"You are the King that God promised,"
answered Peter. His reply pleased Jesus and
he knew that it was time to prepare his disciples
for what lay ahead.

"I must travel soon to Jerusalem," said Jesus.
"The priests and the teachers of the law do not
believe that I am God's Son. They will put me
to death, but, after three days, I shall rise and
live again."

"If you want to follow me, you must expect hardships," Jesus told his friends. "You must expect to suffer, too."

About a week later, Jesus went up onto a hill with Peter, James and John. As he knelt praying, Jesus' face and clothes changed and became dazzling white.

Suddenly, two other shining white figures appeared—Moses and the prophet Elijah. They spoke to Jesus about God's plans for him and about Jesus' own death.

Peter, James and John had fallen fast asleep. When they awoke and saw the figures, they were very frightened. Then, a cloud passed across the sky and from it, a voice spoke;

"This is my Son. Listen to what he has to say." Then, the vision vanished and Jesus and his friends were alone.

My son
was lost

LUKE: 15

Every day, more and more people came to hear
Jesus speak, including many outcasts and
wrong-doers. The Pharisees, the Jewish teachers
of the Laws, were always complaining to one
another, "Jesus is not a good teacher. See the
bad company he keeps." So, Jesus told them
this story to explain why.

There was once a man with two sons. One day,
the younger son said, "Father, I'd like my share
of our property." So the father divided up his
wealth and gave one half to each son.

It was not long before the younger son left
home and went travelling. He had a wonderful
time and, soon, all his money was gone.

Then, famine swept the country and the younger son could only get a job looking after pigs. He was so hungry that he could have eaten the bean pods that he fed to them.

"What am I doing?" he thought to himself. "Back home, even my father's servants have food to spare. Here I am, with nothing to eat. I will go home and admit to my father that I wronged him and God. I will tell him that I am sorry. I do not deserve to be his son, but he might hire me to work for him."

So, he packed up the few belongings that he had and went back home.

The son was still a long way from home, when his father saw him. The father was overcome with happiness and rushed out to meet his son. He threw his arms around him and hugged him. The son said sorry, just as he had planned, but his father just called for his servants.

"Bring new clothes," he ordered. "Kill the best calf and prepare a celebration meal. I thought my son was lost, or even dead. But he's alive and he's home again! Let the feasting begin!"

Meanwhile, the elder son had been working away in the fields. As he neared home, he heard the sounds of music and laughter coming from the house.

"What's happening?" the son asked a servant.

"Your brother has come home to us and your father is celebrating," replied the servant. The elder brother was so angry, that he refused to go into the house.

His father came out to see what was wrong.

"All these years, I have worked for you like a slave," he told his father. "And I have never disobeyed you. You have never had a celebration for me, but you do it for that useless brother of mine!"

"My son, you know everything I own is yours," his father said, "but we must celebrate. Your brother was lost and now he's found again."

The good Samaritan

LUKE: 10

Jesus was so popular with the people that the religious leaders became jealous of him. They wanted to get rid of him and some even wished for his death. Others tried to catch him out with difficult questions, such as, "What do I need to do to have eternal life?"

"What does God's Law say you should do?" Jesus asked the leader in return.

"I must love God with all my heart and strength and mind," answered the man. "And I must love my neighbor as much as myself. But what does that mean? Who is my neighbor?"

To answer the question, Jesus did what he often did. He told a story.

"There was once a man, who was on a journey from Jerusalem to Jericho. On the way, he was attacked by robbers. They beat him and left him for dead. Soon after, a priest passed along the road. When he saw the man, he walked by on the other side.

"Then, a teacher of the Law came along," said Jesus. "He did nothing to help the man, either. He, too, crossed over and continued his journey.

"Later, a Samaritan came along. He saw
the man and immediately felt sorry for him.
He gently cleaned up the man's wounds.

"And with great care, he placed the man on
his own donkey and took him to a nearby inn.

319

"Next day," continued Jesus, "when the Samaritan had to leave, he gave the innkeeper some money and said, 'Take care of this man. When I come this way again, I will pay you any extra that you have to spend.'

"The Samaritan did all this, even though the man was a Jew and the Jews did not like the Samaritans."

Jesus looked at the leader who had asked him the question and said, "Who would you say behaved like a real neighbor?"

"The good Samaritan," replied the man.

"Then go," said Jesus, "and try to be more like him."

The raising of Lazarus

LUKE: 10; JOHN: 11

Jesus liked to visit some friends, who lived in a place named Bethany, near Jerusalem. There were two sisters called Mary and Martha and their brother, Lazarus.

Once, Martha was bustling around, preparing food, while Mary simply sat at Jesus' feet, listening to what he had to say.

"Why don't you tell Mary to come and help me?" Martha said to Jesus, angrily.

"Mary is quite right to listen to me," replied Jesus. "You should not worry so much about worldly things and come and listen to what I have to say, while you can."

One day, Jesus received a message from the two sisters.

"Lazarus is very ill," it said. "Please come to us soon."

Jesus loved Lazarus and his sisters very much, so, naturally, the disciples expected that he would hurry to Bethany. But Jesus stayed where he was for two days, before setting out. He knew that Lazarus, by then, would be dead.

Jesus' friends did not want him to go anywhere near Jerusalem. They knew that his enemies were there, plotting against him. But when they realized that he was determined to go, Thomas said, "Let us all go. We will die together."

As they arrived in Bethany, Martha rushed out to meet them, but Mary stayed in the house.

Martha spoke to Jesus, "If only you had been here, my brother would not have died." By then, Lazarus had been in his grave for four days.

"Your brother will live again," Jesus told her.

"I know that he will live again on the last day," said Martha.

"I am the Resurrection and the Life," replied Jesus. "Whoever believes in me will never really die. Do you believe this?"

"I do, Lord," said Martha. "I finally understand.
I believe you are the Christ, God's Son.

"I believe that you have come to give new and
eternal life to all who believe in you."

Mary and Martha were so upset that they
wept bitterly.

Friends, who had come to comfort the two sisters, were crying, too. When Jesus saw this, he was moved and also wept. He had loved Lazarus very much. Seeing Jesus so upset, some people wondered why he had not come sooner and stopped Lazarus from dying.

Then, Jesus made his way to the grave, which was a cave, with a stone covering the entrance.

"Take the stone away," ordered Jesus.

"But, Lord, he has been dead for four days now," said Martha. "There will be a bad smell."

Jesus began to pray. "Dear God. I know that you are my father. But for the sake of the people here, show them a sign that you have sent me."

Then, he commanded, "Lazarus! Come out!"

329

Immediately, Lazarus walked from the tomb. He was still covered in the cloth that had been wrapped around his dead body.

"Unwind those grave clothes and set him free," said Jesus.

Many people, who were present at this scene, now truly believed that Jesus had been sent by God. But some people did not. They went to the chief priests and told them about the raising of Lazarus. The priests held a meeting.

"Before long," they said, "everyone will believe in this man and follow him. Then, the Romans will think we have started a rebellion."

So, from then on, the priests began to plot Jesus' death.

Have mercy on us

LUKE: 17

On his way to Jerusalem one day, Jesus came across ten men, who had a terrible skin disease called leprosy.

"Have mercy on us, Jesus," the men cried.

"Go and let the priests look at your bodies," Jesus told them. Only the priests could certify that they were truly healed.

As the men hurried to the priests, their skins were healed. One man, a Samaritan, came back to thank Jesus.

"Why has only one man come to thank God, when ten men were healed?" commented Jesus to his disciples. Turning to the man, he said, "Go, your faith has cured you."

Zacchaeus, the chief tax collector

LUKE: 19

Soon, Jesus passed through Jericho. Zacchaeus, the chief tax collector, lived there and he was among the crowd that was trying to catch a glimpse of Jesus. Zacchaeus was quite short and couldn't see over the heads of the crowd. So, he decided to run ahead and climb a tree to get a better view.

When Jesus passed by, he said, "Come down, Zacchaeus. I wish to stay at your house today."

People were shocked! How could Jesus mix with people like that?

But meeting Jesus changed Zacchaeus.

He offered to give half of his money to the poor and to repay four times as much to those from whom he had taken wrongly.

Jesus turned to the crowd and said, "The Son of Man seeks and saves that which is lost."

Entering Jerusalem

MATTHEW: 21; MARK: 11; LUKE: 19; JOHN: 12

On the outskirts of Jerusalem, Jesus spoke to two of his disciples.

"Go on ahead of us," he said. "At the edge of the next village, you will find a donkey. Bring it to me and, if anyone asks you why you are taking it, tell them that I sent you and that I will return it to them."

The men found the donkey, threw their cloaks over its back and helped Jesus to climb on.

When the people realized that Jesus had arrived in Jerusalem, they came out to greet him. Some threw their cloaks down in front of him, as he rode along. Others laid down palm branches. "Praise God," they shouted. "God's King is coming!"

On entering Jerusalem, Jesus went straight to the temple. He found it full of men buying and selling doves. Others were exchanging money for special temple coins.

Jesus was furious and began to drive them out. "This is a place of prayer," he cried, "and you have made it into a den of thieves!"

After this, Jesus healed people who were ill.

When the chief priests heard what he had
done, they were really angry. With so many
people following Jesus, the priests saw him as
a real threat to their power. They were now
even more determined to kill him than before.

339

Thirty pieces of silver

MATTHEW: 26; MARK: 14; LUKE: 22

It was nearly time for the Feast of the Passover.
As the disciples bought food at the market,
Judas Iscariot crept quietly away to see the
chief priests. Evil had entered his heart and he
no longer believed that Jesus was from God.

When Judas told the priests why he had
gone to see them, they were very happy.

"How much would you pay me to give Jesus
over to you quietly?" Judas asked the priests.

The priests counted out thirty pieces of silver
and gave them to Judas.

"I'll take you to him when he is alone, so that
there is little trouble," Judas promised. And
from then on, he started to look for the right
moment to betray Jesus.

The last meal

MATTHEW: 26; MARK: 14; LUKE: 22; JOHN: 13

On the day before the Passover, Jesus told Peter and John to prepare for the meal.

"But where shall we eat?" they asked him.

"As you enter Jerusalem," replied Jesus, "you will meet a man carrying a water-jar. He will take you to a house with an upstairs room. Prepare everything there for us."

That evening, before the meal, Jesus knew
that the disciples had been quarrelling about
which of them was the best. So, Jesus calmly
took a basin of water and began to wash their
feet. Peter was shocked.

"I can't let *you* wash my feet," he said.

"I want you to follow my example," said Jesus.
"Whoever wants to be great in the Kingdom of
God, must learn how to serve others, as I am
serving you."

Then, they sat down to eat.

During the meal, Jesus said, "One of you is going to betray me, one who is eating with me now."

Peter whispered to John, "Ask him who it is." And John did.

Jesus replied, "The one who I give this bread to," and he gave each of them a piece of bread dipped in herbs.

So, still they did not know, but later, John remembered that Jesus gave the first piece to Judas and had said, "Go and do what you have to do."

None of the others realized at the time what this had meant. The disciples thought that Jesus was telling Judas, who looked after their money, to go and buy more food. They saw Judas leave the room and knew it was night.

345

Then, Jesus promised the disciples that God's spirit would always be with them and not to be afraid. He knew that this would be the last meal he shared with them. He took a piece of bread, thanked God for it and broke it into pieces.

"This is my body," he said. "Like this bread, I will be broken. I will die for you. Do this in remembrance of me."

Then, he lifted a cup of wine, thanked God
again and passed it round.

"This is my blood," he said. "It will be spilled
for many people. Drink it in remembrance of
me, we shall not drink together again until we
are in God's Kingdom."

A garden called Gethsemane

MATTHEW: 26; MARK: 14; LUKE: 22

After the meal, Jesus climbed up the Mount of Olives with his friends, until they came to a garden called Gethsemane.

As they walked, Jesus spoke to them, "This very night, you will all run away and leave me."

"I would never do that!" protested Peter.

"Before the cock crows," said Jesus, "you will say three times that you do not know me."

"Even if I have to die, I will never say that!" cried Peter. The other disciples agreed.

At Gethsemane, Jesus took Peter, James and John with him, leaving the rest to wait outside.

"My heart is full of sadness," said Jesus. "I must go and pray. Stay here and keep watch." He went a little further and knelt to pray.

"Father," Jesus prayed, "if it is possible, save me from this death, but only if it is your will."

Then, he went back to Peter, James and John and found them fast asleep. He woke them up and asked them again to keep watch. This time, Jesus went deeper into the orchard to pray. Twice more he came back to the three disciples, only to find them asleep again. As he woke them for the third time, Jesus heard the sound of voices and saw the light of torches coming nearer. The temple guards and the chief priests were heading towards Jesus, they had come to arrest him – Judas was leading them.

"The man you want, is the man I kiss," said Judas to the guards. He walked over to Jesus and kissed him on the cheek. The guards quickly closed round Jesus, but he did not resist. Peter drew his sword and cut off the ear of the chief priest's servant.

"That's enough!" said Jesus and he reached out and healed the man's ear. Then, he turned to the priests and guards.

"Why have you come armed with swords, as if I were a criminal?" he asked. But the priests and guards marched him off into the night, without a word. Then, all of Jesus' friends ran away, just as Jesus had said they would.

I do not know him

MATTHEW: 26; MARK: 14; LUKE: 22, 23; JOHN: 18

The guards took Jesus to the High Priest's house. Peter followed and slipped into the courtyard. He joined a group of people around the fire. Suddenly, a servant girl noticed him and began to stare.

"Weren't you with Jesus?" she asked.

"No, I do not even know him," replied Peter.

Then, a short time after, another person asked him, "Weren't you a follower of Jesus?"

Again, Peter denied it.

An hour later, a third person said, "You come from Galilee. You *must* know Jesus."

"No, I do not know him!" cried Peter.

At that very moment, the cock crowed and Peter remembered what Jesus had said. He left the courtyard, broke down and wept.

Meanwhile, the Jewish Council was trying to find evidence to convict Jesus and put him to death. Many false witnesses came forward and told lies, but this was not enough. Finally, the High Priest questioned Jesus himself.

"Aren't you going to answer these charges?" he demanded. Jesus did not reply.

"I am putting you under oath," said the High Priest. "Are you the Son of God?"

"You say that I am," said Jesus. "From now on, you will see the Son of Man sitting at God's side."

Furious, the High Priest spoke to the Council. "The prisoner claims to be equal with God," he said. "We do not need any more witnesses after this outburst. What do you think?"

"Guilty!" the Council all shouted. "He must die!"

As soon as Judas heard that Jesus had been sentenced to death, he was overcome with guilt and grief. He went to the priests and threw the thirty pieces of silver onto the floor. "I have sinned!" he cried. "I have betrayed an innocent man." The priests laughed at him. Then, Judas went away and hanged himself.

Meanwhile, Jesus was taken before the Roman governor, Pontius Pilate. The Jews could not execute Jesus without the governor's agreement.

"He claims to be a king," they told Pilate.

"Are you the King of the Jews?" asked Pilate.

"That's what you say," replied Jesus and then
he kept silent. He refused to answer any more
of Pilate's questions. Pilate could find nothing
that Jesus had done wrong and wanted to set
him free.

Father, forgive them

MATTHEW: 27; MARK: 15; LUKE: 23; JOHN: 18

It was a Jewish custom to pardon and set free a prisoner at the time of the Passover. Pilate wanted to free Jesus, but the Jewish leaders were determined to get their way.

"Jesus must die," they said. "He claims to be the Son of God, which is against our law."

When he heard this, Pilate was afraid. He ordered that Jesus be whipped. The soldiers made a crown out of thorns for his head and mocked him, saying, "Hail, King of the Jews!" Then, Pilate presented him to the crowd.

"Do you want me to kill your king?" he asked.

"Crucify him!" came the reply. "Crucify him and free Barabbas, instead!"

Then, crying, "Jesus' death is on your hands," Pilate freed the murderer, Barabbas and the soldiers led Jesus away.

Jesus was forced to carry a huge wooden cross through the streets to Golgotha, the place of execution. As he passed, people mocked him and spat at him. He stumbled and fell and the soldiers ordered one of the crowd, a man called Simon of Cyrene, to carry the cross for him.

A group of weeping women followed Jesus. He turned to them, saying, "Do not weep for me, rather weep for yourselves and your children."

At last, they came to Golgotha. There, guards nailed Jesus' hands and feet to the cross. They nailed a notice above his head, which read, "This is Jesus, the King of the Jews." Jesus was in great pain. The guards offered drugged wine but he refused. Then, the guards set up the cross, with a thief on either side of him. "Father, forgive them," he prayed. "They know not what they are doing."

The Son
of God

MATTHEW: 27; MARK: 15; LUKE: 23; JOHN: 19

People jeered at Jesus, calling out, "If you are
the Son of God, come down from the cross and
we will believe in you." One of the thieves joined
in with the jeers as well.

But the other thief said, "We deserve
our punishment. This man has
done nothing wrong.
Remember me, Jesus,
when you come again
as King."

"I give you my promise,"
replied Jesus. "Today, you
will be with me in paradise."

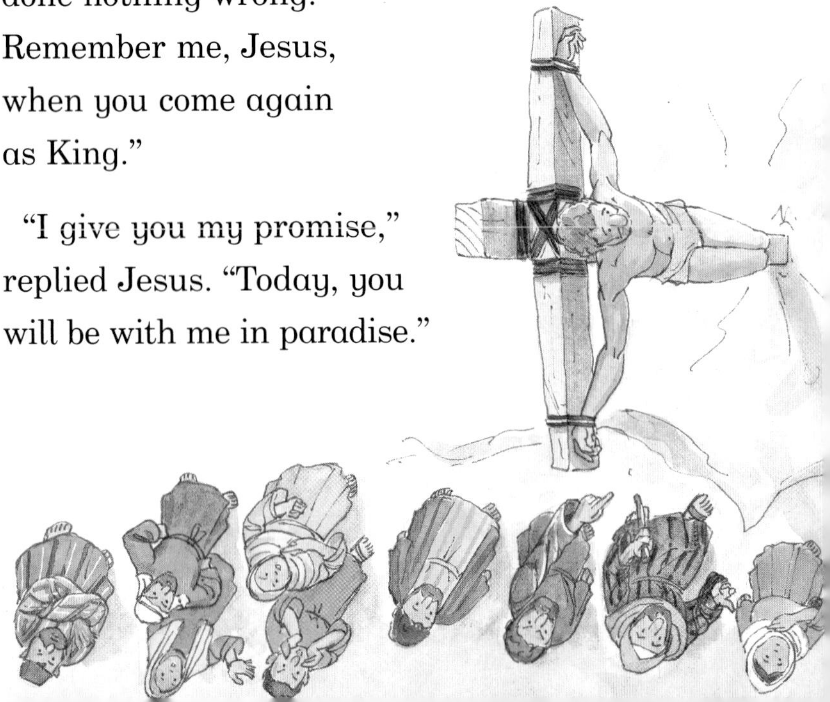

Jesus looked down at Mary, his mother, who was leaning on John's arm and said, "Mother, here is your son." Jesus looked at John and said, "Here is your mother." Then, John took Mary away to live in his home.

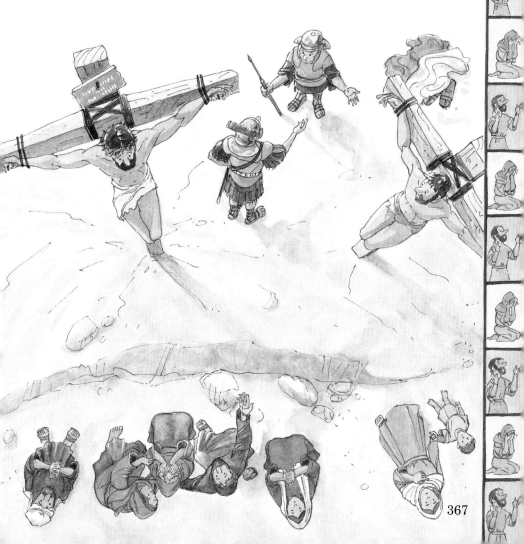

Beneath the cross, the soldiers were throwing dice to win Jesus' seamless robe.

Suddenly, at twelve o'clock, the sky went dark and a great shadow blotted out the sun. For three hours, there was barely any light. Jesus cried aloud, "My God! My God! Why have you left me?" A little later, he called out, "I thirst!" and a soldier soaked a sponge in wine, stuck it on a stick and held it to his lips.

At three o'clock, Jesus gave a terrible cry and said, "It is finished! Father, into your hands, I place my spirit!" Then, he died.

A Roman soldier, who was standing nearby, heard Jesus and said, "This man was truly the Son of God!"

Another soldier pierced Jesus' side with a spear, to make sure that he was dead. Finally, they gently lowered his body down from the cross.

The tomb

MATTHEW: 27, 28; MARK: 15, 16; LUKE: 23, 24; JOHN: 19, 20

Later that day, Joseph from Arimathea arrived. He was a follower of Jesus and had permission from Pilate to take Jesus' body away for burial.

Joseph and Nicodemus prepared Jesus' body, according to Jewish custom. They wrapped it in fine linen and special spices and took it to a tomb, that had just been dug out of the rock. Mary Magdalene and some other women watched, as a large stone was rolled across the entrance and the tomb was sealed.

The next day was the Jewish Sabbath and the Jews asked Pilate to have the tomb guarded. They remembered only too well what Jesus had said, about rising from the dead!

At sunrise on Sunday, Mary Magdalene and some women returned to the tomb.

When they reached it, they found that the stone covering the entrance had been rolled back and the guards had disappeared.

Inside, the women found an angel.

"Do not be afraid," said the angel. "Jesus is not here. He is risen from the dead. Look, this is where his body was. Go and tell his disciples the good news. You will see him soon in Galilee, just as he promised."

The women, filled with fear and happiness, ran back to tell the disciples.

On hearing the news, John and Peter ran to the tomb and saw the burial clothes lying there. They believed what had been said to them and hurried away, leaving Mary Magdalene weeping by the entrance.

Then a voice asked her, "Why are you crying?"

Mary thought that it must be the gardener.

"Sir, if you've taken my Lord, please tell me where to find him," she said, "and I will go and take him away."

"Mary!" came the reply. It was Jesus! She was overjoyed.

"Go and tell my friends you have seen me," Jesus told her.

375

Risen from the dead

MATTHEW: 28; MARK: 16; LUKE: 24; JOHN: 20, 21

Later that same day, Jesus appeared to two of
his followers, as they were walking home from
Jerusalem. They did not recognize him and
asked him if he would like to eat with them.
As Jesus blessed the bread and broke it, the two
men realized who he was. Then, Jesus vanished.
The two men rushed back to Jerusalem, to tell
their friends what had happened.

As the men were telling their story, Jesus suddenly appeared to them all, saying, "Peace be with you." The disciples were really afraid, as they thought they were seeing a ghost.

"See and touch my hands and feet," said Jesus, showing them the nail marks. "Ghosts are not made of flesh and blood."

Then, he sat and ate with them and they knew that this really was Jesus, who was risen from the dead.

377

Thomas wasn't there that night and when he was told what the disciples had seen, he did not believe it.

"Unless I see and touch the wounds myself," he said, "I will not believe."

A week later, the disciples were gathered together again. Jesus appeared to them and all Thomas' doubts vanished.

The next time Jesus appeared was in Galilee.

The disciples had been fishing on the lake all night, but had caught nothing. In the morning, a man called to them from the shore. It was Jesus.

"Throw out your nets on the right," the man said. "You will make a catch." And he was right!

Then, they ate a breakfast of bread and fish with him on the shore. Three times, Jesus asked Peter, "Do you love me?"

And three times, Peter replied, "You know I do." He knew he was forgiven.

"Then look after my followers," Jesus told him.

The Holy Spirit

ACTS: 1-2

For forty days, Jesus appeared many times to his disciples. They now knew that Jesus had come back to life. But now it was time for him to leave them. So, Jesus led his friends to the Mount of Olives.

"Soon," he said, "God will send you his Holy Spirit. You will be given the power to tell the peoples of the world what I have done and what I will do for them."

As he finished speaking, Jesus was taken up to heaven and a cloud hid him from their view.

Then, two men appeared, all in white. "Jesus has gone to heaven," they said. "He will return one day in the same way you saw him leave."

When the day of Pentecost came, all Jesus'
friends met in a house in Jerusalem. Suddenly,
the sound of a strong wind came from heaven.
It seemed as if flames appeared and touched
each of the disciples. They were filled with the
Holy Spirit and could speak in languages they
had never spoken before. Now they could spread
the news about Jesus to everyone.

Jerusalem, then, was full of people from many
countries, who had come to celebrate the festival.
To their amazement, they heard these men from
Galilee, speaking to them in their own languages,
about Jesus who had risen from the dead.

Peter stood up and addressed the crowd.
He promised that if they were baptized in Jesus'
name, God would forgive them their sins.
About three thousand people were baptised
that day – the Christian Church had begun.

Jesus' friends continued to spread God's word. Their lives were often in danger, but, they prayed to God for help and He answered their prayers. Many people came to listen to them and were baptized in Jesus' name.

And today, all across the world, people still gather together to hear God's message.

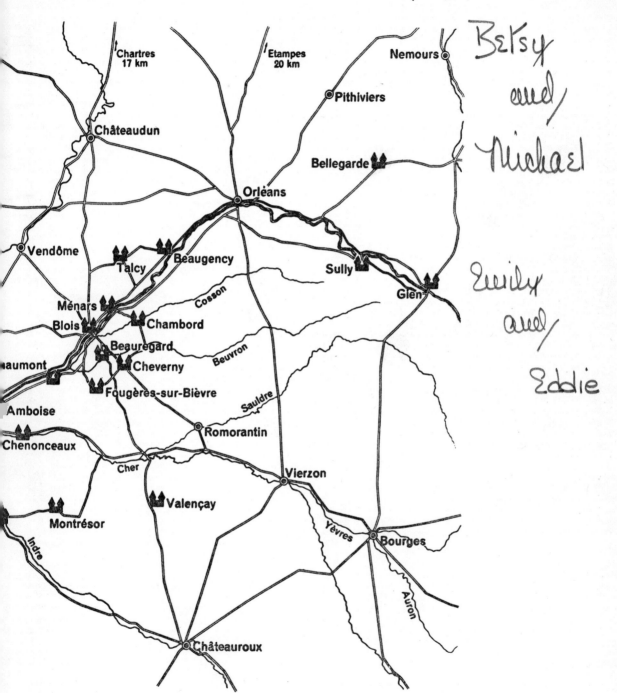

THE LOIRE VALLEY AND ITS TREASURES

1. *Drawbridge and Arms of Charles of Amboise, Château de Chaumont*
2. *Château of Chambord, By Night*
3. *Façade of the Trinité, Vendôme, By Night*

THE
LOIRE VALLEY
AND ITS
TREASURES

BY

JEAN MARTIN-DEMÉZIL

RAND McNALLY & COMPANY

PRINTED IN GREAT BRITAIN

Contents

FOREWORD   page 9

   I   *Landscapes*   11

  II   *History*   15

 III   *Birth of a Renaissance*   23

 IV   *Renaissance in the Val de Loire*   33

  V   *Sleeping Beauty*   42

 VI   *Men of the Loire*   49

VII   *Towards the Future*   54

VIII *Pilgrimages*   61

 IX   *Sologne of my Childhood*   66

EXPLANATORY LIST OF ILLUSTRATIONS   71

NOTES ON BIBLIOGRAPHY   121

PHOTOGRAPHIC SUMMARY   125

4. Orleans – The Town and the Loire
5. Chinon, From the Left Bank of the Vienne
6. House of Adam, Angers, Detail of Carving
7. Wooden Houses at Tours, on the Corner of the Place Plumereau, The Rue du Grand-Marché and the Rue de la Monnaie

ROMORANTIN

8. The Chancellery, Romorantin
9. The Carroir Doré, Romorantin

10. Bas-relief from a House in the Rue Fontaine-des-Élus, Blois
11. Drawing of Francis I, Condé Museum, Chantilly
12. Francis II, Portrait by Clouet. Bibliothèque Nationale, Paris
13. Château of Azay-le-Rideau
14. Catherine de' Medici, Drawing by Clouet, Bibliothèque Sainte-Geneviève, Paris
15. Henry II, Drawing by an Unknown Artist. Museum of Rennes
16. Diane de Poitiers, Attributed to Clouet, Cabinet des Estampes, Paris
17. The Loire at Candes
18. Porte Saint-Georges, Vendôme

7

AU PETIT MOKA

8 9

10

11

12

6

5

13

14

15

16

Foreword

*Where your treasure is, there
will your heart be also.*

MATTHEW, VI, 21.

'I DO not know how the idea of small and gentle slopes can arise in regard to the two great and majestic lines which accompany the Loire. There is no question of gentle slopes! . . .' so says Paul Claudel, a poet seeking to reform the geography of the geographers.

It is indeed true that nature here is proportioned to man, but I would rather describe the countryside as 'well-tempered' in the fashion of Johann Sebastian Bach: the cliffs receding into the distance, the curving river with its green islands, the golden sands and the rustling poplars providing the modulating and superimposing themes of an age-old fugue which has fashioned this land of Renaissances.

Here Saint Martin preached the gospel, the humanities flourished under Charlemagne and Alcuin, Joan of Arc freed the kingdom of France, and the themes of Italian art were interpreted by French hands. Renaissances of religion, literature, politics and the arts here intertwined, just as Martin, a soldier of Christ come from Pannonia, entwined the old pagan trunk with Christian vines; or the Northumbrian monk, working his interlacing around antique initials, grafted latinity to the barbarian stock; or a young girl from the Marches of Lorraine restored faith and authority to the king of Chinon and Bourges; or Cassandra, born of a Florentine father and a Blésois mother, awakened French poetry in the heart of Ronsard.

The Val de Loire, cradle of rebirths, is also a meeting point for native genius and inspiration from abroad. Rabelais had just been born there when Leonardo came there to die. It is a garden where the flowers of the field mingle with those from far-off places; the Tourangeaux gave it the wonderful name of '*le Jardin de France*', the garden of France.

Its wide evenues, the Loire and its tributaries, control landscapes that are enlivened by architectural motifs; churches and châteaux speak their memories of the past:

Orléans, Beaugency,
Notre-Dame de Cléry,
Vendôme. . . .

But there are even more secret places off the beaten track: the Garden of France has a false symmetry; the maze used to play a part in the décor

9

(there is one still at Poncé), and the only way to savour its charming surprises is to steer a zigzag course.

Why write yet another book about the châteaux of the Loire, when so many have been written already? In this one I have attempted something else. I have on occasion received requests from abroad to talk of the Val de Loire where 'more than anywhere else, one feels oneself to be in France.' I would be sorry to seem a chauvinist; besides, this phrase, which was put to me as a question by a young lady from Canada when contemplating a prospect of the Loire, is answered, I feel, by the phrase of Claudel. In short, in compiling this book, if one can call it a book – these remarks rather, written about a picture album – I shall remember faces from Arnhem, Florence, Brussels, Rome, and especially Turin and Naples – for the Val de Loire and Claudel were present there; I shall think above all of my old friends of Neuchâtel and Lausanne, to whom I am bound by the close ties of twenty-five years of friendship in which their two lakes, my river and our common vineyards have played their part. I shall think of those in France – some, alas, no longer with us – to whom the country of the Loire has given human warmth and inner happiness in their meditations or actions, and of those who, like myself, mindful of their own ignorance, are less ashamed to ask themselves questions than to suppose them finally resolved, and finding no humiliation in seeking to understand things, are not afraid to be moved by beauty.

Many of us cherish memories of visiting the treasure of an abbey or cathedral with its reliquaries, ivories and illuminated manuscripts; similarly, Chambord and Chenonceau, Fontevraud and Saint-Benoît-sur-Loire, the Carolingian gospel books of Tours, the tapestries of Angers, the statuary of the Sainte-Chapelle of Châteaudun, the Romanesque paintings of the valley of the lesser Loir, and the works of Leonardo da Vinci could be considered as belonging to a treasury housed in the great nave and side-aisles of the river and its tributaries: a marvellous edifice holding the most marvellous treasures, of which the following pictures and accompanying text are designed to give an account.

Chapter I

LANDSCAPES

ORLÉANAIS, Blésois, Touraine, Anjou: these are our provinces, held together by the thread of the Loire; only the middle reach of the river unites them, for further upstream, in the Massif Central, the Loire is a torrent which flows over rocky shelves, before growing gradually calmer and broader, while soon after leaving Anjou the stately spread of its waters strikes against the granite of Brittany.

As it enters the province of Orléanais, the Loire flows past pleasant woodlands on either bank, but at Orleans the scene changes: the great curve of the river, set at a tangent to the Ile-de-France, seems to emphasize the political rôle of this provincial capital, doubtless foreshadowed by its importance in trade. Orleans made its first appearance with the conquest of the Gauls; waxing strong in the early Middle Ages, it became a corner stone of the Capetian kingdom, and in Joan of Arc's time it stood as the symbol of free France. The boundless swell of the cornfields of Beauce stretches away northwards towards Châteaudun and Chartres, scarcely interrupted by the valley of the lesser Loir; on the opposite bank, looping round to meet the Cher, to the west of the hills of Sancerrois, lies the Sologne, a region of sands and clays – 475,000 hectares of alluvial soil washed down from the Massif Central. The heart of this region is overgrown with scrubby woods and gorse, a land of furze and heather and scattered pools: the *bremailles*, a sort of natural park where red deer and roe deer and also wild boar, find a choice retreat during their migrations, as well as many game birds. The rabbit can be found there too, still the farmer's enemy although myxomatosis has cut this rapid-breeding menace down to size. This land, with its silver birches and heather fading into the autumn mist, is the country of Alain Fournier's *Le Grand Meaulnes*. Maurice Genevoix, born near the edge of the *bremailles* near Orleans, divides his affections between the valley of his book *La Boîte à Pêche*, and the Sologne, the background of his *Raboliot*.

The Beauce plateau with its rustling harvest breaks like an ocean at the foot of the tall flint clay hills of the forest of Blois. West of the road from Blois to Romorantin, the Sologne changes gradually. Deep sand beds and a less porous subsoil make good growing conditions for the flourishing vines, asparagus, bulbs and fruit trees. By imperceptible degrees – for changes in the land and living conditions are not apparent in this open countryside – we enter the province of Touraine without realizing it.

Some signs herald the change, nevertheless. The light grows more delicate between Beaugency and Blois, and from Blois itself we see falling away beneath us the cliffs which will border the river from one end of Touraine to the other, alluvial chalk cliffs riddled with troglodytes' dwellings and caves where the wine ages well. Cliffs like these crop up again in the valley of the Loir near Les Roches and Trôo, and in the valley of the Cher between Thesée and Montrichard. Here, around Bourré, the quarries yield a fine creamy limestone, easily fashioned, which has gone into the building and decoration of the châteaux and has been used for the vine-growers' cottages, stained greenish blue by sulphate from the trellised vines. It is between the rival vineyards of Vouvray and Montlouis, confronting each other on opposite banks of the Loire, that we enter the land of Touraine.

The pleasant many-sidedness of this region may perhaps be considered as an effect of chance, but of guided chance. The ancient sea of the faluns, which lay in the gulf between Brittany and Vendée, left shell-bearing sands along its margins; these, with the alluvium swept down from Auvergne, the wide valleys hollowed by the great river and its tributaries, and here and there the chalk plateaux breaking through, provide the elements of its diversity. North of the Loire the low-lying Gâtine, wet, wooded, with patches of tilled field, links up with the lands of Bas-Vendômois beside the Loir; but beyond, the countryside is definitely Percheron, with its hedges and spinneys; sandstone country, the land of the Chouans. South of the river on the plateau land, cut by valleys, forests grow: Montrichard, Amboise, and beyond Azay-le-Rideau the forest of Chinon. The streams which everywhere flow into the Indre and the river Vienne, making their own valleys, have had their effect on farming, and on their pleasing slopes thrive orchards and vines. The only towns worthy of the name south of the Loire are Loches, Amboise and Chinon, which retained right up until the beginning of the twentieth century the character which Jean Fouquet the painter loved so much. Tours, capital of the plain, sprawling between the Loire and the Cher, can be compared with Orleans. It was an evangelical centre for Saint Martin and those who came after him; thanks to the nearby Abbey of Marmoutier and its many priories, which sprang up throughout Western Gaul from the Carolingian epoch until the ninth century – thanks to their great work in clearing and cultivating the land and establishing farming traditions. Tours occupied an influential economic position which was reinforced by trade, printing, arts and crafts towards the end of the Middle Ages.

Touraine comes to an end at Candes, where the Vienne and the Loire meet. Here was once the cell where Saint Martin took leave of this earth to which he had brought the word of Christ. If we take a sunken road beside the church, which climbs up above the village between the Loire and the cliff, we look out over the limitless wooded plateaux, the river strewn with islands, and the confluence of the two rivers. I know nothing to compare with its harmony

The Loire at Amboise

of masses and curves, with the interplay of the light between water and sky.

At the foot of the slope, and along the cliffs with their cool caves, the monks of Tours and Poitiers quarrelled over Martin's mortal remains. The Tourangeaux drank the Poitevins under the table, and then made their way back up the Loire with the body of their holy bishop, without waiting for them to wake up. Tours, the 'Martinopolis', kept its apostle for the veneration of pilgrims; but these temporal squabbles of a race of vine-growers could not reach the 'thaumaturge of the Gauls', whose spirit is ever present at Candes in the scenery which reflects him so well.

Here we leave Touraine for Anjou. The Saumurois countryside looks scarcely different from Touraine; in its micaceous chalk are caves that shelter the precious wines produced on the local slopes. The forest of Fontevraud clothes the last volcanic outcrops of the Massif Central. Although the provincial capital, Saumur, lost its Huguenot middle classes at the Revocation, and with them its university's brilliance, it has kept its importance in the wine market. Saumur still boasts a cavalry school, the illustrious *Cadre Noir*, and the little old town with its western charm, its churches and mansions grouped at the foot of the château, still recalls Balzac's setting for *Eugénie Grandet*.

Saumurois is different, nevertheless: the valley of the Vienne is left behind at Candes, and that of the river Thouet gives access to Poitou and the lands of the south-west, as the recumbent figures of the Plantagenet King Henry II and Eleanor of Aquitaine, beneath the soaring vaults of the abbey church at Fontevraud, remind us.

The thickly wooded country of Baugeois on the right bank of the Loire also has the same underlying structure as the Auvergne, and pine trees, which grow here in abundance, give a look of the Sologne to this cattle-raising country.

But it is really the Vale of Angers which typifies Anjou. If we go beyond the point where the Maine, itself composed of the Loir, the Sarthe and the Mayenne, flows into the Loire, we are in Segréen, on Breton ground, in the slate and granite country. Trélazé has furnished slate for houses, churches and châteaux all over the Val de Loire; there is cider too, and pig-breeding at Craon. Segréen merges into Armorica just as the Mauges, on the south bank beyond the river Layon with its splendid white wines, merge into Vendée. The Mauges are near Nantais; there they produce – and drink – muscadet.

Thus it is the Vale, centre of the four outlying regions, which creates the unity of Anjou. Its vines, flowers and fruit-laden orchards, the graceful curving of the rivers and the angular pattern of the roads echoed in the tall poplars pointing skywards, make this a Golden Land. The town of Angers itself is overshadowed by its château, whose dilapidated slate-roofed towers recall Segréen, close at hand. The distant past is preserved in the remains of Roman fortifications, and the spirit of tradition witnesses to the continuity of the town's history – Saint-Martin shows Roman building techniques still in use in the

13

eleventh century. The catholic university is of very long standing; the legacy of art treasures, dating from the time of the last dukes, is best represented by the magnificent set of Tapestries of the Apocalypse. The modern additions to the town, which appeared long before it began to grow statistically, are a sign of the vitality and well-being of this fine provincial capital.

Chapter II

HISTORY

THIS open countryside, with a great river flowing through it, was already productive farming land when the Romans arrived. The massacre of the Roman merchants at Genabum in 52 BC – Genabum, capital of the territory of the Aureliani, that is, Orleans – was symptomatic of the times; the chief town of the Carnutes was Autricum, later to be known as Chartres; Beauce was rapidly to become a great granary. Tours, the city of the Turons was to be given the Celto-Latin name of Caesarodunum, 'Caesar's fortress' before it too took the name of the people whose metropolis it was; similarly, the chief city of the Andecavi became the 'market of Julius' – Juliomagos – and later Angers. Twenty years before the birth of Christ, Roman authority seems to have been every-where accepted.

Rome has left far more traces of her presence than is commonly supposed; without going too far north we shall find at Le Mans a Roman wall which is almost perfect to this day. Tours and Angers have Roman remains, while at Thesée, a little village beside the Cher – the Thasciaca of the famous road-maps of the Roman empire known as Peutinger's Table – can be seen the ruins of an impressive building whose function is unknown. A search on the opposite bank reveals traces of what must have been a fairly extensive settlement. The necro-polis of Soings-en-Sologne has yielded many burial ornaments; although we do not know the real nature of a monument near Fréteval in Vendômois, and the presence of the 'Pile' of Cinq-Mars near the aqueduct of Luynes remains a mystery, all these, together with the baths at Angers which have given their name to the part of the town called Esvière, and the baths and amphitheatre discovered at Gennes near Saumur, make up a very concentrated grouping which would be well worth systematic archeological research with financial and scien-tific backing.

These colossal monuments to an expanding Gallo-Roman economy were important in another way : it was certainly not simply from lack of originality that Anjou and the Pays Manceau maintained almost servile traditions of Roman building right down to the early Capetian era; from the fifth to the tenth century invasions tested the solidity of the ancient stone structures in no uncertain way. Thus it was that the keep at Langeais, one of the first stone keeps, built by Foulque Nerra at the end of the tenth century, was thought for a long time to be Roman, and some reconstruction work on Saint-Martin d'Angers done by the same count was held until very recently to be Carolingian.

19. *Château of Valençay. Orangery Court and Jacques d'Étampes Tower*

MUSEUM OF TAPESTRY, ANGERS:

20, 21. *Saint Maurillus as a Gardener, and his Flowers (Detail of one of the Tapestries with Scenes from the Saint's Life)*

22. *The Lady of Rohan*

23. *Border of the Same Tapestry*

24. *The Gardens, Château of Villandry*

25. *Park and Pavilion of the Old Château at Richelieu*

26. *The Marble Basin, Château de Villesavin*

27. *Château de Menars – the Gardens and the Loire*

28. *Apollo Appearing at Issé, by Boucher, Musée des Beaux-Arts, Tours*

29. *The Pagoda, Chanteloup*

30. *Château of Sully and the Loire*

20

21

24

But before the tragic series of invasions came the period which saw the beginnings of Christianity in the Val de Loire, and the formation of dioceses based on the administrative boundaries of the Roman empire. This is significant, for when Roman rule had disappeared from Gaul the Church remained; and alone in a dead world from which, thanks to her, the Carolingian renaissance was to emerge, the Church preserved not only faith but culture and human relations, faint glimmers in a violent world, which were able to blaze up again after a sort of vacillating continuity.

Martin, the apostle of the Gospel coming from Pannonia, died at Candes on November 11, 397, after founding Marmoutiers, the 'great monastery', on the right bank of the Loire outside the walls of Tours, where some vestiges of its former splendour still remain.

The next generation was represented by St Martin's disciples, St Florent at Angers, St Maurille at Chalonnes, St Brice and St Perpet (Perpetuus) in Touraine, St Euverte and St Aignan at Orleans. The intervention of St Aignan against Attila and the Huns, and his appeal to the Patrician Aetius, are pages of history; the fact that Orleans was the meeting place for the Council of AD 511, and afterwards became the capital of the Merovingian kingdom, cannot be ascribed to chance alone.

With the coming of the invasions, the spread of the Gospel continued: in AD 406 there were encroachments on the boundaries of the Roman empire, and Anjou was taken by the Saxons; in AD 428 the Visigoths threatened Tours and won Poitou; the Franks invaded Gaul – it was only later on, after the conversion of Clovis, that they became staunch supporters of the Church. The Bretons resisted, and Clovis drove them out of the region of Blois, where among many others the hermit St Dié probably prepared him for conversion. He reappeared in Amboise and Tours, and we know that he fought, and beat, Alaric. When one of his sons, Clodomir, settled at Orleans, Tours with its own riches and the richness of the surrounding soil became a coveted prize, which was still being disputed in the ninth and eleventh centuries by the houses of Blois and Anjou.

One of the bishops who succeeded St Martin has left us a description of the marvellous basilica which was built in the fifth century by the bishop Perpetuus over the tomb of the saint; his *History of the Franks*, besides being a factual record, gives great insight into the period.

But at the beginning of the eighth century the enemy came from the south, from the countries of Islam, sweeping to victory on the crest of their new faith; the traditions of Touraine commemorate the running battle fought by Charles Martel against the Saracens – he is said to have caught up with them on the heaths of Miré to the south-west of Tours, and finally beaten them near Vieux-Poitiers.

In Orléanais the Christian faith was flourishing: the abbey of Micy already existed under Clovis, Ferrières-en-Gâtinais was founded in the seventh century,

c

and the great abbey of Fleury-sur-Loire was dedicated to St Benoît when his relics were brought back by Aigulfe from the Monastery of Monte Cassino.

It may have lived precariously, but at least the Val de Loire had a life of its own. The era of political renaissance under Charlemagne was approaching, a renaissance which was also to extend to literature and the arts. So Alcuin of York, one of the greatest humanists of the time, adopted by Charles and put by him at the head of the Palatine School of Aix-la-Chapelle, received the Abbey of St Martin de Tours at the hands of the Frankish king in AD 796. Alcuin had journeyed around Italy searching for manuscripts of the holy scriptures and the profane authors of Roman antiquity. Now, with helpers selected by himself, and particularly with the collaboration of monks trained by his friend Benoît d'Aniane at Cormery near Tours, he undertook not only the reform of scriptural research, but reforms in the teaching of grammar, literature, textual research, and in writing.

It might be interesting to take a brief look at this reform, which drew on ancient tradition to renew writing forms which had degenerated considerably. Such was the purpose of the Scriptorium of St Martin de Tours under the direction of Alcuin. There was a sequel to this in another renaissance, when at the end of the Middle Ages Italy decided to abandon the Gothic style of writing which had evolved from the progressive alteration of the Carolingian style, and reverted to the Carolingian style itself.

This incomplete sketch needs elaboration, but evidence handed down to us in other art forms is too fragmentary. Nevertheless, the Carolingian chapel of Germigny near Orleans, even though spoilt in the nineteenth century by a regrettable indifference to style and an even more disastrous 'restoration', has preserved for us some mosaic fragments which are obviously early twelfth century, and possibly even of Byzantine origin.

A few traces of a period which has been well-nigh obliterated by other cultural strata afford us a glimpse of a first renaissance in the Valley of the Loire, where external influences had already produced a new flowering of literature and the arts.

Periods like these are always the legacy of a renewed economy. Our documentation on this point is even poorer, but the great increase in the number of priories about the countryside shows not only that the large abbeys had grown rich, but that more ground was being cleared and lived on – shows, in fact, a state of agricultural expansion which was to be brutally curtailed by the disintegration of the Carolingian empire, and above all by a new wave of invasions.

Anjou especially suffered in this way. Added by Charlemagne to the kingdom of Aquitaine, Anjou was invaded first by the Bretons, then by the Normans from Scandinavia who overran the country in the second half of the ninth century. They sent expeditions up the Loire in swift, flat-bottomed craft, burning and pillaging Tours and Blois (AD 843-854), Orleans and Saint-Benoît-sur-Loire (AD 865), and even occupying Angers for a year (AD 872-873).

This unhappy time saw the exodus of monks, taking with them the relics of their saints; they left Perche to take refuge in the *Castrum* of Blois, founding there the Abbey of Saint-Lomer, and the monks from Saint-Martin went into Auvergne and Burgundy, to Auxerre and Chablis. The Treaty of Saint-Clair-sur-Epte must have put a stop to these devastations, but not to terror; the Hungarian raiders who crossed Champagne in AD 937, and rode as far as the walls of Orleans, show that there was still cause to fear.

The Emperor Charles the Bald had taken steps to protect his territory by giving the country between the Seine and the Loire into the charge of Robert the Strong. The rest is well known: high-ranking offices in the Provinces of the Loire became hereditary, and those in office usurped within their divisions the waning central authority; the dependents gathered beneath their banner to defend their own vital interests; bishops and abbots wielded administrative and political power: all these signs heralded the birth of feudal society, as the family of Robert the Strong ascended the throne – but what a throne! Hugues Capet when he ascended the throne in AD 987 ruled over a kingdom reduced to the domains of Orleans, Étampes and Paris.

Meanwhile, Orleans remained one of the capital cities of this tottering kingdom: Charles the Bald had been crowned in the cathedral church there on June 6, 848; Hugues Capet often went there; in 1108 his grandson Philip I was buried at Saint-Benoît-sur-Loire.

From the end of the tenth century Orléanais, as part of the Royal Domain, existed in comparative peace, but for the rest the Loire Valley was not to be one of those fortunate countries without a history. The rich land of Touraine, where the counts of Blois held the vantage points of Chinon and Saumur, while the Angevins held Loches, Langeais and Amboise, was a golden bait, a jousting ground for the ambitions of its neighbours.

The great forefather of Blois was Thibaud le Tricheur – Thibaud the Cheat – who according to the chroniclers of his enemies (it is unfortunate for his good name that nobody was writing on his behalf) was 'full of deceit and cunning'; and at night in the forests of Blésois, when the north-west wind is blowing, Thibaud the hunter of darkness passes by, condemned by God for his sins to hunt the same deer till doomsday.

In the eleventh century his grandson Eudes I of Blois was the chief adversary of Foulque Nerra, Count of Anjou. These were no mere skirmishes: Eudes, who already held the counties of Blois, Chartres and Champagne, seized Neuchâtel and Morat, was almost made King of Burgundy and perhaps even Emperor, and died before his time fighting the Duke of Lorraine. The Angevin fortunes righted themselves a century later. In 1135 Stephen of Blois, grandson of William the Conqueror on the distaff side, had been crowned King of England. Henry II Plantagenet, who had similar claims by his mother Matilda of Normandy, achieved two prodigious strokes of good fortune: after the annulment of her marriage to Louis VII by the Council of Beaugency, he first carried off and then married Eleanor of Aquitaine, thus extending his domains southwards to the Pyrenees; two years later, on the death of King Stephen, who had granted him the succession on losing his only son, Henry extended his sway as far north as Scotland.

It is for the traces they left that an outline of the events of these troubled times is given here: keeps at Langeais, Loches, Lavardin, Montrichard, Mondoubleau, Châteaudun and Beaugency, the fortresses at Saumur, Amboise and Chaumont which later underwent such pleasant change, fortresses at Chinon and Vendôme – these are there to remind us. For the rest, three hundred years of raiding, pillaging and burning impoverished the land as people fled the countryside, and wrought a transformation as large-scale farming of the Gallo-Roman type gave way to the formation of small towns, like Les Fertés in Sologne, which were strong enough to defend themselves, and contained the population of serfs and free men – 'hôtes' or squatters they were called – who were clearing the land for the priories or the lay lords.

With the conquest by Philip Augustus of the whole of the Loire Valley from Amboise to Nantes, which is one of the highlights of French military history, peace returned, giving ideal conditions for a period of expansion which lasted into the second half of the fourteenth century. In the flat country each squatter soon received his *hostise*, *aireau* or *plessis* – the name varied – a little patch of land enclosed by hedges, where he set up house, cultivated a garden, kept some livestock and soon, if he was in Blésois, earned the right to destroy at any season and at any time of the day or night any game which strayed on to his land. In the bounteous terms of this charter granted at the end of the thirteenth century by a countess of Blois, Jeanne de Châtillon, to the riverains of her forests, any twentieth-century Solognot – for the men of Sologne are born poachers every one – would recognize the credentials of a birthright which, alas, has since been taken from him!

Life in a closed community, moreover, had created friction between the local lords, and even with the royal administration (the revolt of Orleans in 1137). The result of this was that conventions were drawn up, the most famous being the Charter of Lorris in Orléanais, an example which was imitated in the county of Blois at Blois itself, at Romorantin and Châteaudun, at the very end of the twelfth century.

Now the way was clear for a flowering of literature and the arts. Churches rose, the provincial courts grew more refined, and many hunting lodges appeared in the plains. Monastic life in the twelfth and thirteenth centuries attained a very high spiritual level. In 1206 Anjou, Maine and Touraine became part of the royal domain, never leaving it again except when they passed into the hands of royal princes, as did first Anjou, which changed hands repeatedly, and much later, at the end of the Middle Ages, Touraine, which was given to Charles VI's brother, called Louis de Touraine before he became Louis d'Orléans.

Blois, under this rather too free-living house of the Counts of Châtillon, kept its independence until the last years of the fourteenth century. Vendômois – a bite out of the lands of the Counts of Blois – had been annexed to Anjou for almost two centuries, and had gone over to the royal cause soon after the famous battle of Fréteval in 1194, when the English under Richard the Lion Heart had seized the royal seal and archives, which until that time were carried from place to place in waggons in the king's train. Later, under Charles V, Vendômois passed by marriage to the house of Bourbon.

The period of growth and expansion in the Loire Valley which began after the last invasions, and continued until the mid-fourteenth century, is marked by a marvellous crop of churches.

Because it was a place of pilgrimage, Saint-Martin de Tours started off this wave of building with an impressive edifice which has not survived; the lands of Foulque Nerra were soon to bear marks of the frenzy of pious generosity which, for political reasons, attacked the terrible Count of Anjou between campaigns. Churches built by him stand to this day at Saint-Martin d'Angers, Beaulieu-lès-Roches, Château-Gontier. But having said this, may I voice my preference for tiny churches in the early Romanesque style, like Saint-Gilles de Montoire, Meusnes, Cravant and so many more: a picture can impress their simple country beauty better than words could do. Developing religious life embraced on the one hand the abbeys, and on the other the lay clergy; side by side with the monastic schools, the episcopal schools drew benefit from the new literary movement. The economic growth of the country, which greatly enriched the Church, accounts for the scope of architectural programmes; the great minsters and collegiate churches of Fontevraud, Saint-Aignan, Selles-sur-Cher, Loches, Notre-Dame-de-Nantilly in Saumur, Saint-Benoît-sur-Loire, the chancel at Saint-Lomer de Blois, to name a few, are representative of an art which built for the glory of God and for the meditation of the faithful.

The eleventh-century church at Lavardin, and the church of Cunaud dating from the twelfth century, have a special place among my personal 'treasures' for their spiritually uplifting architecture, but I shall also include pictures of the marvellous little painted churches in the Vale of the lesser Loire: Areines, Saint-Jacques-des-Guérets, Saint-Gilles de Montoire, adding the chapel of Le Liget, Saint-Aignan-sur-Cher, and Tavant in Touraine, with its astonishingly modern romanesque paintings in the crypt, and it is only a step from Anjou to nearby Poitou. I shall also include the church of Saint-Savin-sur-Gartempe, which is unique.

In the development of architecture from then on, the episcopal towns, if they were not actual schools of architecture, at least provided distribution centres and points of contact.

In the twelfth century the Angevin Empire – I think we may call it that – was as strong in Poitiers and Le Mans as it was in Angers, and by Eleanor's personal influence the southern civilization seeped up through Poitou into the Angevin territory, where the barons under their Capetian leader soon worsted it; but the domes with which the builders of Aquitaine crowned their naves remain on the banks of the Loire, witnesses to the great marriage with the south which did not quite come off.

The builders of Anjou were just then searching for new methods of vaulting; while their neighbours, at first clumsily and awkwardly, came gradually to adopt the ogival vault, the Angevins supported their rounded arches with a fine network of ribbing, which gave decorative relief. This fashion spread eastwards to Vendômois and Blésois.

But while in Aquitaine the Romanesque architecture lingered on (as an out-worn Gothic style lingered 300 years later in the Val de Loire), Angevin art soon played itself out; from then on the new styles came from the north: the cathedral chancel at Tours, the nave of Saint-Lomer in Blois, a Gothic daughter-church of Chartres Cathedral, just as the marvellous belfry of the Trinité at Vendôme in the preceding century was a twin to the old Chartres belfry. The Valley of the Loire was Capetian, with the exception of the Paris of Philip Augustus, which must already have seemed to the Tourangeaux a rather heavy burden to support. Discipline, which is the strength of an army, has never been the strong point of the men from the Val de Loire.

In 1356, a military incident occurred in the Val de Loire which had wide-spread repercussions. The eldest son of the King of England, the Black Prince, sacking everything that stood in his path, laid siege to the town of Romorantin. The royal army, trying to drive him off to the south-west, suffered defeat at Poitiers; King John was taken prisoner, and Tours had to pay a huge sum before the pillaging bands of English and Gascon troops could be prevailed upon to depart. The war was on again between England and France; who could know how long it would last, except those who came after?

Posterity was to name this particular war the Hundred Years War.

Chapter III

BIRTH OF A RENAISSANCE

IT is apparently agreed by all that the return of Charles VIII from Italy marked the starting point of a 'French renaissance', as it was belatedly called, which seems to have arisen by spontaneous generation. Nothing could be farther from the truth.

To begin with, we could point out an immediate precursor: René of Anjou, 'Le Roi René'. Brother-in-law of Charles VII, who had married his sister Marie, he combined the tradition of humanism with a policy of expansion: his grandfather, the first Count Louis, inherited the kingdom of Naples and Sicily, and died near Bari in the south of the Italian peninsula while attempting to take the tempting prize which had been offered him. René's father, the second Count Louis, met with no more success in his campaign of 1410, though he at least returned to Angers to die. His elder brother, Louis III, was invested by the Pope, and took possession of Naples, but he died soon afterwards in 1434. René, a prisoner at the time of his brother's death, made sure of Provence, where he spent his last years, but failed in Italy, and when Louis XI, who coveted Anjou and Provence, received them from his good uncle at his death in 1480, he also had of him a poisoned gift: his claim to the throne of Naples. Louis XI did not yield to the temptation, but as we know, it was otherwise with his son, Charles VIII. Here, then, is our expansion; here is our legacy of humanism: from the patronage of Louis I of Anjou there remains the admirable tapestry of the Apocalypse which is the glory of Angers; as for René, who was himself a minor poet and a sensitive draughtsman, he surrounded himself with artists like Nicolas Froment, the painter of the cathedral of Aix, a southerner who travelled in Flanders, Burgundy and Italy, and the two Flemish painters, Barthélemy de Clerc and Coppin Delft, who were his close companions at the court of Angers.

This Flemish influence, which was present not only in painting but in music and architecture, was a sign of the times which we find again and again: it is worthy of note, too, that the finest illuminated manuscripts of the house of Savoy in Turin are also of Flemish origin.

Indeed, as far back as the fourteenth century the way was open for Paris, now the seat of power and the capital of a kingdom which had been highly centralized since the time of Philip Augustus (for instance, the archives were kept permanently in the Louvre following the disaster of Fréteval), to become the centre of awakening French humanism. But the Renaissance, to use this convenient

FROM BELFRY TO BELFRY: TREASURES OF RELIGIOUS ART

ABBEY OF SAINT-BENOÎT-SUR-LOIRE:

31. *Chevet of the Church, Seen from the Air*
32. *Under the Abbey Porch*
33. *Early Eleventh-century Mosaic from the Church, Germigny-des-Prés*
34. *Gospel Book Said to Have Belonged to Charles the Bald, Tours Library*
35. *Carving on the Apse, Église Saint-Eusice, Selles-sur-Cher*
36. *Gable Cross with Interlaced Design, Saint-Maur de Glanfeuil*
37. *Capital of the Belfry Porch, Église Saint-Julien, Tours*
38. *Romanesque Arches of the Old Abbey of Saint-Aubin, Now the Préfecture, Angers*
39. *Eleventh-century Façade, Church of Azay-le-Rideau*
40, 41. *Église Saint-Ours, Loches, Capitals of the Great Door*
42. *Belfry and Chevet of the Church of the Trinity, Vendôme*
43. *Église Saint-Ours, Loches, Towers and 'Dubes' of the Nave*
44. *Chancel of the Church, Cunaud*
45. *Nave of the Abbey Church, Fontevraud*

ROMANESQUE MURAL PAINTINGS:

46. *Christ in Majesty, from the Priory Chapel of Saint-Gilles, Montoire*
47, 48. *Lechery; a Holy Martyr; from the Church of Tavant*
49. *Detail of the Tree of Jesse, Chapel of Saint John the Baptist, Le Liget*

ANGEVIN VAULTING:

50. *Abbey of Asnières – Vaulting in the Chancel*
51. *The North Porch at Candes*
52. *Cathédrale Saint-Maurice, Angers; Christ in Majesty, from the Tympanum of the Great Door*

TAPESTRY MUSEUM, ANGERS:

53, 55. *Two Panels from the Tapestry of the Apocalypse*
54. *The Devil – Detail from the Tapestry of the Life of St Martin*
56. *Chevet of the Cathédrale Sainte-Croix, Orleans*

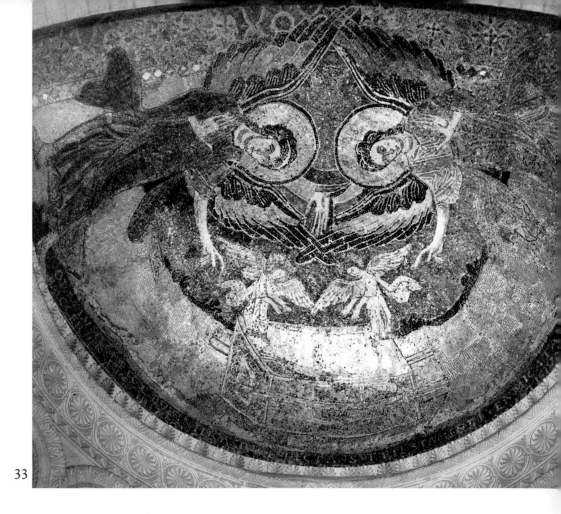

33

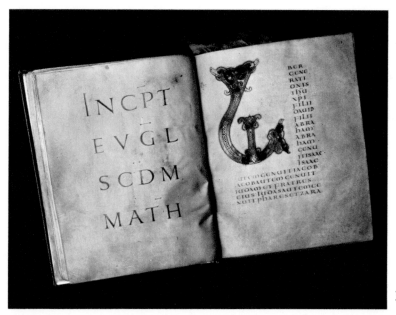

34

35

36

37

39

38

40 41

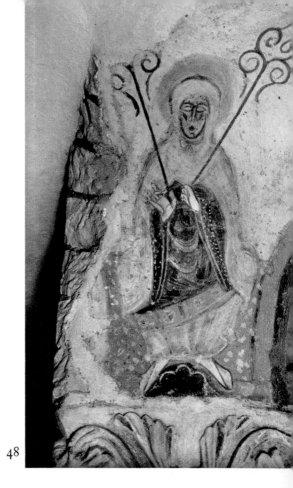

48

47

49

50

52

51

54

55

and customary term, did not come for another hundred years, and when it did it occurred on the banks of the Loire. What curious train of events led to this will provide the theme of the variations which follow.

Too little is said in this connection about the great currents of mediaeval France, and in my view one event of paramount importance was, alas, the Albigensian war in which, under the guise of stamping out a heresy, northern France was in fact asserting its political triumph over the Latin civilization of Toulouse and the Provençal-speaking courts. From now on France was an entity, centralized and Capetian; the Midi was taken over by solid, unsubtle men who showed themselves to be past masters in the art of repression – no longer practised by our contemporaries with the same craftsman's skill since the advent of mechanized arms – only retaining those elements of local tradition which seemed to them directly useful, in this case, the written law; and so the jurists of the Midi went on legislating for the benefit of the reigning dynasty.

This in itself would not be so significant if it did not exactly reflect the lines of stress in fourteenth-century France, which had its centre firmly fixed in the Ile-de-France, and had broken with the Mediterranean. That there should be Angevins in Italy, Jerusalem, or even a little later in Hungary, that Villehardouins should go to Greece, matters little; they had staked their claim in a foreign land, and they were soon forgotten, for the memory of Frenchmen is proverbially short.

Meanwhile, fourteenth-century France continued in close relationship with Flanders, and was much influenced by it in the arts. Thus the county of Blois, before it was amalgamated with the duchy of Orleans in 1398, belonged to the family of Châtillon, who had a mansion in Paris and were on friendly terms there with the Dukes of Burgundy; Guy de Châtillon had married Marie de Namur, and his brother Jean had fought for seven years in an attempt to win back the Duchy of Guelders; their possessions at Avesnes, Thieraches, Guise, Trelon and Landrecy had often brought the Châtillons in on the side of the Counts of Hainault and Flanders, whose allies they were. Thus also the minstrel Watriquet de Couvain came to reside at the court of Blois, and Froissart spent some time there; the connection with Flanders and the low countries establishes and explains a whole series of exchanges in trade, literature and the arts, and the movement remains in evidence right up till Charles VIII's triumphal entry into Amboise, where the sculptors whose chisels had just created the marvellous stone tracery of the Chapelle Saint-Christophe were Corneille de Nesves and Casin d'Utrecht, (whose names certainly did not come from the South).

Things went farther than this: Louis XI's choir-master at Tours rejoiced in the name of Jean Ockeghem, and Louis XII's choir-master at Blois was Antoine de Fevin – again, a good northern name. The step-gabled windows in the gallery which runs the length of the chapel in the Château of Blois, long attributed to Charles d'Orleans, also date in fact from the reign of Louis XII; in other words, at a time when the first motifs of an Italian architecture, refreshed by classical

25

ideas, were being discreetly inscribed on the pilasters of the King's lodge, the Flanders style was apparently still not out of date.

To troubled fourteenth-century France, Italy must have seemed remote; there, the new humanism was gaining ground, bursting the bonds of scholasticism, adapting antiquity to Christian thought, turning its attention once more to a critical study of the ancient texts, seeking inspiration in the plastic arts from the masterpieces of Rome and Athens. This new Italy took up certain themes which had belonged to the Carolingian renaissance, among them the writing reform which I have mentioned.

Some contact between the two countries can be observed, at the end of the fourteenth and beginning of the fifteenth century, in the train of the mad King Charles VI: for instance Louis of Orleans, the new Count of Blois, married Valentina Visconti, a noble lady of Milan; Gontier Col, secretary to the King and the Duke de Berry, visited Florence in 1396, following a journey to Avignon; in 1412, the French diplomat Jean de Montreuil met Leonardo Aretino in Rome and Niccolo Niccoli in Florence. Mention should also be made of the dealers who supplied those patrons of the arts, the French princes: we do not know much about the international art trade in fourteenth-century France, but it is significant to find a Fleming, Jean of Ghent, selling Italian pictures in the shadow of Notre-Dame de Paris in 1338.

All the conditions seemed right to precipitate a French humanist movement in the capital, where the influence of Milan and Tuscany combined with that of the low countries, Flanders and Burgundy; political developments were to prevent it.

The English were on French soil and the country was split into two factions. Louis of Orleans had been assassinated and his mourning widow had fled to Blois, where she later died. She had taken there with her Charles of Orleans, her son, who was himself to be taken prisoner by the English at the Battle of Agincourt. The English now occupied Paris; everything seemed lost. Charles VI's son had only just had time to flee the capital overnight on the night of May 28, 1418, and reach the provinces on the south bank of the Loire, which had remained faithful: Berry, Touraine, Blésois. Here Charles VII retired with his father's heritage, while an English king sat on the throne of France. There, while he was 'King of Bourges', without a throne and penniless, he witnessed the arrival at Chinon of a young girl who had come from the marches of Lorraine to deliver Orleans, and have him crowned King at Rheims.

The deliverance of France, which the pealing bells of Orleans joyfully proclaimed, had made its triumphal progress up the Loire. Setting out from Tours, Jeanne had gathered an army about her at Blois, and met there the Bastard of Orleans who was to be Comte de Dunois, the half-brother of Charles of Orleans, her faithful companion. From there her progress is well known: Chinon, Loches, Saint-Aignan, Selles-sur-Cher, Bourges, through which she passed, still remember 'la bonne Lorraine' whose faith created a national renaissance in the Val de Loire.

When Charles of Orleans won back Blois in 1440 after his long captivity in London, the war was almost over, but France had not risen from the ashes. It was again from the Val de Loire that Charles VII came to her aid, faithful to the province which had given him staunch support in the dark years. It was from the Val de Loire that his son, Louis XI, undertook singlehanded the task of piecing his kingdom together. Charles VIII, brought up in Amboise, elected to be a Tourangeau; all these monarchs counted Chinon, Loches, Le Plessis-lès-Tours, Amboise among their favourite residences. The Val de Loire was to be the haunt of kings for many years to come.

The years of peace which followed the return of Charles of Orleans to France are interesting in more ways than one: at a time when the community, surrounded by the miseries of war, was turned in upon itself, and when it seemed that another civilization was on the brink of destruction, craftsmen arose in the Val de Loire, the exponents of a refined art which with the coming of peacetime was to develop gracefully, delicate without being affected, realistic without exaggeration, its balance and proportion are the very qualities of the land where their style was formed.

The case of Jean Fouquet, whose artistic genius stands upon its own merits, is interesting for other reasons: five years after the return of Charles of Orleans, who himself visited the land two years later but did not seem very impressed – perhaps because his captivity had aged him prematurely – the young Tourangeau painter did a tour of Italy, and met Fra Angelico in Florence. In the absence of more information, this gives adequate proof that relations with the Italian peninsula were being maintained. An amusing example of the literary return to Latin sources – there was virtually no question of Greek in France before the reign of Louis XII – is provided by the rhetoricians of the fifteenth century. This is the period when more and more complex spellings were introduced in the name of etymology, and words of learned formation abounded. The fashion spread apace; until Rabelais, there was no one to quash it. Here is one instance; Jean Robertet, a frequent guest of the Duc de Bourbon, is describing the style of the writer Chastellain:

> '*Ou est l'oeil capable d'un tel objet, l'oreille pour ouïr le haut son argentin et tintinnabule d'or? N'est-ce resplendeur equalle au curre Phoebus? N'est-ce la mercuriale fleute qui endormit Argus?*'[1]

Jean Robertet, for whom the chariot, *char*, of Phoebus becomes a *curre*, followed by a French, ie, non-existent, genitive case, and who manufactures the adjective (mercurial) from the name of Mercury can be considered as the original exponent of a certain style of art criticism, in which the complexity of form

[1] Where is the eye able to see such an object, the ear to hear its high silvery sound, the golden tintinnabulation? Is not its resplendence equal to Phoebus' chariot? Is it not the flute Mercurial which lulled Argus to sleep?

57. *Aerial View of the Keep at Loches*

STATUARY OF THE SAINTE-CHAPELLE, CHATEAU OF CHATEAUDUN :

58. *Dunois*
59. *Saint Mary the Egyptian*
60. *Detail – Saint Elizabeth of Hungary*
61. *A Saint (Unidentified)*
62. *Saint Margaret*
63. *Façade of the Château Overlooking the Loir*

64. *Ruins of the Château at Lavardin*

58

59

60

61

conceals – unconvincingly – the poverty of thought; this self-important person who in 1450 named his son Florimond, (we shall meet this Florimond in Blois and Bury), deserved the sound drubbing which Rabelais' Panurge gave a certain Limousin scholar at Orleans, to help him remember the language of his forefathers.

Be this as it may, the fact was that the men of the Val de Loire had set to work. Jean Fouquet, who died about 1480, painted Étienne Chevalier and Guillaume Jouvenel des Ursins against Italian backgrounds whose polychrome marbles and pilasters with their ornamental foliage anticipate the rest of France by half a century; his pupil, compatriot, and successor, the painstaking Bouridichon, illustrated the *Hours of Anne de Bretagne*; there was also the sculptor Michel Colombe, who lived in Tours from 1470 onwards and built up a flourishing studio: these are only three names, the most famous among many whose work unfortunately is for the most part lost to us.

Two buildings dating from this epoch remain to give a rather simple idea of this style: a church in Orleans, Notre-Dame de Cléry, which contains the tomb of Louis XI, and a castle in Touraine, built in the time of the same king.

As for the civil architecture of the period, setting aside the charming brick and stone gallery at Blois which was erroneously set down by nineteenth-century tradition as a renovation by Charles of Orleans, Jacques Coeur's mansion in Bourges for example, a little too rich and florid (apparently the owner was anxious to show what he could afford) has the decoration and the absence of a regular plan which typify late Gothic architecture.

All the houses of the period have an air of balance and serenity in harmony with nature, like these verses of the poet Prince:

> *Puisque par deça demeurons,*
> *Nous, Solognois et Beaucerons,*
> *En la maison de Savonnières,*
> *Souhaitez-nous de bonnes chères*
> *Des[1] Bourbonnais et Bourguignons.*
>
> *Aux champs, par haies et buissons,*
> *Perdrix et lièvres nous prendrons,*
> *Et irons pescher sur rivières,*
> *Puisque par deçà demeurons,*
> *Nous, Solognois et Beaucerons,*
> *En la maison de Savonnières.*
>
> *Vivres, tabliers,[2] cartes aurons,*
> *Ou souvent estudierons*
> *Vins, mangers de plusieurs manieres;*

[1] *des* = worthy of. Spelling has been somewhat simplified for easier reading.
[2] *tabliers* = table games: chess, backgammon, etc.

Galerons sans faire prières[3]
Et de dormir nous ne feindrons,
Puisque par deçà demeurons.[4, 5]

For Charles of Orleans the years went by; eventually at Blois in 1462 a baby, Louis, was born belatedly. His godfather King Louis XI never forgave him for two misadventures: the first on the occasion of his presentation at the baptismal font, when the unhappy infant wetted the royal sleeve; the second at the ceremonial visit to the happy mother, when the King's feet became so disastrously entangled in the carpet that he interpreted this second accident as an evil portent. '*Et de deux!*' – 'That makes twice!' – he exclaimed, and rode back to Amboise, where he preferred the relaxation of a day's hunting to sumptuous feasting with his cousin in Orleans.

Nor did the matter rest there; the future King Louis XII proved to be an undocile Duke of Orleans, and his good godfather married him off at Montrichard to his own daughter Jeanne, a misshapen and deformed young girl. 'So that,' wrote Louis XI to his co-godfather M. de Dammartin, 'the children they will have will cost them very little to feed!'

But Louis XI's son Charles VIII died without male issue, leaving a widow, Anne, and with her Brittany, a prize for the first comer; of course getting unmarried was a necessary prelude to remarriage, and it is during the wearisome, long-drawn-out law suit of non-consummation put by the new king before the sovereign Pope, that we shall make the acquaintance of Florimond Robertet, son of Jean called as a witness by Louis XII.

He was an able man indeed! Son of a councillor of the Duke of Bourbon, he had no difficulty in insinuating himself into Charles VIII's good graces. When this monarch died at Amboise without an heir, it was Florimond who bore witness to the non-consummation of the marriage of the new king, thus making himself indispensable. When in 1505 Louis XII gave every indication that he would die without a son in his turn, Florimond negotiated the marriage of his daughter Claude with the little Duke of Angoulême. And when the good King Louis XII, belatedly married to a young English princess who was 'most entertaining', eventually left this world for the next, Robertet was still the indispensable man for the new sovereign, who was to outlive him, and see him dead and buried under circumstances which I shall shortly describe.

[3] We shall feast without demur
[4] Charles D'Orleans, *Rondeaux*, CCC XXX VIII.
[5] 'Because we live down here (in the country), we men of Beauce and Sologne, wish us good cheer, as befits the Bourbonnais and Bourguignons. In the fields, in hedges and bushes, we shall trap partridges and hares, living down in the country in the house of Savonnières. We shall have feasting, amusements and cards, and will study wines and victuals in many different ways; we shall not need entreating to eat our fill, and we shall not feign sleep, living down here in the country. . . .'

Robertet married a girl from Blois, and built there the Alluye mansion and the impressive château de Bury, which was a Chambord in all but name, and which was ruined at the end of the seventeenth century. But let us leave the wily negotiator who for thirty long years had managed to make his interests coincide with those of the State, and let us salute the financier who, if we are to believe contemporary accounts, which praise him to the skies even after his death, succeeded in meeting the needs of a treasury which had been encumbered with debt in the first years of Louis XII's reign, while cutting down taxes by half.

Robertet had his final tussle with financial difficulties when Francis I was captured and Charles V demanded an enormous ransom. Did he die of the affair? He did die at any rate, shortly after the king's return on November 29, 1527, in Paris – which brings me to the tale of the 'Return of the Ashes'. Clément Marot, who devotes some five or six hundred lines to Robertet's elegy, tells us how at the gates of Paris he met the funeral procession. On an army waggon draped in black and drawn by six horses fully caparisoned appeared an effigy of the deceased, one of those wax effigies usually reserved for the funerals of kings and princes.

Whose funeral was this? Marot looked at the painted coats of arms adorning the four corners of the funeral cart:

> *O vous, Humains, qui escoutez ma plaincte,*
> *Quel est celluy qui eust ceste esle paincte*
> *En son escu? Vous en fault-il doubter ...*
> *Que c'est le bon Florimond Robertet?*[1]

Let us rejoin the procession as it arrives in '*Bloys sur Loire*'. Here universal terror reigns, even the animals run and hide in their lairs, and – hail Italy! hail mythology! – the fish of the Loire bear the sad tale to the great river:

> *Comment la Mort, qu'ilz avoient rencontree,*
> *Avoit occis quelqu'un de sa contrée;*
> *Le Fleuve Loyre adonc en ses espritz*
> *Bien devina que la Mort avoit pris*
> *Son bon voysin: dont si fort lamenta,*
> *Que de ses pleurs ses undes augmenta;*
> *Et, n'eust esté qu'il estoit immortel,*
> *Trespassé feust d'ouïr un remors tel.*[2]

[1] 'Oh all Mankind who hearken to my plaint, who is he that caused a wing to be painted on his shield? Must you doubt it ... It is the good Florimond Robertet?'

[2] 'How Death, whom they had met, had taken someone from his land; then (in his mind) the great River Loyre, well knew that Death had taken his good neighbour: at which he so strongly lamented, that the waves were swollen with his tears; and had he not been immortal, he had died at the hearing of such grief.'

31

After the animals, the men: lawyers left their practice, merchants their stalls, women their mirrors; laymen came forth from their houses, monks from their monasteries, nuns from their nunneries (Marot, like Robertet himself, was fairly anti-clerical) and the procession of a hundred poor and two hundred ecclesiastics going before the body, and an innumerable crowd following after, came

> *Dedans l'esglise au bon sainct Honoré,*
> *Là où Dieu fut pour son âme imploré*
> *Par Augustins, par Jacobins et Carmes,*
> *Et Cordeliers; puis avec pleurs et larmes*
> *Enterré l'ont ses parens et amys.*[1]

In fact he was not so speedily buried. The king and queen had arranged to send the great master of ceremonies on the day after the solemn service to sprinkle the body with holy water. Their example was followed by the court and town; for forty days the church of Saint-Honoré was hung with mourning, and the tapers in the mortuary chapel were kept burning right up to the celebration of the anniversary of his death. In the course of this same year four thousand masses were said in the diocese of Chartres (the diocese of Blois was not created till the end of Louis XIV's reign) for the soul of the deceased. In his will Robertet had dowered fifty young girls aged fifteen to twenty, had financed the apprenticeship of fifty boys, and had decreed that bread to the value of seven thousand *livres tournois* should be distributed to the poor.

Robertet, of whom we shall now take our leave, was born under Louis XI, and takes us into the century of Francis I: with his lively intellect, not burdened with excessive scruples, combined with a love for the things which make life worth living, he represents the local *grande bourgeoisie* of merchant origin who were taking over key posts in the royal administration round about that time: the Le Breton family in Villandry and Villesavin, the Bohiers in Chenonceau, the Briçonnets and the Beaunes in Semblancay and throughout Touraine, were all of the same stock, '*de la même ancêtre*', as they say in my native Sologne.

[1] 'Into the church of the good saint Honoré, and there God was implored for his soul, by Augustins, Jacobins, Carmelites (Franciscans); then with tears and weeping his friends and relations buried him.'

Chapter IV

RENAISSANCE
IN THE VAL DE LOIRE

So after a long but useful detour we come to the date which is generally supposed to mark the beginning of the French Renaissance: 1496, the year when Charles VIII returned wreathed in glory from his tramontine victory, and leading twenty-two Italians in his suite. Their arrival, however, is more symbolic of the new fashion than an event having a direct and immediate bearing on the art of building. Among these Italians, tailors, parrot keepers, and makers of artificial incubators, mingle with goldsmiths and sculptors like Guido Mazzoni, the gardener Fra Pacello da Mercogliano, joiners like Dominico da Cortone and Bernadino da Brescia, able certainly to do the work of architects, since this was the period when estimates were accompanied by wooden models. Here was also the only architect, properly so-called, Fra Giocondo.

When these Italians came to Amboise the buildings commissioned by the King were virtually completed; the local master masons had undertaken this colossal task, working with sculptors from Touraine, or with Flemish craftsmen like those who had just completed the decoration of the chapel. Damage done at the beginning of the nineteenth century means that we have to look at Du Cerceau's engravings to guess what the Château d'Amboise looked like at the death of Charles XIII: a veritable town in itself, according to the astounded Florentine ambassadors; but it is significant that such an enterprise was the work of local men, for in the years that followed the same teams were called upon to build all the great châteaux of the Val de Loire, and Italianism, when it came, was merely superimposed, so to speak, on the local art of building.

This seems to me to be the crux of the problem; but the passage of time does more to impair our judgement in this matter than to enlighten us; the aesthetic habits which we have today are so ingrained that it is difficult to ignore them in order to imagine the impact and allure of the Italian style for Frenchmen at the end of the fifteenth century. Moreover, the modern habits arise out of the adoption in France, towards the middle of the following century, of architectural theories imported from Italy with no indigenous foundation in France itself: thus the first French translation from the Italian art was necessarily a distortion; only the genius of the locality turned this distortion to artistic effect.

Let me make myself clear: the Italian architects of the *Quattrocento* were men of science; they had read Vitruvius in the original, or in Italian translation;

33

their art of building was an intellectual concept of certain ways of dividing space according to mathematical rules. Their decorations, derived from antiquity, became progressively more chastened and refined, thus enhancing the monumental quality of their buildings. To avoid complicating the issue I shall say nothing here of the different character of the various schools.

As for Frenchmen, Fouquet in Florence or Charles VIII in Naples – a prince in search of a province or an artist in search of a style – they could experience only a sort of blissful amazement at this Italian style which sought to recapture and interpret ancient Rome. These Frenchmen had never read Vitruvius, and the very word 'architecture' held no meaning for them – the master masons of Amboise were inspired empiricists. Thus the French were greatly taken with the antique style so different from what they were used to; but as for those things which were essentially new about the art of Italian building – an orderly plan, symmetrical elevation, the balance of mass, rhythmical spacing – these they were scarcely able to grasp; a period of acquaintance with the Italian style, French translations of the Italian commentators of Vitruvius, and the span of a generation, were all necessary before France could awaken to the idea of architecture in the second half of the sixteenth century.

In 1498 Charles VIII died accidentally in Amboise, leaving no direct heir. He was succeeded by his cousin Louis d'Orléans, the son of the poet – a double succession, as Louis had married Charles' widow Anne de Bretagne. Louis XII was born at Blois and spent his childhood there; under him this little town became the second capital of the kingdom; he too was to campaign in Italy, pursuing his claim to Milan, inherited from his paternal grandmother, Valentina Visconti.

In the early years of his reign Louis XII rebuilt the wing which gives access to the castle at Blois; this retained the form of a fifteenth-century French lodge of brick and stone with high, slate-covered roofs, dormer windows with steep gables and the alternating curves of the Gothic style, together with sculptured scenes the gallic zest of which reflects the flavour of local wine and the spirit of the people. There is a gallery overlooking the courtyard, with flattened arches resting alternately on columns and pilasters; it is here that innovation is apparent, in the pilasters with their Italian design of candelabra in light relief alternating with the fleur-de-lys pattern of the columns supporting the new gallery. Here the Renaissance made its first tentative entry into the Val de Loire, round about 1500.

Louis XII's favourite adviser and minister, the Cardinal of Amboise, had his own contact with Italian artists through his nephew Charles, who was Governor of Milan. While Charles was rebuilding Chaumont, his uncle, who was Archbishop of Rouen, decided to build a château in the new style in his diocese, Gaillon, of which a few ruins and the drawings of Du Cerceau are all that remain today. Taken out of its geographical context, it marks substantial progress in the Italianate style, especially because of the influence it had on later buildings, and because the builders' estimates show that the master masons who were responsible for this château in Normandy came from Amboise and Blois in the Val de Loire. Italy was represented at Gaillon by Solario, who painted the frescoes in the chapel; there was a copy of the *Last Supper*, also by Solario, executed in Milan under the personal supervision of Leonardo da Vinci; ornamental basins brought from Italy at vast expense adorned the gardens, and the gardens themselves were Italian – indeed this was one of the aspects in which the new fashion had first made itself felt in the Garden of France, thanks to the influence of Pacello da Mercogliano, who had been brought to France by Charles VIII in 1496, and had been appointed by his successor to look after the gardens of Blois. Besides, Louis XII had the services in Italy of a genius in hydraulics: Leonardo himself, who had been presented to him in Milan but had refused to follow him to France. The king had admired his 'Last Supper' so much that he had cast about for a way in which it could be detached from the wall and taken to Blois.[1]

Louis XII died, and his cousin and son-in-law, Francis of Angoulême, brought up by his mother Louise of Savoie in Romorantin and Amboise, succeeded him in 1515. Queen Claude, daughter of Louis XII and Anne of Brittany, was fond of the family seat at Blois, and when he came to the throne Francis I began reconstructing the part overlooking the gardens, even before he left for Italy and the glorious campaign of Marignano. The work was cut short in 1524 by the death of the Queen.

This work represents a complete break with previous buildings. Using the old mediaeval rampart as an outer wall, a great façade was erected on one side of the courtyard, two storeys high with a sloping roof; delicate complex mouldings run across its width separating the storeys; a richer cornice surrounded by a balcony runs along the edge of the roof. The window bays with pilasters on either side, one above the other, show the direct influence of the château de Gaillon, and the panels of the wall which they mark out are ornamented with the salamander of Francis I; this whole frontage has a brilliant whiteness which contrasts with the Louis XII brickwork and sets off the architectural feat of virtuosity, the admirable open staircase. From panels of delicate leaf sculpture on the ground floor, very lightly carved, the eye follows an uncluttered balustrade up to the first floor with its statues in their niches; the design of the next two flights is more intricate and deeply carved, making much of royal motifs. Above the higher balustrade, whose decoration echoes that of the roofs, a final storey juts out on a level with the Italian dormer windows, and another decorated cornice crowns this amazing work of art, created for the quality of the light in

[1] We have found an isolated copy of the *Last Supper*, some vestiges of which were left on the wall of the Franciscan refectory in Blois. This is certainly a work of Solario, or carried out under his direction: the *Virgin with the Green Cushion* had been painted by him for the Franciscan memorial chapel of Mary of Cleves, mother of Louis XII.

the Val de Loire, and for the eye which happens suddenly upon it when one passes the castle vault; created for the majesty of kings.

On the outer aspect, overlooking the gardens, the old feudal rampart was a very austere setting. Now two new storeys were built upon it, made to look like galleries, but in fact formed of lodges opening inwards with no inter-communicating doors; it has been suggested that these show the influence of Bramante's rhythmic bays, but I prefer to see them as a superb example of a misunderstanding on the part of the master masons of the Val de Loire, inter-preting after their own fashion an art which was far too 'learned' for these un-lettered men of genius.

Then there is Chambord.

On the banks of a small river on the edge of the forest of Sologne, it had been used as a hunting lodge by the counts of Blois from the twelfth century.

Francis I began by encircling with walls a portion of the forest, together with lands between the river of Cosson and the Loire which rounded off the estate – a park about the size of Paris in the nineteenth century.

Here he built a château, a palace: Chambord.

The plan is straightforward: a rectangle of buildings around a central court-yard. The great façade facing north-west overlooks the river. Access to the château is through the door at the centre of the opposite wing, facing south-east. This wing, like the two lateral wings and the two corner towers, consist of one floor surmounted by a flat roof, but half-way to the main façade they become two-storied structures with sloping roofs flanked by tall lantern turrets. A symmetrical effect is achieved by two narrow galleries of similar height connecting the two wings to the main part of the château over the centre of the great façade: the 'donjon' – to use the old military architectural term which has been preserved at Chambord.

This is a large structure, basically square, intersected by two great halls which form a Greek cross; where they meet rises the famous double spiral staircase upon which – to quote not only the guides but Leonardo da Vinci, who left plans for such a staircase among his notes – two people can go up and down without meeting at any point.

At roof level the single flight around the great lantern turret continues this staircase; this is the centre of the building about which everything turns. The roof itself is prodigious: picture a vast terrace cut across by four groups of pointed roofs corresponding to the plan of the halls below, close to the lantern. Up there bell turrets, chimneys, gable windows and pinnacles, jumbled together, lose all sense of order and perspective from close up, like some strange village hanging in the air – an astonishing piece of fantasy crowning the sober, solid walls beneath; here, transposed into the ordered setting of the Italian style, are the delicate structures which in the late fourteenth century used to adorn the French châteaux of Saumur and Mehun-sur-Yèvre, as we find them painted by Pol de Limbourg in the *Très Riches Heures du Duc de Berry*, with the airy quality of their flamboyant decoration in strong contrast to the austere ramparts under a glowing sky.

There are no ramparts at Chambord of course; broad windows open upon the world of nature, and the interior streams with light. But especially striking is the way that architectural order reigns: this is unmistakably the Italian influence.

How far did this influence go? This we shall never know exactly, as we have no documents. It is certain, however, that the point of departure was an Italian idea. This was 1519: did Chambord, which rose when Leonardo da Vinci was dying at Amboise, owe anything to the venerable exile?

We only know, from chance information given us by some of the bills, that the enterprise was undertaken by master masons from the Val de Loire: Jacques Sourdeau, who had worked in Blois, Pierre Trinqueau, a serf freed by Francis I, and their successors carried out the work under the supervision of royal administrators like the Bastard of Chauvigny. We further know that, except on a very general level, there are only slight resemblances between the *donjon* which we see today and what must have most certainly have been an Italian plan, probably the work of Dominico da Cortone. A close examination of the building reveals countless modifications of a substantial kind which were made during construction. It also tells us how long the construction took: the château was begun in 1519, then after a short interruption due to the defeat at Pavia and the capture of the king, it was far from completed in 1559, at the death of Francis I's son Francis II; the greater part of the staircase attributed to this king, and the vaulting in the chapel, were only finished in the seventeenth century in the reign of Louis XIV.

Let us not jump so far ahead, but go out in imagination on to the balcony in the great lantern turret, and lean over to take a look at the courtyard. We shall be struck by the contrast there: on the one hand, the ebullient style of Francis I, with slate decorations on stone, in imitation of the Italian marble inlays, adding a picturesque note; on the other hand, the pure and uncluttered lines of the wing which was built in his son's time.

At Blois the few years from 1501 to 1515 had been sufficient to transform a Gothic château, with some tentative Italian ornamentation, into a full-blooded classical idiom, chock-a-block with motifs borrowed by fifteenth-century Italy from ancient Rome, and already out-moded in that peninsula when they were adopted by France, where the flamboyant gothic was still in vogue. Another few years – to about 1540 – saw the acquaintance with the Italians passing from the learning stage to the building stage. The Loire valley lost its master masons, and France gained its architects: Pierre Lescot, Philibert de l'Orme were cultivated men, humanists like their Italian colleagues. With them the classical style was born. But the message left between Blois and Saumur by the old master masons of the Val de Loire remains; Amboise and Chaumont, Blois and Chambord, Chenonceau and Azay-le-Rideau reflected in their waters, Ussé and Villandry, without counting the host of modest and charming country mansions which can be found around the dwellings of the king and of the king's lords and treasures. In this extraordinary compromise between two opposite concepts, flourishing in the garden of France for scarcely half a century, lay a link with the past; but art, casting aside its mediaeval verve, became universalized according to the canons of the return to antiquity.

In the same way, in the realm of literature, the humanism of Rabelais was succeeded by that of Ronsard. Born about 1495, Rabelais still belonged to the late Middle Ages; he has their vigour, inspiration and wealth of expression; he is a *flamboyant* writer; he builds up word structures which buttress and sustain each other; his language is robust, diverse and eclectic, a language of curves and counter-curves, whose forms recall the façade of the Holy Trinity at Vendôme. Not so with the content, which reflects the vine-growing humanist from the Touraine, the man who had drunk the Breton wine of Chinon in the glass of Erasmus. Rabelais belonged to the same intellectual family as Leonardo da Vinci; like him, curious of all knowledge, he also used experimental analysis for a minute exploration of the mysteries of life; it was the task of Rabelais to break down the obscuring crust which surrounded mediaeval thought, the armour in which it had gradually become encased, while beneath its apparently solid exterior the vitality was draining away.

Pierre de Ronsard belongs to the next generation. Born in 1524, he was four when Rabelais began writing. Naturally I do not intend to compare the work of a pamphleteer, although this does not truly describe Rabelais, with the work of a poet; but the son of a local justiciary from Chinon and the son of the country squire of Vendôme were both churchmen, and both made contacts abroad, particularly in Italy when accompanying diplomatic missions in the capacity of secretaries. Pierre de Ronsard, a clerk who took only the minor orders, remained respectful of the hierarchies of the Catholic Church, but does not seem to have been divorced from an appreciation of good food and wine or the delights of love, which find expression in his poetry, sometimes (I am thinking especially of certain of the *folasteries*) of a fairly uninhibited kind.

These poems were written for amusement, however; the real significance of his poetical work is that of the Pléiade; it lies in his contribution to the defence and illustration of the French tongue and the use he makes of the language of antiquity, recalling in this respect the composers under the late house of Valois, his contemporaries, who had recourse to 'antique measures' in their music. This literary fashion, whose clumsiness made us smile in the time of Jean Robertet, can still afford amusement from time to time in Ronsard's day; but we should not forget that it laid the foundations of the classical art.

The Val de Loire had had its day. In December 1588 at Blois, above the room of the dying Catherine de Medici, the Duke of Guise and the Cardinal of Lorraine were summarily executed at the order of Henry III, who died the following year. To this last of the Valois succeeded the first Bourbon king; but Henry IV had realized that to restore peace within the kingdom of France and give her back her rightful place among the other nations he must govern from Paris, and the Val de Loire relapsed into the indolence which is its natural state.

In the preceding pages I have tried to put into context the ephemeral flowering of the French renaissance on the banks of the Loire. I shall conclude with a tale which, as a historian, I can tell without a blush, because it respects historical accuracy.

Once upon a time, at the end of the fifteenth century, lived a rich Florentine banker, Bernardo Salvati. For reasons which no doubt had nothing to do with poetry – but in Florence one can never be sure – he came to France; first, on leaving Tuscany, to Lyon, where he spent an unhappy time; then to Blois, residence of the king. There he married a young girl from the town, Françoise Doulcet; they had a daughter Cassandra, and he bought a small château in the Beauce, half farm, half country residence, which he transformed. Standing in an oasis of trees amid the corn, it is the most charming house I know. You enter through a porch under a large square tower, and here the magic begins: there is the paved courtyard, the gallery with its archways, and the well surrounded by columns; in one corner a fig-tree grows, and flowers brighten the foot of an old wall where lizards live in the cracks; beyond, on either side of the walnut trees in the farmyard, rise the out-houses – the gardener's house, which makes you want to be the gardener of Talcy, the dovecote hollowed like a hive inside, still with its tall revolving ladder mounted on a squeaking shaft, and the wine press with master wheel, pulley, wooden vice and a stone basin, which looks as if it must have been taken straight from one of Leonardo da Vinci's note-books for the personal use of Rabelais' giant Gargantua. It is modest and simple, the air breathes poetry:

> Dedans un pré, je vis une Naïade
> Qui comme fleur marchait dessus les fleurs. . . .[1]

writes Ronsard, prior of Saint-Gilles de Montoire and Cassandra's poet elect.

It must have been at a court ball at Blois towards the end of the reign of Francis I that the young bachelor Ronsard first met his Cassandra, playing on the lute and singing a Burgundian *branle*

> Ville de Blois, naissance de ma dame,
> Séjour des rois et de ma volonté. . . .[2]

But I like to imagine that sometimes, in the cool of the simple nave of Talcy, the wings of the romanesque angels from the church of Saint-Gilles would beat in time to their dance. It makes no difference that in the time of the earlier poet

---

[1] 'In a field, I saw a Naiad, like a flower walking upon flowers. . . .'
[2] 'City of Blois, birthplace of my lady, seat of kings and of my own will. . . .'

CHATEAU OF AMBOISE

65. *Balcony of the Conspirators (Balcon des Conjurés)*
66. *The Hurtault Tower and the Chapelle Saint-Christophe*
67, 68. *Ogival Vaulting and Lintel of the Great Door in the Chapelle Saint-Christophe*
69. *Entrance Pavilion Saint-Agil*

CHATEAU OF LE PLESSIS-LÈS-TOURS

70. *Roof of the Staircase*
71. *Louis XI*

CHATEAU OF BLOIS

72. *Main Doorway, with Statue of Louis XII on Horseback*
73. *Francis I Staircase Seen from the Gallery of the Louis XII Wing*
74. *Façade of the Lodges*

66

70

71

they were imprisoned under the lime wash which covered them in the nineteenth century; they will still have a tale to tell, for at Talcy Cassandra's niece Diana fell in love with Agrippa d'Aubigné, but could not marry him because he belonged to the reformed church; Cassandra also had a daughter, who married the Lord of Bonne Aventure and Courtoisie. La Bonne Aventure is at Gué du Loir, the Bonne Aventure au Gué of the song; her husband's name was Musset; this marriage made Ronsard's muse a forebear of the poet (Alfred Musset) who wrote the *Nuits*.

This is what the angels would tell us, coming across the plain of Beauce from the banks of the Loire in Vendôme. Perhaps the angels would even tell us that Diana's great nephew Paul Godet des Marais, Bishop of Chartres, who was born in Talcy, would one day receive as a penitent Françoise d'Aubigné, widow of Scarron and granddaughter of Agrippa, better known as Madame de Maintenon. But let us leave behind, in this country house lovingly preserved by tradition, this story which a Protestant priest, a friend of mine, used to refer to as a quirk of divine humour. Memories of the past, old songs, come to us on the wind. Sit peacefully near the dovecote and the wine press: this haven of greenery is a fit setting to remember the daughter of the Florentine and the woman of Blois whose faint shadow still stands beneath the slate well-cover beside the mossy edge; she is the soul of this land of meetings and rebirth.

Chapter V

SLEEPING BEAUTY

THE court of France had withdrawn; the king now reigned from Paris, and later from Versailles, within easy reach of his capital, and the Loire rested, flowing leisurely between its banks and among its green islands.

The long residence of kings in the region had given rise to a saying that the purest French was spoken between Orleans and Tours. The teachers of Blois were widely known; their grammars with the accompanying dialogues were read by the English, Flemish and Germans. George Villiers, the future Duke of Buckingham, journeyed here as did countless others, and a little later London welcomed under the name of 'Petit Blois' a kind of French institute under the direction of one of these teachers. But on his return to France the man in question settled in Paris. The first editions of his grammar contained this simple dialogue: 'From whom do you learn French?' 'From a master recently arrived from Blois,' 'It is true that it is there one finds the true purity of the language, and not elsewhere;' but now the text was modified thus: 'From a teacher of Paris.' 'It is true that with the proximity of the court. . . .' Here, grammar assumes a symbolic significance.

It is self-evident that the eclipse of this brilliant life must have had an adverse effect on the local economy. On the one hand, the country was picking up the pieces as best it could after the religious wars; with the Catholic Reformation monasteries were springing up everywhere; the Congregation of Saint-Maur took the Benedictine Abbeys in hand, the Génofévains dealt with some others, the Oratiens founded colleges at Vendôme and Pont-Levoy, and the Jesuits at Orleans, Blois and Tours. Meanwhile came a succession of unfortunate events: first the troubles of the Fronde – Marie de' Medici's imprisonment at Blois, her romantic escape via the castle moat, her stay at Angers and the *drôlerie* at the Pont-de-Cé;[1] then the revocation of the Edict of Nantes; and finally several years of bad crops towards the end of the reign of Louis XIV: these were three wounds which would heal only with difficulty; the second, in fact, never. The Huguenot middle class had been much in evidence throughout the kingdom, but especially here; in 1685, Saumur ceased to be an intellectual centre, Tours ceased to be capital of the silk industry and Blois was no more the leading clock-making town; Gien and Baugé were wiped off the economic map; the trade with the low countries, which had been so profitable, ceased abruptly.

---

[1] Victory of Louis XIII over the partisans of his mother, Marie de' Medici, in 1619.

Would a Prince Charming materialize as in the fairy tale to awaken the Sleeping Beauty? To Blois it seemed for a brief time that this might happen.

On his disgrace Gaston d'Orléans, the brilliant mad-cap brother of the duller Louis XIII, had there surrounded himself with a little court of poets and musicians. The botanical garden of Monsieur was famous; the gallery of the château housed his collection of antiques, cameos and medallions; his collection of clocks incorporated many rarities which he found there; he fell in love with the beautiful Louison Roger of Tours for whom Étienne Moulinié created the *Ballet of the Marriage of Pierre de Provence and the Beautiful Maguelonne*. Thus the humanism of the late Valois kings, together with a taste for entertainments, lingered on into the century of Louis XIV with the help of this prince who was at the same time the most turbulent of the *frondeurs* and the last Florentine in the reigning family.

Gaston d'Orléans' overriding interest was architecture, especially contemporary architecture, and François Mansart rebuilt for him one wing of the château at Blois, although he never had time to reside there; he was also interested in Chambord, which he thought charming, and it was there that Mademoiselle visited him when, still a young child, she first came to see her father in the Val de Loire; he preserved it from decay long before his nephew Louis XIV reconstructed and restored it for use as a hunting lodge.

Gaston had already died in Blois when Louis XIV began visiting Chambord; but the presentation there of *Le Bourgeois Gentilhomme* by Molière and Lulli created no precedent, and Chambord fell asleep once more beside the river, with Cheverny, Chenonceau, Amboise, Azay, Brissac and all the other dwellings of kings of France and servants of kings beside the river Loire.

Thus Cheverny and the central part of Menars, together with the Jesuit church in Blois and the château of Gaston d'Orléans, are the last châteaux of the Loire of historical significance, but architecturally they are the first châteaux of the classical epoch, for the local sources had run dry, and French architecture was now tending towards the universal.

The only trace which Richelieu has left in Touraine is a charming little town, but the château which was the Cardinal's pride and joy – he had had the earlier one at Champigny demolished to erect it – has by a kind of poetic justice failed to survive the centuries. The windows in this chapel at Champigny – Renaissance work, postdating the greatest period of the art of stained glass – remain to bear witness to the ambitious and sumptuous designs of the period which gave them birth, the second half of the sixteenth century; while the chapel itself, dating from the first half of the sixteenth century, is one of the finest examples of church architecture of that period.

Already the Val de Loire was welcoming visitors to its silent châteaux.

One of these was the doctor-cum-architect Claude Perrault. Brother of the author of the *Contes*, this translator of Vitruvius had his interest aroused by what he saw, and would have taken a closer look at Blois if the keepers of the château had not been busy with the grape harvest and would allow no visits.

After the brother of the writer of tales came the writer of fables: Jean de La Fontaine admired the town and the pretty women who contrasted strikingly with the great number of humpbacks to be seen there – also frequently met with at Orleans, he says. As for the Château, he wrote, 'There are many galleries and windows, balconies and ornaments, all small and without regularity or order, together making up something large which pleases mightily.'

La Fontaine's next visit, to Amboise, had another meaning for him: his friend Fouquet had once languished in prison there because at Vaux he had dimmed the rays of the Sun King – but that would be another story.

To complete our series of visitors comes a woman of the world, also as it happens a friend of Fouquet. On May 9, 1680, Madame de Sévigné took a boat from Orleans; with her went the chassis of her personal carriage: 'the front window affords us a marvellous view; from those on either side we have glimpses in every conceivable direction. There are only the two of us, the Abbé and myself, in this pretty little chamber, sitting on plump cushions, taking the air at our ease, while the rest are like pigs among the straw. We have partaken of soup and hot boiled beef; we have a little stove, and eat our meals on a plank within the carriage like a king and queen: only see, if you please, how refined our Loire has become, and how vulgar we once were when *our heart was on the left bank*: indeed, my dear, whether right or left my heart is full of you'.

We shall follow one more visitor down the Loire, this time fifty years later. I do not refer to Voltaire who, exiled from Paris on account of some wicked verses he had written, went to Sully where he wrote the *Henriade* and presented *Oedipe* and *Artémis*; our visitor was wise and discreet, brought up by the Visitandines, nuns of Nevers, in the fear of God, and his journey was to their sisters at Nantes. His 'father'[1] was the poet Gresset, who taught at the Jesuit college in Orleans, then Blois, and subsequently Tours, thus himself accomplishing, albeit more slowly, the voyage his son was to make in 1734. I omitted to mention his son's name: he was called Vert-Vert, and he was a parrot who had been entrusted by the good sisters to the boatmen of the Loire for the duration of the voyage.

But the journey was long, and the vocabulary used by the boatmen – which must however have been pure French, as this was the River Loire – was subtly different from the language of the convents, and this did tend to confuse the Visitandines of Nantes, when they came out to welcome their visitors. The education of the unfortunate bird had to begin all over again, but alas, an

---

[1] The 'child' was the poem *Vert-Vert*, of which the hero is a parrot.

44

excessive consumption of sweet-meats brought the career of Vert-Vert to an untimely end.

The Loire flowed on between uneventful banks. . . . Men of Touraine journeyed afar in search of the New France: who in Beaumont-la-Ronce remembers the Choinards, whose statues stand at les Trois-Rivières? Mme Guyon, the heroine of quietism, who died at Blois, is not to be confused with a certain Mme Guyart, an Ursuline from Touraine who founded a convent in Quebec: Tours and Canada have a common memory of the venerable Mary of the Incarnation, and Canadian memories in Anjou, Poitou and all the west country abound.

Meanwhile new bridges were being built over the Loire at Blois and Tours. The bishopric of Blois was created in 1698, and Gabriel designed a commodious lodging for the new Bishop, while in Orleans a great Gothic cathedral was still in the process of construction.

As for the royal châteaux, Chambord, which had been the refuge of Stanislas Leszczynski before he settled in Lorraine, became the property of the Maréchel de Saxe fifteen years later. This victor of the battle of Fontenoy ended his days there prematurely in 1750 amid feasting and revelry, surrounded by his colonel's brigade of Slavs, Germans and Africans.

Soon afterwards Menars was acquired by the Marquise de Pompadour, who enlarged and partially rebuilt it; her brother Marigny, superintendent of the King's Buildings, inherited it from her and surrounded it by magnificent landscaping.

An edict had already been issued for the demolition of the château of Blois, now empty and unwanted, when it was saved by a stroke of military genius on the eve of the Revolution for use as a barracks. The château of Amboise gave shelter to the minister Choiseul after his downfall, but became empty after he finished building Chanteloup, of which after the Revolution only the pagoda remained – the course of events put a sudden stop to the vogue for *chinoiserie*. Amboise too was preserved at a price; Napoleon gave it as a senatorial residence to his former colleague Roger Ducos, but the treasury had their eye on it, and although Blois survived the château of Amboise was partially demolished. The Préfet Pommereul, a friend of Balzac's father, had the old Basilica of Saint-Martin in Tours pulled down because it was on the point of collapse; thus disappeared the finest example of pre-Romanesque architecture. A similar but less drastic fate befell Saint-Martin d'Angers; of Saint-Martin de Vendôme only a bell tower remains: 'time which destroys all, and forgetful man,' wrote Honoré de Balzac, a former pupil of the old college of Vendôme, a few years later. And did not Paul-Louis Courier of Touraine, who died under tragic circumstances, advocate the demolition of Chambord?

Shortly after the Revolution, in the now silent Château of Chenonceau, a very old lady, Mme Dupin, was living out her days beside the Cher. Here she remembered the 'Bear of Geneva', Rousseau, the tutor of her stepson who at

45

Chenonceau had 'written several trios for singing, with a fairly strong sense of harmony' and had become 'as fat as a monk'. At Chenonceau, too, the Abbot of Saint-Pierre had meditated upon his spelling reforms. Then the storm of the Revolution broke. Rumours of the successful royalist and catholic uprisings in the Mauges, Vendée, and the country of Segré poured into fearful Touraine; the names of M. de Charrette, Bonchamp, Stofflet, and Cathelineau flew from mouth to mouth; Saumur, la Flèche, even Chinon had been taken. Then Cathelineau was killed before Nantes, the monarchists of Vendée were beaten at Cholet, the harsh repression was at an end. Silence returned, and with it forgetfulness, except in the country of the Chouans.

And Mme Dupin, protected from the revolutionary storms by the villagers, who loved her well, and by her priest the Abbé Lecomte, President of the Committee for Public Safety for Amboise, was allowed to depart in peace, bequeathing Chenonceau intact, a legacy of the old France.

One of her step-son's descendants, also descended from the Maréchal de Saxe, made a pilgrimage here in later years – the woman novelist Georges Sand.

Let us leave the so-called 'Monne Dame de Nohant' to her black valley full of legends, and while we are on the subject of literary women let us leave 'le camarade Sand', as Balzac called her, for another 'tom-boy' (Balzac's expression again), Mme de Staël.

While M. de Chateaubriand, dressed in black, bowed before Chambord, which he pictured as a woman with wind-tossed hair streaming upwards, or as Clarinda reclining on the ruins of Monarchy, another enemy of the Emperor Bonaparte had been banished to the banks of the reposeful Loire, where Chambord was her pleasant abode. M. Le Ray had invited Franklin here, and as his son and heir was in America at the time, Mme de Staël sought refuge here with her literary court, Juliette Récamier, Hegel, Mathieu de Montmorency; she also had a friendly understanding with M. de Corbigny the Prefect, who was responsible for keeping an eye on her and who was himself, unbeknown to him, under the watchful eye of an informer in the military police, who eventually found him too kindly disposed towards her. Then Le Ray, who was supposed to be paddling in the Mississippi, came back and claimed his home. A local lord of the manor, M. de Salaberry, took Mme de Staël into Fossé. It was there that an officer from the local police came and informed her discreetly that her book De l'Allemagne had been seized, which piece of advance information allowed her to save, with equal discretion, a set of the proofs.

At the same time the son of M. de Corbigny, named 'Corcyre' after his birthplace – his father had been a Commissary of the Republic at Corfu – was studying at the Collège de Vendôme with the son of a high-ranking government employee, Honoré Balzac. His mother would pay him a visit whenever she had the time, which was twice in seven years; in the interests of education, parents were asked not to take their children home for holidays.

The pupils went for long walks in the surrounding countryside, as far as

Rochambeau, where the victor of Yorktown was living in retirement, and even to Montoire; and while the future author of the *Comédie Humaine* was reading solidly through the college library in secret (he was withdrawn abruptly by his parents soon afterwards, suffering from 'mental congestion'), M. de Talleyrand, the new owner of Valençay, was entertaining the Spanish Bourbons in his château by imperial request, and keeping an eye on their movements. Feminine attachments could be of use in such cases, so the Emperor recommended that Mme de Talleyrand and several ladies should be present. It was at Rochecotte in Touraine shortly afterwards, lovingly cared for by his enchanting niece Mme de Dino, after a career which had come to a close under Louis XVIII at the French Embassy in London, that this limping genius, a former Bishop of Autun, ended an existence in which he had not put a foot wrong.

From the terraces of Rochecotte he could still look out over the Loire, and see the tall sails of the flat-bottomed barges weaving in and out on the water in a scene of peaceful prosperity, which was scarcely troubled by a fresh Chouan uprising, led this time by the Duchess de Berry.

It is worth remembering the July Monarchy and King Louis-Philippe, who was such an object for the scorn and ridicule of his subjects because his reign saw the end of pillaging of France's monuments by the '*bande noire*'. Between the reigns of the Citizen King and Napoleon III, an Inspector General of Historical Monuments, Prosper Mérimée, was set to work classifying and preserving châteaux and churches; Chambord had just been purchased by a nationwide subscription and given to the '*enfant du miracle*', the count of Chambord for whom, after the fall of the Empire, the throne, bed and royal tapestries and coronation coaches were to be assembled in the rooms of the château—assembled, but never used.

Meanwhile the flat-bottomed barges ploughed their way less and less frequently up and down the Loire; in 1852, at Amboise, they witnessed Napoleon III's liberation of the Emir Abd El-Kader; then there were rumours of projects for improving the Sologne, an old eighteenth-century economist's dream which the Emperor had taken up. But in 1846 the Paris-Orleans railway reached Tours; the few brave attempts with steamships came to nothing, and the boatless waters of the Loire flowed on between meandering banks – having proved of little use to man, it retained its beauty.

At the beginning of the present century Charles Péguy of Orleans, poet of the Beauce, Notre-Dame de Chartres, and Jeanne d'Arc, could write that the *ancien régime* came to an end once and for all with the economic renaissance arising out of the July Monarchy, with the industrial transformation and the appearance of the railway.

Three more whirlwinds were to pass over the Loire; today the last eyewitnesses of the 1870 war are disappearing, but the marks of the Prussian bullets were still there when Chambord narrowly missed being razed to the ground by the retreat of the defeated Nazis. Many wounds will never heal, but history cannot be rewritten, and if military achievements in their turn become monuments to our past, some memories should be lovingly preserved—the heroic resistance of the Cadets de Saumur, and the sacrifices of all those who lost their lives in combat or in concentration camps. Every province had its heroes and martyrs; ours were silent men and women who set more store by their duty than their lives.

Chapter VI

MEN OF THE LOIRE

La terra molle e lieta e dilettosa
Simili a se gli habitator produce.
Impeto fan nelle battaglie prime;
Ma di leggier poi langue e si reprime.
TORQUATO TASSO, *Gerusalemme liberata* I, LXII

THESE lines of Tasso are too often quoted. Is the race born of this earth, which the poet describes as 'soft, gentle and delightful like the land from which it comes', really so impetuous at the first onslaught of battle, but so quick to lose its impetus?

This statement is undoubtedly false on a military level. Too often have the men of the Loire shown lucid calm in battle – I am thinking especially of the 1914-18 war – to substantiate this description. But if the saying is applied to daily life it might be another story. . . .

Examples from our time seem to prove otherwise; for instance:

A northern industrialist had bought a pretty eighteenth-century house – there are still some left – overlooking the valley, with a garden in the French style.

A local gardener tended the garden.

The new master was a meticulous man.

Having observed over a period of several months that his orders were never carried out at once, but put off to a more convenient day, he exclaimed angrily:

'I'll have to get a lad down from the north *(un gars de ch'Nord)*; he'll set things right in a trice!'

'As you please, sir,' replied his gardener, 'but once he gets acclimatised you'll have to send for another.'

The climate certainly has a lot to do with it; at the right season of the year the climate of the Loire valley is agreeable in Orléanais, sweet at Blois, delicious at Tours, pleasant and gentle in Anjou, not yet spiced with a tang of the sea, and although it has nothing exhilarating about it, it produces a lot of centenarians.

Besides, this is, generally speaking, wine-growing country, and therefore possessed of a pleasant scepticism; one can understand the author Anatole France feeling at home at La Béchellerie.

One of the good things of life is leaving other people to do what you can get

49

F

out of doing yourself, while reserving the right to criticize their efforts. In this pursuit everyone here is actively engaged, if actively is the right word.

This is a country of individualists. Maurice Bedel would smile blissfully when he heard a communist from Chinon or Chissay talking about *his* cows, *his* field and *his* wine – the only ones which really meant anything to him.

Sologne is above all a tolerant country. This virtue is not to be confused with Christian charity. It is polite, convenient, even useful to agree with what some-one says. But the speaker should be warned about the real meaning of the response he will get. '*V'avez ben raison*' ('You are quite right') is only a manner of speaking; '*ben sûr*' ('certainly') is a bit dubious; '*p'tête ben qu'oui* ('almost certainly yes') is definitely against, and '*ça se pourrait*' ('it could be')[1] is an example of a tense particular to the grammar of Sologne – the conditional nega-tive.

A visit to the Sologne takes place in two stages. First stage: the visitor arrives. If you have any taste for good living you go to fetch a bottle before a quarter of an hour is out. Glass in hand, you converse about the drought, the neigh-bours, the livestock, the vines, taking all the time in the world. Then the visitor gets up and goes towards the door: end of the first stage.

At this point a linking phrase opens infinite prospects: '*A propos . . .*' ('by the way . . .').

It is only now that your guest will reveal the reason for his visit.

The Beauce is different.

A farm in Beauce is a fortress guarding its central well, isolated in a bound-less sea of corn.

The well is used in Touraine and Anjou to chill bottles of wine; it furnishes water to cool the vine farmer's casks, and he may even use it for his ablutions.

The Beauceron drinks the water from his well.

One day in a gale-force wind I arrived at the door of one of these farms (this was during the occupation, and the farmers of Beauce often received calls from not disinterested visitors); I was met by a rabidly angry dog. Now, you can always calm a dog with a friendly word even if he is defending a farm on the Beauce, but this one took a dislike to my raincoat flapping about his nose, and showed it in no uncertain terms. There was an ominous rending sound. While I was contemplating the damage his master appeared:

'*C'est le chien qu'a fait ça?*' ('did the dog do that?').

And as I continued to gaze sadly at the tear – for, however thread-bare, my old mackintosh was irreplaceable – I received this consolation: '*C'est vieux, ça ne tire point à conséquence!*' ('It's old, it's of no consequence!').

If you visit a little country town in Sologne, the children on their way back

[1] These phrases are not easily translated; the English given is only an approximation.

from school give you a polite good-day, you return the greeting and their mother smiles from the doorway where she stands waiting. In a market town in the Beauce, if a child were to say hello you would hear his mother telling him

'Qu'est-ce que tu lui causes, à celui-là? Tu ne le connais seulement point.' ('What are you saying to that one, you don't even know him.').

The Beauceron is about as welcoming as his farm, a hard worker and a hard paymaster; he is notwithstanding steadfast in his friendship and in his word, once it is given. He helps his neighbour without advertising the fact. The Beauce has given the church a number of priests, vigorous in their faith and works, and the large-scale agriculture here makes the men leaders with the ability of command and an aptitude for problems of productivity. The virtues of the Beauceron are those of an isolated man; he is not used to public relations, as the industrialists term them, but he has a far stronger community sense than a first encounter would lead one to suppose.

Having read this, you will probably smile at this postcard sent by a young Beauceron recruit to his father and mother: 'My dear parents, this is to tell you that I have just arrived in a beautiful country: not a single tree.'

You will come across intellectual curiosity in the valleys, allied here and there with tendencies to the Left, which seem to have remained constant ever since it has been possible to gauge local opinion by consulting the *'cahiers de doléances'*, (complaint books) and following the various electoral régimes.

I would like to point out the very real sense of historical curiosity in Vendômois; one instance, one among many, is the occasion when a mayor, an honest vine grower able to read and write, one day furnished a passing archaeologist with a full and accurate iconographic description of the wall paintings in his church, and informed him that an American publisher had just brought out a book on them.

Archaeology sometimes poses problems for the expert. One evening a friend of mine was gazing in perplexity at a building which was certainly very old but very difficult to date; an inhabitant of the town came up and, having contemplated his puzzlement in silence for a time, said:

'You are looking at the church?'

'Yes. . . .'

'Why, that's been old for a long time now. . . .' (*'Dame, il y a longtemps que c'est vieux. . . .'*)

This wise counsel, which I sometimes take to heart, could warrant many a long speech.

But the thought of Vendômois brings us back to the vine-growing country and to Montoire. Little is known of the inside story of an encounter which, alas, is now well known. Some days before the event, which was shrouded in secrecy, the little town of Montoire was more than usually agitated. The astounded mayor received an order to obtain four litres of milk. The next day, the officer of the occupying army came to collect the order and, asking for a glass, held it out to the mayor and said quite simply:

'*Buvez, monsieur le Maire.*'

That day, for the first time in his life, the septuagenarian Louis Renard, wine merchant by profession, drank a glass of milk. The next day he was made to repeat the performance.

And he died of it – fifteen years later.

Not that I wish to condemn milk: it is used – and goats' milk in particular – to make delicious cheeses in Touraine, in the valley of the Cher, in Sologne and in nearby Berry. As for the wine, which *un chèvre*, a goat's cheese, complements so perfectly, its virtues are great. A *vigneron* of Touraine, whom I complimented once on his fine old age, gnarled as the vines over which he had laboured all his life, but like them restored to vigour each spring, admitted:

'My health wasn't always as good as this, you know. When I was about fifty I had to go and see the doctor; he even forbade me to touch another drop of wine.'

'What did you do?'

'What do you think, I changed my doctor. . . .'

This roguishness is typical of Anjou or Touraine, and there is something akin to it in the men of Sologne.

I have a friend who was sitting one day with one of the local farmers, a bottle and two glasses on the table between them. At this point there appeared a farm machinery salesman whose mother must have suffered from terrible nightmares before giving birth to him, because he was repulsively ugly—and unfortunately equally voluble.

I have already mentioned the extreme politeness of my countrymen, the men of Sologne. Sitting patiently with their glasses in front of them, the host and his visitor waited for him to make an end, but as he went on and on the farmer leaned forward slightly, and in the confidential tones usually reserved for horses at plough, which do not carry above a distance of fifty feet, he remarked:

'*Monsieur Bernard: quand y sera mort, y fera un ben vilain défunt!*' ('Monsieur Bernard – when he dies he will make a pretty ugly corpse!')

In this area which has remained so essentially rural, there seems to be little to say of the industrial working class. When the workers are local and not imported, managerial opinion praises unanimously their conscientiousness, good humour, rapidity and good returns which, I quote, 'hardly falls short of Parisian workmanship, so widely reputed.'

It is evident that these few real life illustrations can only give a fairly superficial picture – one could differentiate more finely between regions, record the superstitions which still flourish in out-of-the-way corners of Sologne and even more in Perche; the *birettes* and *rabâteaux*, spirits which trouble the nights on lonely farms, the sorcerers and the *marcous* – for there are still some left.

One could tell how the country of the Mauges is still Chouan country, belonging to the Vendée in the same measure that Segré belongs to Brittany; but this geographical psychology would need a book to itself.

Here finally is a well-known little nineteenth-century poem about the towns:

> *Orléans, âpre au gain,*
> *Garde son Saint-Frusquin;*
> *Blois, ville de parvenus,*
> *Mange chichement ses revenus;*
> *Tours, ville de carnaval,*
> *Dépense intérêts et capital.*[1]

There is no mention of Angers – perhaps the unknown author of the maxim was an Angevin?

[1] Orleans, eager for gain keeps its worldly goods to itself; Blois, town of the newly rich, ekes out its revenues; Tours, town of carnivals, spends interest and capital.

Chapter VII

TOWARDS THE FUTURE

MY main object in this book has been to give account of treasure handed down from the past. This heritage must be safeguarded and prized for what it is; it must be a *raison d'être* for the Val de Loire, and our modern efforts at artistic creation must achieve continuity with the glories of the past – while avoiding, naturally, mere fruitless imitation. These are truths which should be recognized by all who are in some way concerned with inherited cultural wealth, or with its continuation.

Let it not be thought that these are empty words; although to be specific here would take too long and be beside the point. I shall say only that the basilica of the Capucins of Blois, next door to my own house, gives encouraging examples of contemporary sculpture and stained glass. As for the presentation of old treasure, the tapestry display at Angers and the meticulous restoration work on the château of Châteaudun are instances of a highly satisfactory results, obtained in the first case by a happy contrast which blends with the setting, and in the second by successful use of the old building techniques combined with the invisible use of modern methods.

All this is part and parcel of the work of archaeologists, museum keepers, historians, architects and town planners – indeed all these gentlemen ought to have a general grasp of the facts; but these facts cannot be isolated in a little world set apart from present-day activities.

Let us suppose for a moment that a choice had been possible. If, with the aim of preserving the traditional occupations – building, carving and painting just as much as joining, vine-growing and farm labouring – one had opposed any form of industrialization, a region which was still alive, but only just, (the mid-nineteenth-century dip in population is only now being ironed out) would have been transformed into an unreal countryside of folk operetta, or at best would have become a museum-case for past glories, with the inevitable trappings and touristic futility.

This poses the problem of tourism and its dual aspect in the Val de Loire – firstly, as an increasingly important source of income, the tourist industry promotes the life of the region; but although this is a desirable, in fact an essential aim, its development needs to be very closely controlled. The tourist industry brings vulgarity and ugliness – wealth and ugliness often go together – and is a fact which cries out for the attention of administrators and town planners. They must be constantly on the alert, and nothing is more difficult. To this is added the complication of investment policies, which presuppose a choice, and must be carried out consistently and with constant supervision.

It seems appropriate here to applaud the intelligent common plan of information bureaux, town councils and departmental tourist committees in welcoming the species of visitors which has been on the increase in recent years: campers. The camping site of the Ile d'Or in Amboise is one attractive example of what can be done. But I find possibilities in a new idea which was introduced in Sarthe last year and is gradually gaining ground: the *stations vertes de vacances*. Keeping away from tourist-crammed areas, these will offer visitors simple but attractive accommodation, as well as leisure pursuits which can be placed at the disposal of the local people; thus they provide a ready-made meeting point for the latter, and for the city dwellers an opportunity to re-establish contact with the calm of nature which, tragically I think, escapes them more and more.

Secondly, of prime importance in this region, is the cultural aspect of tourism. *Son et lumière* originated at Chambord: it is a medium which can only succeed if it fires the imagination of the spectators; in other words, it must be poetic. Let me mention quite disinterestedly the charming spectacle at Le Lude, which is both informative and very moving; one would wish always to see such taste and discretion, together with all those qualities which can create art from this counterpoint of architecture, light and words merging convincingly with the shadows of night.

Museography is implicated here. The tapestries at Angers, the paintings of Perroneau and Mantegna in Tours, are famous, and have now at last received the setting they deserve. Châteaudun can be considered as a château-cum-museum, but the nationally owned tapestries and the superb statuary in the chapel there are too little known. The château of Blois, ultimate victim of the assassination of the Duke of Guise and of a disgraceful nineteenth-century interior decoration which is now slowly disappearing, requires and will require attention; but here perhaps the paintings of Corneille de Lyon and Antoine Caron, to mention only two, deserve their share of the attention which seems to have been more than necessarily fixed on the criminal record of the building. The little museum of Sologne at Romorantin, the Musée du Cheval at Saumur, the museum of hunting at Gien and the fishing museum at La Buissière in Loiret are the main examples of specialized collections – there are others – which are gradually building up; they have a useful contribution to make. I shall even draw attention to certain tiny local collections like the 'museum' (in a room of the town hall) of flints at Meusnes: an intelligent and sensible display of a local craft, however modest, whose products were used throughout the world, cannot be lacking in interest.

Lastly, in a world which is changing before our very eyes it is high time that open-air museums made an appearance; the Scandinavian countries have made a success of these – I am thinking particularly of the Lillehammer museum in

CHATEAU DE CHAUMONT

75. *Main Gate, Seen from the Park*
76. *The Courtyard and the Well*
77. *Terra-cotta Medallion of Franklin, Made at Chaumont by Nini (Museum of Blois)*
78. *Fireplace*

CHATEAU DE CHAMBORD:

79. *Aerial View from the South-west*
80. *The Great Staircase*
81, 82, 83. *Details of the Great Staircase*
87. *Roof of the Great Staircase*
88. *Detail of the Roof*

84. *Detail of a Stall in the Chapel at the Château d'Ussé*
85. *Roof of the Staircase, Château de Poncé*
86. *Roof of the Staircase, Azay-le-Rideau*
89. *Decorative Carving on the Staircase Tower, Château de Montsoreau*
90. *Arms Above the Main Gate, Château of L'Islette*
91. *Detail of the Façade, Hôtel Gouin, Tours*

CHENONCEAU:

92. *Avenue Leading to the Château*
93. *Aerial View of the Château and Its Surroundings*
94. *Château of Ussé*

77

76

78

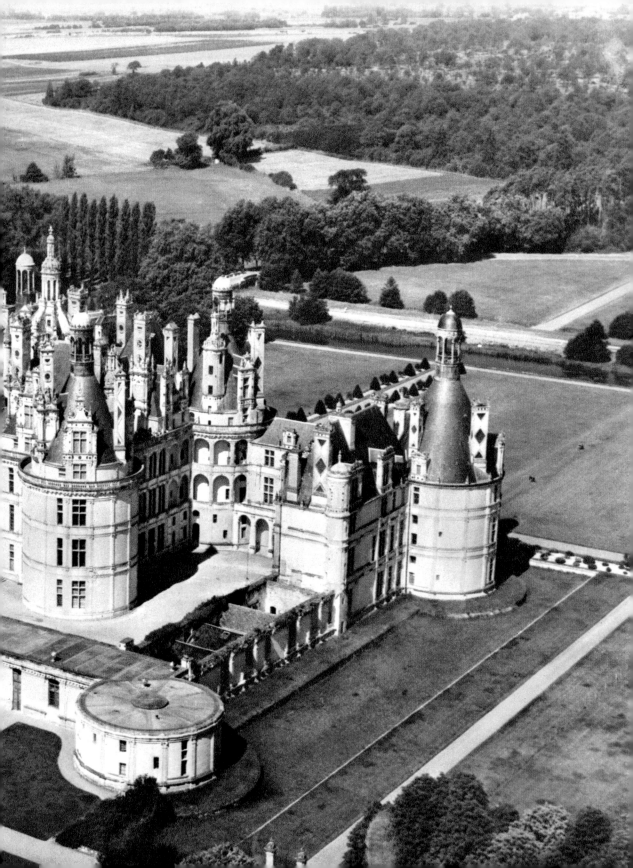

82

83

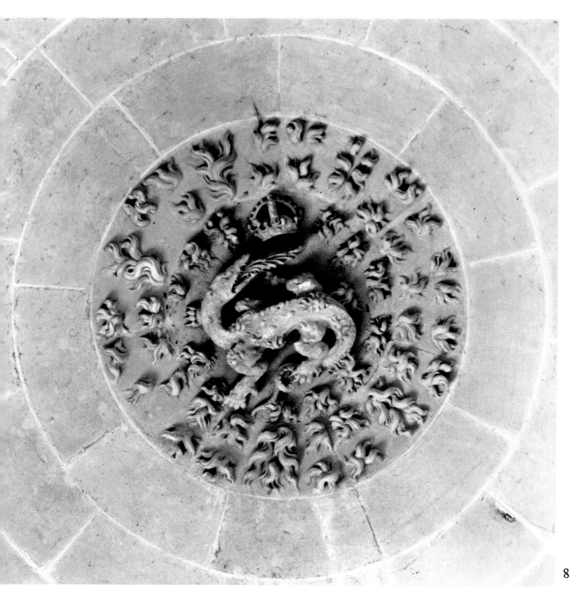

81

87

86

85

84

89

90

91

Norway. Here the old living conditions are reconstructed in a well-chosen natural setting, providing a background for the traditional crafts and display of workmanship.

There is one more aspect to consider before we have done with tourism in the Loire valley: we have been concerned up till now with the tourist passing through rather than with the tourist who comes to stay. There is a rather unfortunate but long-standing tradition which consists of visiting châteaux and nothing but châteaux, crowding as many as possible into one day. But let us pass swiftly over the nature of the visit.

The rule with tourism is that of the majority; it is a rule merely because they are the majority, but some of us are free to have a more aristocratic conception of tourism. By this I do not mean that tourists are a privileged class of society, but that they are men and women of goodwill who, irrespective of their origin and their knowledge of French or lack of it, speak the common language of a love of beauty, which they worship with a sort of contemplative curiosity and a sense of joy.

To these unknown friends of mine for whom this book was written I should advise a visit, *hors saison* as we say; that is, in May or June, or September or October, if possible. They will be able to wander off the beaten track and see the furniture and interiors at Brissac and Langeais otherwise than over a sea of shoulders; they will be alone with Balzac in Saché, they will dream on the banks of the Loir unspoilt by picnickers. When they search out some little market town among the fields and woods for their stay, and go and sample the wine in the caves hewn from the rock, hob-nobbing with the good people of the neighbourhood, they will not be strangers any more, even if they come from Delft, Copenhagen, Verona, or Munich. Gourmets too will be gratified by what they find.

Tourism is only mentioned here, however, as one modern activity of the region.

The most traditional pursuit of farming is in a period of radical change. Mechanical methods and international competition are dictating more and more the course of events, and it is the small farmers and vine growers, so passionately attached to their independence, who will suffer first.

Although agricultural training has developed already and continues to grow, if somewhat slowly, and although the powerful steps taken by the *Caisses Régionales de Crédit Agricole* (the provincial farmers' savings banks) are helping along the essential effort towards contemporary farming, the amalgamation and redistribution of land, which conflicts with the farmers' individualism, is sadly lagging; for instance, the process in the *Département* of Indre-et-Loire has so far affected only 15,000 hectares out of an operating area of 500,000. There are a certain number of wine co-operatives, but at present there are few associations of farmers pooling modern equipment for cultivation. The *Département* of Loir-et-Cher, with its two large farming co-operatives among the half dozen flourishing co-operatives in France, is an example to emulate.

Plantations and nurseries still flourish in Orléanais, and grain all over Beauce – the area sown with cereals diminishes from time to time, but the yield increases steadily. Fruit and vegetables are grown in the Loire valley and in western Sologne, together with bulbs and especially asparagus – in the Loir-et-Cher around Vineuil and Contres is concentrated almost half of the total asparagus output of France. Fruit and vegetables are grown in all the valleys from Touraine to Anjou; livestock is reared in Perche, Beaugeois and Segré, that is, north of the Loire exclusively, except for the sheep and goats on the plateaux of Touraine and Sologne. Goats are also found throughout the valley of the Cher: I have already mentioned the goat cheeses.

As for vines, the growers are aiming more and more at quality. From Sancerrois to the great muscadet vineyards of the west, the best known are Vouvray and Montlouis, Chinon and Bourgueil in Touraine, and the vineyards of Saumur and Brezé, Layon, La Roche-aux-Moines in Anjou, but countless others have a place in the cellars of connoisseurs for their distinctive character: the *gris-meunier* of Orléanais, now so rare, the *romorantin* of Mont and Cour-Cheverny, the remarkable *Sauvignons* of Oisly and the Cher valley, the white *pinots*, akin to the wines of Vouvray, the rouge and rosé of Mesland, the Jasnières of the valley of the Loir, beloved of Henry IV, so it is said – these are the amiable squires of the noble company of wines, often no less worthy of esteem for not having received the accolade.

As the Loire goes forward to meet the future, the problem of industry remains.

A problem familiar to the economist is the migration of populations. Let us say, making a gross over-simplification, that workers finding no employment in the country become concentrated in Paris – a seemingly inexhaustible source of employment, a city with golden pavements. Nevertheless we must add that before there was any concerted policy about this, the country towns and smaller towns when they were lively enough, gained, though not as much as one might wish, from this exodus from the fields. In a France which could become top-heavy with the slightest relaxation of vigilance regional economy needs, and is beginning to receive, a complete overhaul. As for the region which concerns us, Indre-et-Loire and Loir-et-Cher, together with the Loiret, belong to the economic demarcation known as the *Région Centre*, with Orleans as administrative centre, while Maine-et-Loire is attached to the *Pays de Loire* region, whose economic capital is Nantes.

Here are a few figures which shed some light on the development of the local population problem: the lowest ebb was reached just after the First World War, and today the population of Loiret slightly exceeds the figure for 1850 (390,000, as compared with 353,000), while Loir-et-Cher, which has long been held back by a county town too modest in size and ambition, has not even come up to the corresponding figure (258,000 now; 269,000 then). Indre-et-Loire shows a steady increase (403,000 from 324,000), Maine-et-Loire is more thickly populated than Loiret but shows a similar trend (560,000, compared with 526,000). The population figures for county towns have risen to twice that of 1850 for Orleans (88,000), three times for Blois (44,000), Tours (112,000) and Angers (122,000). If I add that the town of Blois had only 30,000 inhabitants in 1950, this says a lot for the results of planned action.

In Loir-et-Cher, which I have chosen as an example, the campaign has consisted in fixing the population with the aid of industrial expansion balanced between the county town, the sub-prefectures, and a number of secondary points, and appealing largely to decentralized labour from the Parisian area – Blois is less than 120 miles from Paris. Heavy industry was avoided, and for preference industries were adopted which could make use of natural products of the region.

Industrial development, and constructional development to echo the industrial expansion, were the two points on which this plan hinged. Here are the results in brief:

In Maine-et-Loire electronics has been added to the traditional industries of liqueurs and spinning in Angers, weaving and the shoe industry in the Choletais. A canning factory in Saumurois absorbs the local farming resources.

In Indre-et-Loire, Michelin and Hutchinson in 1957 developed a rubber industry in Joué-lès-Tours; a metallurgy industry has arisen in Saint-Cyr-sur-Loire, Saint-Pierre-des-Corps, La Riche, and at La Haye-Descartes and Azay-le-Rideau outside the suburbs of Tours. Electronics has also taken its place among the traditional industries of Touraine, of which printing, with the allied industries of paper manufacture, publishing, and the press were the oldest and most important; there are also plastics at Château-Renault, which have put new life into the local leather industry, and elsewhere pharmaceutical laboratories, building concerns, and public works.

Loiret already had a rubber factory at Montargis, earthenware at Gien, and the various concerns of the region round Orleans: Thermor, Saint-Gobain, clothes, vinegar, canning and farm machinery; and now a national experimental tobacco farm has grown up, and there is a great movement towards decentralization in which IBM plays a major part.

Until very recent times Loir-et-Cher was just scraping by; a cloth industry at Romorantin was losing momentum, there were shoes and chocolate at Blois, a tannery and traditional glove-making in Vendômois. But in the last ten years a committee for economic action, founded by M. Sudreau, at the time Préfet of Loir-et-Cher, and organized by André Boulle, a man of courage and strength of will, whose death was untimely, has succeeded in introducing 115 enterprises, mostly of small or medium importance, and mostly coming from the Parisian region. In this way 4,500 jobs were created, in addition to 2,500 new posts offered by the traditional industries. Dairy plants and cheese-making around Vendôme and Blois are typical of processing industries introduced into the producing country; printing and metallurgy together are the most important; as for the rest, they are intelligently distributed around the *Département*.

Finally Chinon and Saint-Laurent-des-Eaux have been selected by Electricité de France as future sites for two new nuclear centres.

It is unnecessary to prolong this account by giving the details of urban planning and development with a complete context of industrial and teaching requirements and leisure facilities. Sometimes the architectural result is devoid of feeling or imagination, sometimes it is a total success: undoubtedly an effort has been made, although it could perhaps have been more reflective, more co-ordinated. Successful attempts in the traditional style to repair the ravages of war are to be seen at Blois and Gien, among other towns; an impressive project for the future is the bold plan of Orleans, which envisages a new town of population 50,000 south of the Loire, covering 700 hectares – a town where the university will play an important part. Thus the middle Loire faces the future and preserves its heritage.

The gain for the region is easy to assess – it is more difficult to say what it might lose. To put the point more clearly, a *reductio ad absurdum*: if the day were to come when a materialist civilization kept only Chambord, the Château de Blois, Azay-le-Rideau and the tapestry museums at Angers from their regional past by reason of some co-efficient of productivity, the land would have lost its soul.

I shall not be melancholy, for this point has not been reached. One could also reverse the facts and dream – need it be only a dream? – that the enrichment of the land might help, for instance by restoring monuments, to safeguard its cultural purpose, might help to embellish the natural park of which the Loire, winding through the Garden of France, is the main avenue. This is country where we can travel alternate paths of sun and shadow to visit Rabelais and Leonardo da Vinci, King René, Joachim du Bellay, Ronsard and Charles d'Orléans, Balzac's Touraine, the Beauce of Péguy and, guided by Alain-Fournier, the Sologne of *Le Grand Meaulnes*.

Château of Azay-le-Rideau, and the Indre

Chapter VIII

PILGRIMAGES

IN the Sologne of my childhood there were curious traditions arising from a mixture of superstition and the religion of the country folk, like the 'Voyages en pied de marmite'. These were triangular pilgrimages to country churches, undertaken by mothers for their children. In one or other of these churches a gospel against fear would be declaimed before the statue of the good Saint Loup – a reminder of the time when the register of deaths made mention of children, sometimes even of adults, 'péris du fait de la beste'.[1]

Mine is a different kind of pilgrimage; I would say a literary one, if it did not have another aim : to rediscover, in the places where they lived, three men whose presence lives silently on in the countryside they loved.

The first stage of our pilgrimage will bring us to the Anjou of Joachim du Bellay, to Liré and the banks of the Loire; it is a pilgrimage to the sources, one which was undertaken by Joachim himself when he came back from Italy. He had learnt beyond the mountains to paraphrase Petrarch, but the decadent themes which flowed from the pen of this poet who died young were more than a literary device. He returned *Plein d'usage et raison*, but on the way home he sang of the call of his native land :

> *Quand revoyrai-je, hélas! de mon petit village*
> *Fumer la cheminée, et en quelle saison*
> *Revoyrai – je le clos de ma pauvre maison,*
> *Qui m'est une province, et beaucoup d'avantage . . .*[2]

Du Bellay, Baïf, Jodelle, Remy Belleau :

> *Te concevant, Belleau, qui vins en la Brigade*
> *De bons, pour accomplir la septiesme Pléiade . . .*[3]

'The *Brigade* became the *Pléiade* and to Ronsard, now back in Vendômois, his river Loir became a river of antiquity, while the forests of Gâtine wove the poet's crown :

[1] The registers of Anjou have many similar entries.
[2] 'When, alas ! shall I see again the smoking chimney of my little village, and in what season shall I again see the garden of my poor house, which for me is a province, and much more than that . . .'
[3] 'In conceiving you, Belleau, who entered the Brigade of the good, to become the seventh of the Pléiade . . .'

Sainte Gastine, o douce secrétaire
De mes ennuis, qui responds en ton bois
Ores en haute, ores en basse voix,
Aux longs souspirs que mon coeur ne peut taire;

Loir, qui refreins la course volontaire
Des flots roulans par nostre Vendômois,
Quand accuser ceste beauté tu m'ois,
De qui tousjours je m'affame et m'altère:

Si dextrement l'augure j'ai reçeu
Et si mon oeil ne fut hier déçeu
Des doux regards de ma douce Thalie,

Maugré la mort, Poëte me ferez,
Et par la France appelez vous serez
L'un mon Laurier, l'autre ma Castalie.[1]

Indeed, the transposition from the fount of Castalia at the foot of its rocky walls and the olive groves of Delphi clinging to the slopes of Parnassus, to the softly mellow landscapes of the valley of the Loir surrounded by gentle hills, is an entirely literary one:

Si quelque pèlerin arrive
Auprès de ta parlante rive,
Dy-luy à haute vois
Que ma Muse première
Apporta la lumière
De Grèce en Vendômois[2]

But when Ronsard writes of his own land:

En tes bras m'as reçu
Quand la belle lumière
Du monde j'apperceus;
Et toi, Braye, qui roules
En tes eaux fortement,

[1] 'Sainte Gastine, gentle minister to my cares, replying now loud, now soft, to the long sighs that my heart cannot restrain; Loir, you who cannot hold back the headlong course of the waters running through Vendômois, when you hear me speak of this beauty after which still I hunger and thirst: if I have construed the signs aright, and if my eye was not yesterday deceived by the gentle glance of my sweet Thalie, in spite of Death you will make a Poet of me, and by France you will be named, one my Laurels, the other my Castalia.'

[2] 'If some pilgrim comes to your chattering banks, tell him clearly that my Muse first brought the light of Greece to Vendômois.'

Et toi, mon Loir, qui coules
Un peu plus lentement, . . .[1]

when he wishes his friend Gaspard d'Auvergne to drink the Prépatour wine, from a golden cup ('may its vines flourish'), we are reminded of La Poissonnière, his birthplace, where *avant partir*,[2] Pierre de Ronsard, sitting before the marvellous fireplace which the sculptors had decorated in the Italian style, with delicate leaf patterns, blazons and canting arms, held to the light his glass of clear wine, newly brought from the cellars hollowed in the rock on the other side of the yard. There the wines of the Loir stood side by side with wines from foreign parts – *vina barbara* said a new device – and one of the other cellar doors bears this wise council: '*Cui des videto*' ('Consider whom you give it to').

Near La Poissonnière, in the church of Couture are the tombs and effigies of Ronsard's father and mother. Nearby flows the Loir, and a little further upstream is that green island, Ile Verte, where the young Ronsard had 'chosen his grave'. But that was a long time before departing this earth, and it was near Tours, in his priory of Saint-Côme, with its romanesque ruins, echoing in their Frankish style the precision and purity of the Greek lines, that Ronsard fell into his last sleep.

After Joachim du Bellay's Anjou, and Ronsard's Vendômois, the last stage of this pilgrimage takes us to the acropolis of Amboise.

Not far away, but outside the town in the time of Francis I, the little manor house of Le Cloux received Leonardo da Vinci, who spent the last years of his life there, accompanied by his pupil Melzi and his servant Villanis. Prematurely old, he was still asked to prepare festivities and devise machanisms – like the roaring lion whose breast opened, scattering abroad the lilies of France. As a painter he seems to have been content to live among his favourite works, contemplating universal Beauty for the last time, but as a hydraulic engineer he was busy with the fountains of Blois, and was doubtless consulted by the King about canalization in the Sologne, and about the plan to construct at Romorantin, a palace in two main sections on either side of an expanse of water on the river Sauldre, with steps leading down to the waterside from which spectators could have watched jousts on the water.

This project was set aside in favour of a palace to be built in the middle of a forest: Chambord, which if it is not Leonardo's own (and this we shall never know), remains in its proportions and in the double staircase which dominates the building a Leonardesque conception.

Then Leonardo, feeling death approaching, summoned his lawyer and expressed his last wishes. He looked into his soul, confessed his sins and received

---

[1] 'You, who took me to your arms when I first saw the beautiful light of day, and you, Braye, whose waters roll strong and swift, and you, my Loir, flowing a little slower, . . .'

[2] 'Before departing': this was a device which he read as a child and meditated upon later in maturity.

the last sacrament with pious humility, the final humility of a man of genius whose life had been an unceasing search for the truth of all things.

The rest was peace: the procession of chanting monks, the service in the collegiate church of the château. Today the collegiate church no longer exists, but it may be that the chapel which rises like a ship towards the east preserves Leonardo's ashes mingled in this high place with the earth of Touraine.

Du Bellay, Ronsard, Leonardo: three circles linked in the manner of the humanist symbol as it is found mysteriously inscribed on a canopy over a fire-place (see Plate 78) in Chaumont: these are the three saints of our pilgrimage.

But there are many more pilgrimages to be made – merry ones around Chinon, to Rabelais' house and to the ford, the Gué de Vède, where it is good to rest in the shadow of the hedges beside the stream: think of Gargantua's great mare who, when she wallowed in the river, 'so swelled the waters downstream that all that band of enemies were horribly drowned, save those few who had taken the path towards the slope on the left'.

We could visit the Sologne of Alain-Fournier, of *le Grand Meaulnes*, wild and mysterious, but I shall reserve that till last, because it is my country. Balzac's Touraine, teeming with life like himself, reaches out its tentacles in all directions: to Vendôme, where according to his sister Laure he 'meditated upon the *Comédie Humaine*', and where he pursued his singular studies; to Saumur, home of le Père Grandet; Vouvray, home of Gaudissart, with its old town around the cloistered cathedral reminding us of *Le Curé de Tours*; La Grenadière, and especially the valley of the Indre – *Le Lys dans la Vallée*, one of the finest titles of French literature. Balzac's refuge in Touraine was the rustic château of Saché, where M. de Margonne would welcome Balzac when he fled Paris, illness and his creditors: ('Touraine had cured me . . .'). Here the idea of *Séraphita* came to him, and it was at Saché, where he found 'the sky pure, the oaks so fine, the calm so vast!' that he completed *Maître Cornelius, Louis Lambert, Le Père Goriot* and *Les Illusions Perdues*.

There is the Pégny's Beauce, out of whose spreading harvest rises Chartres cathedral on the horizon, the cathedral of the *Pèlerinage*.

There is one pilgrimage in the work of Charles Péguy which we shall adopt, though it is not presented by him as such:

> Le long du coteau courbe et des nobles vallées
> Les châteaux sont semés comme des reposoirs,
> Et dans la majesté des matins et des soirs,
> La Loire et ses vassaux s'en vont par ces allées.
>
> Cent vingt châteaux lui font une suite courtoise,
> Plus nombreux, plus nerveux, plus fins que des palais.
> Ils ont nom Valençay, Saint-Aignan et Langeais,
> Chenonceau et Chambord, Azay, le Lude, Amboise.

64

Et moi j'en connais un dans les châteaux de Loire
Qui s'élève plus haut que le château de Blois,
Plus haut que la terrasse où les derniers Valois
Regardaient le soleil se coucher dans sa gloire.

La moulure est plus fine et l'arceau plus léger.
La dentelle de pierre est plus dure et plus grave.
La décence et l'honneur et la mort qui s'y grave
Ont inscrit leur histoire au coeur de ce verger.

Et c'est le souvenir qui'a laissé sur ces bords
Une enfant qui menait son cheval vers le fleuve.
Son âme était récente et sa cotte était neuve.
Innocente, elle allait vers le plus grand des sorts.

Car celle qui venait du pays tourangeau,
C'était la même enfant qui quelques jours plus tard,
Gouvernant d'un seul mot le rustre et le soudard,
Descendait devers Meung ou montait vers Jargeau.[1]

---

[1] Along the curving hillside and the noble valleys, the châteaux are strewn like as many altars, and through these avenues, in the majesty of the mornings and evenings, move the Loire and her vassals.

One hundred and twenty châteaux follow courteous in her train, more numerous, sturdier, and more delicate than palaces. Their names are Valençay, Saint-Aignan and Langeais, Chenonceau and Chambord, Azay, Le Lude, Amboise.

And I know one of these châteaux of the Loire which rises higher than the château of Blois, higher than the terrace where the last of the Valois would contemplate the sun setting in its glory.

Its moulding is finer, its arches lighter. Its stone tracery is harder, sterner. Modesty and honour and death graven there have inscribed their story within the heart of this orchard.

It is the memory left on these banks by a child who led her horse to the river. Her soul was fresh, her coat of mail was new. Innocent, she was going towards the greatest of destinies.

For she who came from the land of Touraine was the same child who, some days later, governing country churl and trooper with a word, was passing down towards Meung, or up towards Jargeau.

G

Chapter IX

SOLOGNE OF MY CHILDHOOD

BEFORE taking my leave I should like to speak of the Sologne of my child-hood.

The year 1918 was approaching and I was five years old, the age of first dis-coveries; five more years, and I would only be revisiting Sologne during school holidays. Already it was changing, and had been since the early years of the century, but the process was suddenly arrested by the war – as the frost some-times interrupts the first rising of the sap.

That was still the ancestral Sologne, wild and unspoilt. The roads were simply metalled and the sound of a jolting cart, a trotting pony or a shoe striking flint carried far at dusk.

A child's memories are at ground level; I remember silk-skinned mushrooms growing by the path, or scattered in fairy circles in the fields; a hedge which sheltered from the *vent de galerne*[1] the peasant woman keeping her goats, or rather doing needlework or knitting while the dog ran importantly round the nanny goats, with his hackles up, barking loudly. Then there was the scent of the gorse flowers and the green smell of the broom, massed with gold when it was in bloom, the earthy tang of heather and the resinous scent of the pine woods where the crackling floor yielded underfoot. On the plain, a covey of partridges calling to each other, or the cry of pheasants going down to the pool from the woods to drink; swifts swooping low before rain and, with the appear-ance of the woodland flowers, the first song of the cuckoo from a hidden perch, perhaps in a white-beam tree – then we would turn our pockets inside-out, and if we found a single coin we could be certain not to run short of money all the year.

The child running through the thickets or crouching there as an onlooker could make countless discoveries: rabbits playing in the wild oats in a clearing; the track leading from a bramble bush to a stinking trap where animals rotted; the glimpse of a graceful marten or weasel, a supple fox in flight, a couple of squirrels flirting overhead. Then there was the wild boars' wallow, and the haunts of the larger animals – hart and roe deer, which could sometimes be seen vanishing under the trees; and then their signature on the ground, the *vol ce l'est*[2] as hunters call it, which I had to learn to identify with the help of my

---

[1] The wind from the west-north-west.

[2] Pronounced 'vocelet' (word for word, '*vois-le, ce l'est*') 'see him, it is he': the trace left by the animal's foot.

father or a gamekeeper, or even one of those poachers of Sologne whose mysterious activities awoke in me admiration mixed with awe as for some secret cult – for when I met them they were going about their daily business, hoeing the garden, or at the plough late in the afternoon, with a few litres of *noah* inside them against the great heat, urging their horses on with irreverent but reiterated invocations of the name of the Lord.

In those times the old women wore their flat-crowned bonnets of Sologne whose snowy whiteness was their sole coquetry in dress. The men wore velvet and wooden shoes, or gaiters if they were working in the fields – the soil was Sologne clay, the kind which a seven- or eight-year-old thinks it manly to bring back, a pound of it on either foot; they had already discarded the *biaude*, a blue smock which was still in general use at the beginning of the century, but they kept for winter wear the cap with ear-flaps which was, I think, a fashion of the times, because I never saw any of the hats which must have been worn previously here, and were still being worn in Berry.

The room of the farm house had a tiled floor, or more rarely one of beaten earth; if the top of the Dutch door was closed it meant there was no one at home, and the barking dog would be straining at his chain at the farmyard gate, while hens clucked on the dung heap and two or three fine pigs rooted around the midden pit.

The two focal points of the living-room were the *lit à langes* – a canopied bed with curtains – and the fire place, this last surmounted by a gun, a holder for resin candles (*chandelier à oribus*) and a farming almanack; beside it ticked a clock with hanging weights, while the bed stood in shadow behind its drugget curtains. In between stood a large table which gave the measure of the housewife, sometimes shining and spotless, sometimes strewn with crumbs and bearing a half-empty bottle of red wine and a dirty glass. Soup would be simmering in a pot on the hearth over the ashes where embers still glowed, and the whole room would be smelling of washing, skimmed milk and meals.

These were the farms I knew as a child, with their walls of wattle and daub, or wood with bricks arranged in a herring-bone pattern, or even of stone in western Sologne, towards Touraine.

Now times have changed, and the reconstruction rooms in the museum of Sologne at Romorantin, informative and well presented, preserve a vanished aspect of the recent past. The improvement in living conditions may sometimes manifest itself in the country towns in regrettable ways, but while the hunting is being exploited, Sologne by and large has kept its old face and its subtle but distinctive charm.

At the pool of Montpercher in the heart of the forests of Boulogne, with the château of Chambord, masterpiece of the royal craftsmen, rising from the woodlands nearby, one can picture equally well Francis I riding to hounds, or the phantom hunt of the accursed Thibaud le Tricheur.

95. *Sainte-Chapelle, Château de Champigny*

96. *View of the Lantern of the Gaston d'Orléans Wing, Château of Blois*

CHATEAU DE CHEVERNY

97, 99, 100. *The Staircase and its Decorative Carving*

98. *Ornamental Details from the Façade*

101. *Aerial View of the Château in its Setting*

102. *Château de Brissac from the East Side, with the River Aubance*

99

Chambord, and the smaller châteaux of nearby Villesavin and Beauregard in the forest of Russy, are the outposts of Sologne. Further to the south and east are the wilder regions of woods, pools and silver birches growing in the heather, where one can drive or wander at will, enjoying the solitude.

Here is a simple country château, surrounded by pines soughing in the autumn wind. Sologne is at its best in the autumn; the carp leap in the pools, and the paths which vanish into the woodland seem to lead away from the present.

Philip, lord of the manor, rescued Charles XIII at the battle of Fornoue and then built the château of Le Moulin. The coloured brickwork is mirrored in the moat where two swans glide through the motions of a languid ballet, while assorted silhouettes of slate-covered towers and lodges rise against the sky.

To tell all would be to tell too much; speaking of Le Moulin brings two more names to my mind. One is Cheverny, where the same family has resided for six hundred years. The château standing today dates from the end of Louis XIII's reign, and everything about it – paintings, tapestries, furniture, beams and wood-work – preserves some of the charm of *la vielle France*.

But Cheverny is not a repository for past graces; the sound of the hounds and the horn reminds us of that most French of traditions, hunting. It is hoped that the nonsense which appears in print from time to time will not misrepresent hunting to the uniformed reader: the contest between the animal, and the hounds trying to anticipate his ruses, is one of our last links with nature in its wild state and the fast disappearing world of instinct. Besides, all the crafts which hunting keeps alive contribute to the economic balance of a region which tends – all too readily – to depopulate, and the fame of the night banquets held here, one might say, in honour of Diana and Saint Hubert jointly, has spread much farther afield than France.

I shall not say the last name. In his old house of brick and stone surrounded by sleeping water, glimpsed from afar beyond the great pool, lost from sight, glimpsed and lost again among the bronze of October leaves, lived a man who seemed to me as a child an extraordinary being: painter and poet in the *patois* of the Sologne, which he wrote about in moving terms, depicting the country people with malicious wit; sculptor, musician among other things, he was also the last bargeman of the Loire.

No doubt he was uneven in his various talents – I was neither of a mind nor of an age, thank God, to judge it – but he was prodigiously alive, an omnivorous critic, sharpening his teeth as a rule on all classes of society, and especially the *bourgeoisie*. He was a bourgeois himself, and not unrelated to those men of Orleans whose intellect he heartily despised. Full of contradictions, a prey to Homeric wrath but deeply and unassumingly a humanist, his features when I knew him resembled those of Ronsard in old age, as he appears in the drawing in the Hermitage museum.

Much later I learned that in the sixteenth century this house had belonged to Ronsard's aunt – and this is my last story.

Two young orphan girls, Jeanne and Renée Chaudrier, had been entrusted to Louis XII. The elder, who had been sent to stay with Mme de la Trémoille in the country to recover from an illness, was carried off by a young lover and married in secret. '*Dont ne sommes contens*' said the king, and he showed his displeasure in no uncertain way. Louis XII was quite capable of breaking a marriage, and the elder of the Chaudrier sisters, who not unspoilt but dowered, found a husband in the old Guyot des Roches, while Renée became her sister's niece by marrying René des Roches. Marriage between a young girl and an old man has its pitfalls, as Louis XII was to discover for himself. While the young widow took a second husband, Louis de Ronsard, René des Roches lost his father and inherited his estate. A lock on one of the doors of the château bears the date 1548: this, then, must have been the house rebuilt by the uncle and aunt of Ronsard.

My tale is ended.

I shall give the last word to a very old lady, a friend of my grandmother's, whom I had never seen, nor indeed ever did, and who one day wrote me a charming letter of the kind which old ladies used to know how to write. She was spending her old age in another province of France, beautiful Périgord, the province of her husband whom she had lost. He was a Hellenist, and he used to say to her, '*Vous qui êtes d'un pays de gens civilisés.*'

This phrase, which one would like to be as true tomorrow, is addressed to the men of our time, and beyond them to their land of renaissance and encounter.

Explanatory List of Illustrations

The following explanatory list relates to the illustrations to be found all together at the end of this book, except for the colour plates and maps which are placed as indicated below.

1. 75-76. 78. CHÂTEAU DE CHAUMONT. The late tenth-century fortress of Chaumont, overlooking the Loire downstream from Blois, together with Saumur, Chinon, Montrichard and Amboise, were 'vantage points' in the struggle between the counts of Blois and Anjou for the possession of the Touraine, which passed from hand to hand. For five hundred years Chaumont belonged to the house of Amboise. The participation of Pierre d'Amboise in the League of Public Good led to the château's demolition, but Louis XI personally ordered it to be rebuilt. This new château was completed by Charles of Amboise, Lieutenant General of Louis XII in Milan, who died in 1511.

Immediately after the death of Henry II, Catherine de' Medici, who coveted Chenonceau, forced Diane de Poitiers to exchange it for Chaumont even before the deeds were signed. She had also neglected to pay the succession duty, and when Diane took possession of the château it was seized by the Treasury; the Duchess of Valentinois kept it nevertheless until her death in 1566. Among the many owners of Chaumont was Jacques Donatien Le Ray; it was he who installed the Italian Nini, whose terra cotta medallions depicting celebrities of the time were executed at Chaumont between 1772 and 1786. For a few months in 1810 Mme de Staël lived there after her downfall, a rather difficult guest. In 1938 the Princess Amédée de Broglie (née Say) who after Viscountess Walsh was responsible for the extensive restoration work carried out in the nineteenth century, sold the château to the State. About 1740 the mediaeval wing overlooking the river had been demolished, opening up the inner courtyard to magnificent views of the Loire.

1 and 75. Charles of Amboise's reconstruction was carried out between 1498 and 1510. Chaumont still kept its fortified appearance, but great windows were pierced in the outside walls: the introduction of the cannon into warfare had rendered anything but a token defence against a determined attack impossible. There is decorative carving on either side of the main entrance, which is still guarded by a drawbridge. Also there are the emblems of Louis XII and Anne de Bretagne and the cardinal's hat of Charles' uncle, George of Amboise, with the coat of arms of the owner borne by two savages and crested by a helmet with lambrequins, surmounted by a head.

The heraldic motif is inserted in a niche crowned by a scallop shell; this and the console with ovolo mouldings are borrowed from Italian style.

The frieze running round the walls and towers at mid-window level on the ground floor has alternating motifs: the intertwined Cs of Charles de

71

Chaumont, and the 'chaud mont', a sort of burning mound manifesting the fifteenth-century Frenchman's taste for puns. The same motif is used at the Château de Meillant in Berry, another of Charles of Amboise's domaines.

76. The courtyard owes far too much to nineteenth-century restoration. The gallery built by La Morandière is flush with the staircase which used to project into the court and has a modern upper storey. The fine well in the foreground has been brought from elsewhere.

The fireplace on the first floor of the St Nicholas tower (flanking the chapel to the north-east) is intact. Its hood has a design of colonnettes and arches enclosing shells resting on a lower section decorated with arabesque panels. The design, which has been restored to its original colours, is completed by a central motif of a triangle in three interlaced circles, which is repeated on the outside of the towers. Delta (△) is the Greek initial for Diane de Poitiers; it recurs elsewhere in the tapestry hanging The Story of Diana, which was woven for her.

The Duchess of Valentinois is also recalled in the panels decorating the base of the battlement walk, where the machicolations, bear two carved Ds intertwined and the horn, bow and quiver of Diana the Huntress.

2. Chambord By Night. The Très riches heures de Chambord created in 1952 was the first example of son et lumière, the interplay of history and architecture in the nocturnal countryside creating for visitors a new poetic truth. This art form, if it is one, has a large following, but sometimes virtuosity has stolen a march on the interpreter. See also notes on 79 to 83, and 86.

3. 42, 130 to 132. 135. VENDÔME: THE TRINITY. One evening looking down on Vendôme from his Castle above Count Geoffroi Martel, son of Fulk Nerra, saw three fiery lances descend into a spring in the middle of the fields: this is the traditional story of the founding of an abbey dedicated to the Trinity. The dedication took place on May 31, 1040, ten days after his father's death had made Geoffroi Count of Anjou.

Only in the transept can the original walls and capitals still be seen. The twelfth-century bell tower stands to the south-west apart from the church – the thrust of its masonry rising towards the spire achieve a kind of formal perfection (No. 42).

The choir of the abbey church, with its ambulatory giving access to five radiating chapels, dates from the early fourteenth century. The eight bay nave with side aisles, has a triforium and was under construction from the fourteenth to the early sixteenth century. The façade, a masterpiece of flamboyant Gothic art, has curves and counter curves arranged with a skill which gives the illusion of simplicity; the effect is completed by flying buttresses on either side of the building (No. 3).

One should also mention the 'Ma Dame Saincte Larme' (Weeping Madonna) in the main abbey church of the Trinity at Vendôme, a precious relic given to Geoffroi Martel in the Orient; its authenticity was questioned in the eighteenth century by Jean-Baptiste Thiers, the turbulent Curé of Vibraye.

The rood screen has gone, but some of the late fifteenth-century choir stalls were put back into the chancel after the Revolution; a delicate Renaissance screen of stone separates the chancel from the ambulatory. Several of the misericord seats are carved with lively scenes depicting work at different times of the year (No. 130, 131, 132, 135).

There is a fine collection of stained glass, mostly dating from the Renaissance, set in the flamboyant windows, one in particular, a twelfth-century scene of the Virgin and Child, is indescribably beautiful.

4. THE LOIRE AT ORLÉANS.

5. CHINON 'the white' – this is the origin of the Celtic name – was occupied from very early times. Roman conquerors camped here, Saint Martin preached the gospel here, Saint Brice built a church here in the fifth century. At Chinon the Visigoths resisted Egidius, and Saint Mexme founded a monastery.

The counts of Blois and Anjou held it in turn in feudal times; here Henry II of England died, abandoned by all, in 1189, as according to tradition, did Richard the Lionheart, ten years later. In 1205 after a siege lasting a year King John of England surrendered Chinon to Philippe-Auguste. There are two tragic memories connected with Chinon in the fourteenth century: passage of Jacques de Molay and three dignitaries of the order of Knights Templar on their way to Poitiers where they were taken to be executed by Philippe le Bel, and burning alive in 1321 of 160 Jews, found guilty of poisoning wells.

In the fifteenth century Chinon provided a refuge for Charles VII when he was south of the Loire, and on March 9, 1429, Joan of Arc, after waiting three days, was admitted to the great hall of the château and recognized there her 'gentil dauphin'.

Chinon was then abandoned; the fort of Le Coudray, the château du Milieu and the fort of St Georges form a ruined acropolis from which one can gaze down on the Vienne and distant horizons, and the town with its picturesque streets and houses closer at hand. Between the town and the château are the 'caves pintes', cool cellars hollowed in the honey-coloured tufa containing the vin breton (from the vine so named) which is ruby red, almost purple. Rabelais came from Chinon; the giant Gargantua must have originated in this wine-growing country which enlarges everything.

6. ANGERS: THE HOUSE OF ADAM. Time has effaced the original parents of mankind who were portrayed naked, as was fitting, near the tree of good and evil. This fine house dating from the second half of the fifteenth century, of brick with timber framing, still has some very fine carving, often with lively motifs.

7. TOURS: WOODEN HOUSE. In spite of the incidents of 1940 Tours still has some picturesque timber houses, often slate-roofed like the one on the left, with an abundance of interesting carving on corner posts and window frames. These houses are in the Place Plumereau, on the corner of the Rue du Change and the Rue de la Monnaie.

8 and 9. ROMORANTIN. The Chancellery and the Carroir Doré (or D'Orée?) These two timbered buildings decorated with sculptured motifs were both known to Francis I, who would also have distinct memory of the Hôtel Saint-Pol, a

73

neighbouring house which is still standing. In 1521 on the day of Epiphany, *le jour des Rois* (The Day of Kings), while participating in a mock combat which was a traditional part of the festivities, Francis was burned by a flaming torch which somebody threw: the resultant scar on his chin gave rise to the fashion of beards!

10. BLOIS: BAS-RELIEF OF THE HÔTEL DE JASSAUD IN THE RUE FONTAINE-DES-ELUS. Placed over the door leading to the staircase, this carving decorates a house which has otherwise lost nearly all its interesting features; it seems to belong to the end of the reign of Louis XII.

What union is symbolized in this group? Who are the shepherd and shepherdess with their crooks on their shoulders? Which family is represented by the shield supported by a family tree? Possibly the union is that of Jacob and Rachael, as local tradition has it, but certainly it has a specific allusion – maybe to the marriage of Bonne Cottereau, daughter of Louis XII's personal secretary, to Guillaume de Beaune, son of Semblançay? Cottereau's story is interesting. After amassing a considerable fortune as a cattle-dealer he started a butchery business in Blois and married into the Doulcet family, themselves butchers there, from whom the mother of Cassandre Salviati was descended. He won the favour of the Duc d'Orléans who became King Louis XII, whom as his secretary he had followed to Italy, and between the years 1509 and 1514 rebuilt the little manor house of La Vicomté near Blois and, above all, the château of Maintenon. He became owner of the house after his brother Pierre who, thanks to him, had obtained the position of Keeper of Water and Forests of the Comté of Blois and the duchy of Orléans.

But what does it matter? While contemplating the beauty of this old carving with its Italian feeling, its air of fragility and timeless perfection, one can forget the circumstances in which it was made.

11. FRANCIS I – A drawing in the Condé Museum at Chantilly.

12. FRANCIS II – A portrait by Clouet, Paris, Bibliothèque Nationale.

13. 86 and colour plate II.
CHÂTEAU D'AZAY-LE-RIDEAU. Without dwelling on the former owners of Azay, counts of Blois in the tenth and eleventh centuries, counts of Anjou who soon afterwards became kings of England, and Philippe-Auguste under whom it became the property of the Capets etc., we must mention the Burgundians whose occupation of the château came to a bloody end in 1418, when the whole garrison was hanged, the château pulled down and the town burnt. It then became known as Azay le Brulé until the thirteenth century when the family de Ridel took possession and gave it their name.

Towards the end of the fifteenth century Gilles Berthelot, son of a Master of the Chamber of Finance to Louis XI and Charles VIII, owned the land. In alliance with the Keeper of the Seals, Adam Fumée, with Cardinal Guillaume Briconnet and with the General of Finances, Semblançay, Berthelot soon became Treasurer of France. The Semblançay affair, which ended on the gallows at Montfaucon where, as Marot reminds us, the condemned man showed himself 'such a firm old man', brought disgrace and imprisonment upon all his associates. Berthelot died soon afterwards at Cambrai, victim of the hatred, no doubt unjustified, of Louise of Savoy.

The supervision of the present château's building is largely attributable to Philippe Lesbahy, wife of Gilles Berthelot – (the name is used here as a woman's christian name). Azay was built quickly; started 1518, confiscated 1528. It is incomplete, yet homogeneous, consisting of two main parts forming a right-angle. In the Romantic period a turret was added to the eastern portion, and a tower, replacing one that was too out-of-date for a sixteenth-century château – it was necessary to re-establish the 'unity of style'! With its towers, crenellations and machicolations, Azay is still a fortified château, but two storeys of mullioned windows topped by dormers give light and decoration to the top storey: overlooking the waters of the Indre, diverted into moat, Azay's gracefulness reminds one of a charming woman's face reflected in a mirror.

As is usual in châteaux built during the reign of Francis I, the storeys are separated by horizontal courses, and flat pilasters emphasising the vertical lines of the bays are set regularly along the façades which are decorated with antique medallions. On the ground and three upper floors the staircase has twin bays of projecting basket-handle (basket-handle means nothing in English though it is a descriptive term in French) arches topped with a tall decorative gable; columns, pilasters and niches, together with a profusion of Italian motifs complete this structure, which dominates the building, as do the staircases at Blois and Chambord. All three staircases are quite different, however; the one externally built in the manner, but not in the style, of fifteenth-century staircase towers, the other with its two concentric spirals constituting the centre of the building; the staircase of Azay, built simply into a façade to give it interest, consists of two straight flights broken by landings; it has an exceptional coffered ceiling with depressed arches and pendant keystones. All these serve to express an art which, while preserving the architectonic principles of late Gothic and adopting the decorative ideas imported from Italy, shows the continuing taste of early sixteenth-century France for an abundance of decorative carving.

14. CATHERINE DE' MEDICI, a drawing by Clouet: Bibliothèque Sainte-Geneviève, Paris.

15. HENRY II – An anonymous drawing. Rennes Museum.

16. DIANE DE POITIERS, attributed to Clouet. Cabinet des Estampes, Paris.

17. CANDES: The Confluence of the Loire with the Vienne.

18. VENDÔME, ST GEORGE'S GATE. Built in the second half of the fourteenth century and altered at the beginning of the sixteenth century, the Porte Saint-Georges was given in 1467 by the count of Vendôme to the inhabitants for use as a town hall, which it remained until the bombardment in 1940. It has been very carefully restored.

The present archway was made in 1809 to allow Napoleon's artillery to pass through on its way to Spain.

19. 153. 154. CHÂTEAU DE VALENÇAY. Jacques d'Etampes was in possession of the château when reconstruction was begun. There are two wings set at right angles: the west wing was built in the seventeenth and eighteenth centuries.

The great corner tower shown here, and fluted basket-work capitals of the pilasters may be compared to those being built at Chambord in the last years of Francis I's reign. M. René Crozet has also pointed out borrowings from other buildings, especially the château of Veuil whose owner, Jean Hurault, was the uncle of Jacques d'Etampes. But at Valençay one looks for grandeur rather than refinement.

M. le Duc de Talleyrand, the most famous owner, I have mentioned elsewhere both in the text and in the illustrations (Nos 153 and 154).

20. 21. 22 and 23. ANGERS: TAPESTRY MUSEUM. The famous Tapestry of the Apocalypse (cf. Nos 53 and 55) is an unrivalled masterpiece, but the hangings in the chapel and in the governor's lodgings are also major works of art. It is appropriate here to draw the attention of the visitor to Angers to the Museum of Fine Arts, the Archeological Museum of Saint-Jean, the Musée Turpin de Crissé in the Logis Pincé, and the Treasury of the Cathedral, all of which contain important works.

20. 21. THE GARDENER, AND ANOTHER DETAIL FROM PART OF THE TAPESTRY OF THE LIFE OF SAINT MAURILLE.

22. CONCERT. A lady, sumptuously dressed, is seated at the keyboard of a portable organ, the bellows of which are worked by a page; she accompanies the singing of a man who is standing in front of her, while two children are teasing a cat and a dog. The dark blue ground is scattered with flowers and animals.

This tapestry with a flowered background is the product of a charming fashion favoured in the residences of the Val de Loire in the reign of Louis XII, but there are no precise proofs to suggest that this series (scenes from seignorial life, pastoral scenes, the Lady with the Unicorn, legends of Saint Florent and Saint Julien, etc.) were manufactured on the banks of the Loire.

The tapestry shown here has been called the tapestry 'de la Dame de Rohan': according to this hypothesis the people represented are Pierre de Rohan, marshal of Gié, counsellor of Louis XII, who fell from favour through the influence of Anne de Bretagne in 1508 and died in 1513, and his second wife Marguerite d'Armagnac, whom he had married in 1503. According to this theory it came, like another concert scene which is now housed in the Musée des Gobelins, from the Château du Verger in Anjou, the Angevin residence of the Rohans. Nevertheless, the lower portion bearing the arms of Pierre and Marguerite de Rohan (No. 23) is not part of the tapestry to which it has been sewn, but belongs to the now incomplete tapestry of the Angels carrying the Instruments of the Passion.

23. Flowered border sewn to the same tapestry.

24 and colour plate 3. CHÂTEAU DE VILLANDRY. Like Villesavin (No. 26), Villandry was rebuilt for Jean le Breton, who bought the domaine in 1532.

Only the medieval keep was preserved. The sixteenth-century building was disfigured in the eighteenth century, and in recent times the whole has been energetically restored. This château is much larger than Villesavin, but it still has three wings around a rectangular courtyard, and two square pavilions. M. Gébelin believes that this arrangement, dispensing with the old corner towers, could have been derived from Ecouen.

Architecture in the Val de Loire ceased to exploit new forms: after Pavia, Francis I returned to the Ile-de-France and Paris; the Château de Madrid in the Bois de Boulogne (1528), Saint-Germain (1539), the Louvre (1546), sprang up to mark his return.

But Villandry today offers the unique attraction of its gardens.

Indeed, its twentieth-century owner Dr Carvalho had the idea of re-creating the gardens in the style of the sixteenth century as a setting for Villandry. These extend on three levels, the kitchen garden, the ornamental garden, and on the highest level the water garden with its cascades and arbours.

In the ornamental garden, shown here, the box hedges arranged geometrically, contain the vivid patches of floral colour, while the vertical lines of clipped yews cut across the flower beds rather like men on a chessboard. This art of gardening was skilled and refined; we are fortunate to have a living example of it before our very eyes.

25. 126. RICHELIEU.

25. This château was built for Armand-Jean du Plessis, Cardinal-Duc de Richelieu, according to the plans of the architect Le Mercier. It was begun in 1625.

In 1631 Richelieu was authorized by the king to construct near his castle the curious little town which bears his name (No. 126), and which, like the port of Brouage, he believed to be sound economic ventures. These failed in both cases.

The enterprises of the great are sometimes 'short-lived': all that remains of the château de Richelieu is the pavilion pictured here. Also at that time the cardinal decided to join to his duchy the estate of Champigny-sur-Veude, which belonged to Gaston d'Orléans, and razed the entire château there to the ground. Of this there remains the Sainte-Chapelle (No. 95), saved by the Pope Urban VIII, and the outbuildings (110), now promoted to the status of château.

26. CHÂTEAU DE VILLESAVIN. The creation of Villesavin is linked to that of Chambord. Nicolas de Foyal, the builder of Herbault, had been the King's commissioner at the construction of Chambord (cf. No. 79-83); towards the end of his life, Jean Le Breton, or Breton, appears to have exercised similar functions in which his widow certainly succeeded him. According to Bernier, the historian of Blois, who was writing in the reign of Louis XIV, the estate of Villesavin had been given to him for his services. The work must have been virtually finished by 1537, a date which is inscribed on one of the dormer windows. At one time President of the Chambre des Comptes of Blois, and after sharing Francis I's captivity at Pavia, Jean Le Breton later appeared at Villandry (No. 24).

Villesavin is a charmingly modest building of one storey beneath a roof pierced by dormer windows with high carved gables. There are corner towers;

the main block has a square pavilion on either side; a wing lies to the right, and to the left simply a decorated wall both of which connect with other pavilions, the one on the left containing the chapel. Originally the courtyard was bounded by a moat. From the centre of the façade two small projections have been inserted rather clumsily, one on the courtyard and the other on the garden side, this last forming a sort of loggia with an oratory above.

All that remains of the interior decoration are the paintings of the chapel, the earliest of which dates from the beginning of the seventeenth century, the time when Raymond Phelyppeaux owned Herbault and his brother Jean, Ville-savin.

The clear glass 'round the borders of which are depicted the metamorphoses of Ovid and the Arms of the Lords of the Court of Francis I', mentioned by Bernier, have disappeared.

On the other hand the marble basin in the courtyard, decorated with dolphins, chimeras and lion masks, is an Italian work reminiscent in some ways of Leonardo, and of exceptional quality.

27. 119. CHÂTEAU DE MENARS. The central portion dates from about 1645, the same time as the wing built by Gaston d'Orléans at the château of Blois, the church of the Jesuits (Saint-Vincent) and Cheverny. This first castle of Menars was built by Guillaume Charron, Controller of the Wars, son of a wine-merchant of Saint-Dyé, of which the church tower is visible on the opposite bank of the Loire. Charron left Menars to his nephew, 'le Président de Menars', and his niece, Marie, married Colbert. Saint-Simon has left us this portrait of the Président de Menars : 'Menars was a very fine figure of a man and a very good man too, not very capable, but full of honour, probity, equity, and modest ! A marvel protégé in a high court president.'

In the next generation Stanislas Leszczynski, who lived at Chambord from 1725 to 1732, spent the last five summers of his stay in the Val de Loire at Menars.

In 1760 the château was acquired by the Marquise de Pompadour four years before her death.

In 1763-64 Jacques-Ange Gabriel added the two lateral wings and outbuildings which surround the court of honour. Then the Marquis of Marigny, Director of the Royal Buildings, who succeeded his sister, commissioned Soufflot to build the orangery and the circular temple, the charming ornamental lake and grotto, together with the terraces and flower gardens.

In the Romantic period it is quite amusing to find the châtelaine of Menars, the Countess of Brégode, née Pellapra, illegitimate daughter of Napoleon, marrying the Prince of Chimay, whose mother had been married to Tallien (opponent of the Girondins). Passing over other owners who in the eighteenth and nineteenth centuries gradually emptied Menars of its furniture and statuary, it is interesting to point out that the Saint-Gobain Company, who acquired the château in 1939, tastefully restoring to order the château and the gardens, is none other than the Manufacture des Glaces which had made for Menars the mirrors ordered by Mme de Pompadour.

Here are shown the flower beds of Soufflot, their successive terraces leading to the view of the Loire. In addition there is the park surrounding Menars with its arbours and quincunxes, a delightful walk where one can stroll in the quiet contemplating the prospect of the Loire.

28. F. BOUCHER – APPOLLO APPEARING TO ISSE, from the Musée des Beaux Arts at Tours. This painting, which comes from the château de Chanteloup (cf. No. 29), is one of numerous works representing the collections of the French school in the Museum at Tours. The foreign schools are also well represented especially Italy: the two panels of Mantegna (*The Agony in the Garden* and *The Resurrection*) are famous. The museum of precious stones *(le musée lapidaire)* is also well worth a visit as much for its collections as for the magnificent Renaissance house, the Hôtel Gouin (cf. No. 91), which contains them.

29. PAGODA OF CHANTELOUP. Choiseul, Louis XV's minister, who in 1761 acquired the land of Chanteloupe and Amboise, combined into a duchy in 1764, altered the château built in the early eighteenth century for the Princesse des Ursins and had an admirable series of gardens made. The Duke and Duchess of Choiseul lived there after their disgrace in 1770.

The '*Bande Noire*' annexed the château in 1823, and of so much pomp only the pagoda remains. The piece of *chinoiserie* conceived by Le Camus and built between 1775 and 1778, rises more than 120 feet above the surrounding countryside.

30. CHÂTEAU DE SULLY. This château, connected with the defences which the bishops of Orléans raised in the twelfth century at the bridge-head on the Loire, dates in its present form from the fourteenth or early fifteenth century – Joan of Arc stayed there in March 1430 – and was sold by Claude de la Trémoille, a convert to the reformed religion, to Maximilien de Béthune, Marquis de Rosny. This minister of Henry IV was himself descended on the distaff side from the former lords of Sully. This land was elevated to a duchy in 1606.

After retiring from affairs of state on the death of Henry IV, Rosny lived alternatively in his *hôtel* in Paris and his châteaux, Villebon and Sully.

It is here that he undertook, with the help of a whole staff of secretaries and printers, the publication of his memoirs, the Œconomies Royales, written to enhance his own and his master's fame. The first two volumes appeared in 1638; Sully died in 1641 at Villebon.

In the eighteenth century the château received a famous guest: in 1716 Maximilien-Henry de Sully entertained there Voltaire, who was then twenty-two years of age. The author of the *Henriade*, which was begun at Sully, and the tragedy *Artémise*, performed in the theatre of the château on the first floor of the keep, returned to Sully in 1719, the year when his host married the daughter of the famous Mme Guyon.

The château remained in the possession of Maximilien de Béthune's descendants and was recently acquired by the Département of Loiret.

31. 32. SAINT-BENOIT-SUR-LOIRE. The Abbey of Fleury-sur-Loire was founded in 651 by Leodebold, Abbot of Saint-Aignan d'Orléans. It comprised two churches, Saint-Pierre and Saint-Marie, of which only the second remains today.

At the beginning of the eighteenth century the monk Aigulf's expedition to Monte Cassino in the south of Italy, from which he returned with the relics of Saint Benedict, started the long era of pilgrimages. In spite of pillaging and burning, the abbey grew under abbots like Saint Odo who introduced the Cluniac reform there in the tenth century; Saint Abbo (988-1004); and his successor, the illegitimate son of Hugues Capet, Gauxlin, who was later archbishop of Bourges, abbot from 1004-1030.

The so-called 'crypt of Saint Mommolinus', which does not date from the seventh century, and is not a crypt but was probably the treasury which the cantor Godefroi wanted to build in stone and which was no doubt finished in the early years of the ninth century, is the oldest part of the building as it stands today.

The West Tower, unquestionably the most original part of the abbey church, is next in the chronological order of buildings and will be studied separately. The fire of 1026 destroyed the two churches, and was the occasion for general rebuilding. The new chancel and transept were begun under Abbot William (1067-1080), and their consecration was performed by the bishops of Orléans and Auxerre on March 21, 1108.

The apse is over a crypt, and the ground level there is much higher than that of the choir. It is surrounded by an ambulatory and has only two radiating chapels. To the north and south two more chapels make a false transept; each of these has a low tower and an absidiole facing east. The interior elevation of the apse comprises great arches supported by columns, and above them a storey of blind arcades and then a clerestory.

Beneath the church and roughly reproducing its plan extends the crypt designed for the veneration of the reliquary of St Benedict. If pilgrims were unable to go down, they could venerate the body of the saint through six narrow bays opening on to the choir.

The choir continues the design of the apse, except that the difference in floor level has left a blank wall between the top of the great arches and the base of the blind arcades.

The crossing of the transept is roofed with a cupola on squinch-vaults; each arm of the transept (the south arm has been rebuilt) has two absidioles facing east.

The construction of the nave, which began in the mid-twelfth century, was held up by another fire (1184), and not completed until 1218. The nave has side aisles and seven bays; the square piers with four engaged half columns support great pointed arches. It is lit by tall splayed windows and covered with pointed rib vaulting, while the side aisles have groined vaults. The north door, dating from the thirteenth century, is flanked on either side by three columns carved to represent prophets. The tympanum shows Christ in Majesty surrounded by the Evangelists; the lintel shows the translation of the bodies of St Benedict and his sister St Scholastica.

The west tower of the abbey church of Saint-Benoît forms a square; its two storeys have three aisles and three bays with groined vaulting; entirely open to the outside at ground level, it rests on massive piers, with engaged half-columns, the capitals of which have dosserets, supporting semi-circular arches with an internal order borne by its own half-columns. The blind arches on the west face of the church are divided by decorative arches resting on central engaged columns. Additional reinforcement is provided by corner buttresses, the eastern ones containing the staircase which gives access to the upper floor.

The plan of this floor is identical to that of the ground floor, but the springing of the arches on each face of the square piers is from the capitals of twin engaged columns without dosserets. Moreover, the light on this floor is provided by sets of three windows in the north, west and south faces; three semi-domed apses occupy the east section of this tall chapel, whose central altar was probably dedicated to St Michael.

On the exterior of the north wall are several re-used low reliefs, inserted haphazardly. They are of very early workmanship and reminiscent of those at Lavardin. The lantern roof which covers the tower only dates from the seventeenth century.

So far only the building has been described, but the carving of the capitals is of superb quality : acanthus leaves, animals and historiated capitals, especially on the ground floor, have helped considerably to date the building.

Without entering here into a detailed discussion, it is difficult to see in this building anything other than the 'tower built in stone from the Nivernais' – as indeed it is – which Gauzlin wanted to show as 'an example to the whole of Gaul', although death forestalled him before he completed the enterprise. If this is so, the construction could have been begun after the great fire of 1026, as the use of older motifs on the north wall would indicate, or four years before the death of Gauzlin, and in all probability it was finished before the church of Abbot William (1067).

To date the St Benedict tower as late as the last third of the twelfth century, it has been necessary to base the estimate not only on a doubtful interpretation of texts, but above all on arguments which relate to the monumental aspect and to the quality of the decoration – arguments which turn against their users as soon as they are forced to admit to 'clumsiness' and 'archaism' in the masonry and sculpture : how can one suppose that an edifice built 'to be an example to all Gaul' would have been entrusted to men who were behind their times, rather than to up to date builders?

33. GERMIGNY-DES-PRÉS. The theologian, sage, and poet Theodulf, most probably of Spanish origin, and who was honoured by Charlemagne, became bishop of Orléans and subsequently abbot of Fleury (Saint-Benoît-sur-Loire), had a villa built for himself at Germigny in the early years of the ninth century; the present church embodies the remains of the old chapel, where radical restoration in the nineteenth century has not entirely destroyed its character. A nave had already been added to the small centrally planned building; the mosaics had been whitewashed over, and apart from the one illustrated here, which was skilfully exposed and restored by the Italian specialist Ciuli in 1841, there were other important elements of interior decoration, mosaic and stucco that the restorers removed without a pang of conscience. In yet another way

the restoration done in 1869 ruined the effect of the great mosaic, by replacing the missing golden tesserae by pieces of Sèvres porcelain.

This mosaic shows cherubim and the Ark of the Covenant, at which two archangels above are pointing; between their wings the hand of God is extended. A Latin inscription around the scene reads roughly as follows: 'Look here at the Holy Oracle and the cherubim, and, while admiring the splendour of the Ark of God strive to touch by thy prayers Him who thunders, and join I pray to thy vows the name of Theodulf.'

34. Traditionally called the 'GOSPELS OF CHARLES THE BALD', without any apparent foundation, this extremely fine manuscript of the four gospels (Library of Tours, No. 23, f. 11 V° and 12) comes from Saint-Martin de Tours, and seems to have been executed in the eleventh century in the scriptorium of the abbey itself. Shown here is the beginning of the gospel according to St Matthew *(Incipit Evangelivm Secvndvm Mathevm)*. The calligraphy is of a very high quality, for instance, on the title page, executed in golden letters, and at the beginning of the text (geneaology of Christ), in uncial script beautifully arranged around the double illuminated letters (the 'L' and 'I' of *liber*). This illumination incorporates the animal kingdom (two heads) and an interlaced design in a skilful composition of remarkable balance and restraint.

35. SELLES-SUR-CHER. DECORATION OF THE APSE OF THE CHURCH. The abbey of Selles was founded in the Merovingian epoch by St Eusice. Pillaged and ruined by the Normans, it was rebuilt by the archbishop of Bourges, Pierre de la Châtre, who in 1145 entrusted it to some regular canons. In 1562 Coligny left the collegiate church in a sad state. It was very carefully restored by the architect A. de Baudot.

The choir, which lies above a raised crypt reconstructed almost entirely by Baudot, has an ambulatory and three radiating chapels; the transept with its two absidioles, together with the west front and the wall of the south aisle, belong to the romanesque church (second quarter of the twelfth century). The nave, which never received the vaulting intended for it, and the side aisles each of which has seven bays with ribbed vaulting, belong to a late-thirteenth-century reconstruction.

This church, where Joan of Arc prayed, has an apse with radiating chapels, and derives remarkable balance of proportion from its buttress columns, its modillioned cornices and the two bands of carving framing the windows with external colonnettes.

The lower frieze shows scenes from the Old and New Testaments, where we can see Christ being seized; the upper frieze contains the miracles of the legendary life of St Eusice, like the episode at the top of the illustration where demons who tried to disrupt the building of the church were employed by Eusice to quarry stone and draw a cart.

The marble columns and colonnettes used in the façade and in the choir are not Roman as had been suggested, but may very probably have come from the basilica built by Eusice thanks to the generosity of King Childebert in the second quarter of the sixth century.

36. GABLE CROSS AT SAINT-MAUR DE GLANFEUIL. This magnificent gable cross with an interlaced design incised in low relief on a background of diamond-shaped stones is similar to the cross decorating the south wall of the church of Esves-le-Moutier. The Abbé Plat suggests that both of these should be placed in the first half of the tenth century, but in illuminated books the 'Carolingian' interlaced designs were employed until the twelfth century. The art of building was very conservative in Touraine and Anjou; the eleventh-century builders there made use of the lozenge shape: these are a number of reasons why, as precise dating evidence is lacking, we should be cautious in our estimates.

37. A CAPITAL OF THE BELFRY PORCH, SAINT JULIEN OF TOURS. The present abbey church of Saint-Julien, founded by Gregory of Tours to house the relics of the saint brought back from Brioude, consists almost exclusively of thirteenth-century restoration work, but the tower built in 966, and extensively altered by the Abbot Gerbert in 1080, has not been altered since. This lively eleventh-century carved capital showing two wild beasts holding a man upside down by the legs makes use of a very rough technique to provide decoration of a kind which is to be found in the liturgical manuscripts of the eleventh and twelfth centuries; the similarity is seen more clearly when, (as in the case of the crypt of Saint-Aignan of Orléans in particular, where the columns were incorporated into square piers soon after their execution) the capitals have kept their original colours.

38. ROMANESQUE ARCHES IN THE CLOISTER OF SAINT-AUBIN, ANGERS. The cloister of Saint-Aubin in Angers (now the prefecture of Maine-et-Loire) comprises, to the right of the chapter house, a great door and arcades which may date from the beginning of the time of the abbot Robert de La Tour-Landry (1127-1154).

The great arch shown here, which has every voussoir carved with an angel, contains two arches supported centrally by twin colonnettes. Between the intrados of the great arch and the extrados of the lesser arches the Virgin in majesty is represented in a glory held by two angels. There are still traces of colour on the sculpture.

About the beginning of the thirteenth century the theme of the Virgin and Child was used by the painter who decorated the two lesser arches. The dimensions of these paintings are not much greater than those of a large manuscript; they are made to be viewed from close up, and are executed with precision. Here only two of the subjects are shown: on the right the wise men appearing before Herod seated on his throne with three counsellors near him; on the left the wise men coming to adore the Child, bringing him their gifts. In the centre can be seen the towers of Jerusalem depicted between the two arches as a fortress.

This work is of high quality; two different reds, a light blue, a yellow and a green are harmoniously combined in the figures seen against a slate blue background.

39. CHURCH OF AZAY-LE-RIDEAU. Roughly speaking, the church of Azay-le-Rideau consists of a Renaissance and a Romanesque nave joined together.

83

The west front of the Romanesque nave is curious: the old gable is inserted into more recent masonry, and bands of small stones, a row of billet moulding and a diagonally-laid infilling make a setting for two rows of seven figures. The lower row has been altered, if not mutilated, by the insertion of a gothic central window. Only the Christ, who has a halo with crucifix and occupies the central position in the upper row, is certainly identifiable. The arcades enshrining the figures, the style of the carving, which has been somewhat defaced by the weather, and particularly the decorative stonework, which is found in a number of other churches in the Loire Valley have sometimes caused people to overestimate the age of the front of Azay-le-Rideau. In fact, the old tradition of stonework was maintained in various ways (brick-courses, blind arcades, small stone infillings, *opus reticulatum* and herring-bone masonry) until the beginning of the twelfth century. The church at Azay was ruined when the Abbey of Cormery received it as a gift *circa* 1026-1040; the church as it stands today is mainly the mid-eleventh-century reconstruction which followed directly afterwards.

40. 41. 43.   LOCHES: THE COLLEGIATE CHURCH.   The church of St Ours, formerly the Collegiate Church of Notre Dame, is interesting on various counts. One of the most striking is the method of roofing the nave. The aisles were a later addition, and can be ignored. In the eleventh century, the church consisted of a western porch, with belfry-tower over, the original lower storey of which exists today, and an unvaulted nave and transept. At some time earlier than 1150, the crossing was given a cupola on squinches, and its square tower buttressed with small columns and topped with four bell-turrets and an octagonal spire. Eastwards from the crossing extends one bay of the choir, barrel-vaulted and ending in a semi-circular domed apse with absidioles. The transepts were also given barrel-vaults.

As to the nave: in either side wall were set three great piers carrying early pointed arches across the width and ribbed ones on the wall face, these forming at their intersection pendentives carrying octagonal pyramids to roof the two compartments thus created – a method closely related to the string of cupolas covering an unaisled nave, of which Fontevraud is only one example. The strange arrangement at Loches dates from just before 1168.

The porch added to the west of the original one during the last third of the twelfth century has a curved gothic vault of the Angevin type; a portal without tympanum; and carved decoration (Nos 40 and 41) reminiscent of the north portal of Bourges and the cathedrals of Le Mans and Angers.

42.   *See No. 3.*

44.   CUNAUD: THE CHOIR.[1]   The church of Cunaud poses a number of archaeological problems which need not be discussed here. The reader may be referred to the study by M. Francis Salet in the report of the Archaeological Congress of France, Session CXXII, 1964. (Anjou.)

[1] Rather than the official spelling: 'Cunault', 'Fontrevrault' the forms: 'Cunaud', 'Fontrevraud' have been adopted, in accordance with their etymology.

Villandry – the château and the gardens

From the staircase descending into the nave one is struck by the quality of the architecture: the narrowing of the nave from west to east creates an astonishing impression of depth, in spite of the flat wall of the sanctuary which, in the thirteenth century replaced the axial opening into the ambulatory with its radiating chapels. The indirect lighting from the windows of the tall aisles gives the architecture its full value. If the Choir is itself the result of two campaigns fought out during the first half of the twelfth century, that of Cunaud, with its central unlit space, its early pointed arches buttressed by the cross vaults of the aisles, shows the influence of Poitou in the land of Anjou; 'but Cunaud', concludes M. Salet, 'surpasses the churches of Poitou by the severity of its design, the audacity of its slender pillars, the beauty of its proportion, its varied rhythm and its technical perfection'.

45. 117. ABBEY OF FONTEVRAUD. (See Note p. 84.)

45. NAVE AND CHOIR OF THE ABBEY CHURCH. Early in the twelfth century, Robert d'Arbrissel founded the monastery which, combining two communities of men and women, was to have considerable importance in the monastic life of the West. The site is in Anjou and local building materials were used: limestone from the district of Saumur, slate carried down the Loire for the Breton who had assembled these monks, and was to die in 1117. Used until recently by the Prison authorities, the great complex of buildings, as it now stands has received many successive additions. The masterpiece is the Abbey Church, the choir and transept, built under d'Arbrissel, being 270 feet long, 120 feet wide at the transept and 50 feet across the nave.

Over the crossing is a dome on pendentives, and a barrel-vaulted ambulatory with three radiating chapels runs from the transepts round the choir. The transepts have each an apsidal chapel on its eastern flank. This arrangement with the tall columns supporting the great arcades, and the smaller ones carrying the intermediate arches, all with undecorated capitals, has a pure and austere beauty of its own.

As to the nave, the lower part on either side has been reinforced by robust wall-arcades with double mouldings, some being carried on triple engaged piers others on piers with dosserets, ending below the windows in a triforium walk without balustrade. Square piers with engaged rounded columns carry cupolas on pendentives covering the four bays of the nave.

In layout, dimensions, carving, one is reminded of Angoulême Cathedral.

The Abbey of Fontevraud, however, is not merely a fine example of the South-Western Romanesque, it has also much historic interest. From 1189 to 1204 it was the burial place of the English Plantagenets, and here are the tombs of Henry II and Eleanor of Aquitaine and of their son, Richard Lion-Heart and their daughter, Joanna of England. Then, in the middle of the thirteenth century, Isabel, widow of King John (Lackland) who married Hugh de Lusignan as her second husband, Raymond II of Toulouse, son of Joanna came also to rest in the Abbey. The heart of Henry III, whose body was transferred to Westminster Abbey in 1292 remains at Fontevraud. Here in peaceful assembly are the four surviving effigies, those of Henry II, Richard, Eleanor and Isabel, the latter carved in wood.

46. MONTOIRE : CHAPEL OF THE PRIORY OF ST GILLES. CHRIST IN JUDGMENT. This is a deeply moving place for two reasons : the mural painting and the associations with Ronsard, who was the Prior here.

The chapel is a small eleventh-century building, with a partially ruined nave. The choir and arms of the transept have each a short barrel-vaulted bay, the transepts ending in a semi-circular apse set in a straight wall, while the apse of the choir is semi-circular inside and out. The crossing whose arches rest on flat piers with moulded imposts, is covered by a small dome and the lines of jointing painted on here appear to be original.

The oldest and finest of the mural paintings (first quarter of the twelfth century) is in the apse. On the intrados of the western arch is shown the Lamb between two seraphim, recognizable by the three pairs of wings. On the ceiling of the apse is the 'Christ in Judgment' of the Apocalypse, seated, framed in a double mandorla, His head surmounted by a halo with cross, His right hand raised in blessing and His left holding a book. On either side, the symbols of the evangelists alternate with dancing angels. The whole is very light in feeling and picked out in shades of white, yellow, ochre, grey and green on a white background. Some of the details, particularly on the face, have vanished.

'Christ sending the Holy Spirit to the apostles' and 'Christ giving the keys to Peter' in the semi-domes of the transepts, which have been covered over by later paintings have not the simplicity of line or the refined elegance of the painting shown here. These scenes are complemented by a bust of Christ, on the intrados of the chancel arch, inscribed in a medallion surmounting two Virtues triumphing over two Vices, the Virtues shown as knights-Patience transfixing Wrath and Chastity overcoming Lechery. All these paintings can be dated from about 1150 to 1170.

47. 48. TAVANT : PAINTINGS. St Nicholas at Tavant is a parish church once belonging to the Abbey of Marmoutier. Noteworthy traces of the paintings in the upper church remain, but it is those in the crypt that have made the church famous. Their great vivacity, the skill of the drawing and the successful use of a restricted scale of colours – ochre, green, white and black – make them most appealing. They can be considered as mid-twelfth century. The iconographic themes are highly varied; to the hagiographic group belongs the martyred saint shown here; a cosmic group (the caryatids) one of morals (the vices), of which the figure of Lechery is the best-known, and a biblical set of the Old and New Testament all of which represent, says Abbot Josef Sverina, 'an inventory of Romanesque universalist thought, samples of that period's ideas of the world.'

49. ST JOHN-THE-BAPTIST'S CHAPEL OF THE LIGET, IN THE COMMUNE OF CHEMILLÉ-SUR-INDROIS. One of the remaining buildings of the ancient Carthusian Monastery. This small circular edifice, probably of the second half of the twelfth century, contains a remarkable, though poorly preserved, set of mural paintings. M. Marc Thibout assigns them to the extreme end of the twelfth century, say between 1197 and 1201, at the time of the enlarging of the Chapel with a nave now vanished. The Tree of Jesse (shown here) is on the left as you enter the South Door and is symbolised here by a simple plant held up in the

right hand of Jesse, whose name is inscribed above his head. The whole is completed by a Virgin, holding the Child above her head between two branches springing from her halo, and the heads of seven doves, representing the seven gifts of the Holy Spirit. 'Sweetness and nobility, says M. Thibout, are the qualities best describing these mural paintings, and these place them among the most remarkable of our medieval examples.'

50. THE ABBEY OF ASNIÈRES has come down to us in a sadly mutilated condition, but the Choir with its square chevet, its delicately ribbed vault carried on slender pillars with their carved capitals and, above all the bosses where are portrayed in a most expressive and animated way scenes from the life of Christ, make it the most dazzlingly successful piece of Angevin architecture of the first quarter of the thirteenth century.

51. THE NORTH PORCH AT CANDES. Here St Martin died in 397. At this meeting place of the Loire and the Vienne (*condate* was its Celtic name) in one of the most beautiful landscapes that exist – just climb up the slope and look – Martin founded a church dedicated to St Maurice having, says tradition, brought from Agaune (now Saint-Maurice in the Swiss Canton of Valais) a flask containing the martyr's blood. Though knowledge of the Theban massacre was thus brought through St Martin from the Swiss Rhône to the Loire, nothing remains today of the building he must have known.

A Romanesque choir with three conjoined apses, and transepts which bear traces of various reconstructions, were ineptly matched in the thirteenth century by a triple nave of the Poitevin type (as at Notre Dame, Le Puy).

However, the north porch, facing the Loire, is quite out of the ordinary. It is surmounted by a chapel of St Michael, which was normally reserved by Romanesque builders for western porches. Here, however, for topographical reasons, the principal entrance has been transposed. This powerful, massive piece of architecture, clumsy in parts, with carvings uneven in quality, torn between Romanesque tradition and a more elegant realistic art, gathers on one central soaring column the whole bunch of slender ribs from the Angevin domed vaults.

After the simple uniformity of the exterior with its wall-arcades, its series of canopied statues which loads the fairly heavy gallery cutting the façade in half, what a pleasant surprise is given to the eye by the delight of the play of light and shadow on the colonnettes, pointed arches and domed vaults of this porch.

52. ANGERS CATHEDRAL : TYMPANUM OF THE WEST DOOR. This dates from about 1170-1180. Christ in Majesty, surrounded by the symbols of the Evangelists, and the charming angels which decorate the voussoirs make a well-known iconographic theme. Regional influences here are apparent; the influence above all of the great portal of Chartres, noticeable in the smaller figures, but there persists, however, as can be seen in particular in the fine line of the folds in Christ's robe and the way they are arranged over the knee, a trace of the Romanesque tradition which reflects the western provinces' attachment to their past.

103. *Château of Langeais, overlooking the gardens, at night*

104. *The Denial of St Peter, by Georges de la Tour. Musée des Beaux-Arts, Tours*

105. *The Gallery at the Château of Amboise*

106. *Detail from the Tomb of Agnes Sorel, Château de Loches*

107. *The Children of Charles VIII and Anne of Britanny: Charles-Orlando and Charles. Detail from Their Tomb in Tours Cathedral*

108. *Château de Chenonceau, by Night*

109. *Son et Lumière at the Château of Le Lude*

110. *The Drawing-room, Château of Champigny-sur-Veude*

111. *Polychrome Statue of Saint Catherine, Château du Moulin*

112. *Guard-room in the Château de Brissac*

PANELS AND PAINTINGS:

113. *Secret Cupboards in the Château of Blois, Catherine de' Medici's Private Room*

114, 115. *Details of the Ceiling in the Guard-room at the Château of Le Plessis-Bourré*

116. *Detail of the Bell Room at the Château de Beauregard*

106

105   107

104

113

114

115

116

117

118

119

MARIE JOHANNE
DE SAVMERY
MARQVISE
DE MONTGLA
COMTESSE DE
CHEVRE
✶ 172

122

123

121

124

KITCHENS AND FIREPLACES:

117. *Fireplaces and Kitchen Roof at the Abbey of Fontevraud*
118. *Fireplace of the Château of Le Plessis-lès-Tours*
119. *Kitchen of the Château de Menars*
120. *Esau Selling his Birthright, by Michel Corneille, Museum of Orleans*

INTERIORS:

121. *Drawing-room in the Château of Le Lude*
122. *Marie de Johanne de la Carre, wife of Louis de Clermont, Count of Cheverny (Grandson of Henri Hurault de Cheverny) – a Portrait by Mignard at the Château de Cheverny*
123. *Hérault de Séchelles as a Child, by Drouais, Château de Montgeoffroy*
124. *Madame Chevotet, by Perronneau, Museum of Orleans*
125. *Drawing-room at the Château de Montgeoffroy*

I

53. 54. 55.   ANGERS: MUSEUM OF TAPESTRIES. THE APOCALYPSE.   The tapestry of the Apocalypse at Angers is the oldest known French one to come down to us. Louis I of Anjou commissioned the cartoons, probably about 1374, from Hennequin of Bruges, painter to Charles V – at this period Flanders was the great art-centre. The artist must have been inspired by several manuscripts such as the one that had been drawn from the king's library and lent to Louis I 'pour faire son beau tappis'. The Duke of Anjou entrusted the execution to a famous Parisian weaver, Nicolas Bataille. It was to be finished in 1380.

When René of Anjou went to live in Provence, he made a gift of the Apocalypse to 'the Church of Monsieur saint Maurice' and it decorated the Cathedral of Angers on great occasions until 1767, when it was noticed that it deadened the voices. From then onwards it was used for all sorts of purposes: protection of orange trees in the winter; hanging on the stable stalls and was even taken to pieces. In 1843, the Estate administrator put up for sale what remained of it, among other rubbish, and the then bishop, Mgr Angebault saved the tapestries and left them to the Cathedral, the Chapter undertaking the first restoration. By virtue of an agreement in 1952 between Mgr Chappoulie and the Education nationale it was decided to put them permanently on display. Two years later, in the newly restored and appointed Château of Angers, the opening took place in the great hall, the work of M. Bernard Vitry, architect and head of the Department of Historical Monuments, where the surviving portions of the tapestry – seventy-two scenes out of the original 105, divided into seven pieces – are set off to perfection.

As far as a reconstruction is possible, it seems that on each piece a scene read vertically shows a tall figure reading under an architectural canopy; perhaps these are the seven bishops of Asia to whom St John dedicated his work? To the right of this initial scene are fourteen, representing the visions of the apostle, arranged on two levels. Above the upper row a long band carried angel musicians crying to Heaven; beneath the lower one, earth is represented by a flowery meadow, the home of little rabbits. It is known that there was once a yet lower band showing legends, texts of the Apocalypse or commentaries, but this has completely disappeared. The backgrounds are of alternate red and blue; they are plain in the first three pieces and the first scene of the fourth, but from then on are decorated with various motifs.

53.   SCENES 5 AND 13 OF THE FIRST SECTION.   In the upper scene the Elders bow down before Christ in glory . . . 'they worship Him who liveth for ever and ever, and cast their crowns before the throne, saying, Thou art worthy, O Lord, to receive glory and honour and power . . .' (Revelations, IV, X, XI)

In the lower scene the Martyrs, robed in white, are receiving the honours of the Triumph, without waiting for the end of persecution (fifth scourge of the Apocalypse): '. . . I saw under the altar the souls of them that were slain for the word of God, and for the testimony which they held . . .' (Revelations, VI, 9-11.) On the left is St John.

55.   SCENES 1 AND 8 OF THE FOURTH SECTION.   In the upper scene the Apostle is receiving the tapered reed: this is the rod of the medieval master-mason: 'And there was given me a reed like a rod: and the angel stood, saying, Rise, and

measure the temple of God, and the altar, and them that worship therein . . .'
(Revelations, XI, 1-2.)

In the lower scene, St John contemplates St Michael and his angels fighting
the dragon. (Satan). (Revelations XII, 7-12.)

(*Cf.* R. Planchenault, *L'Apocalypse d'Angers*, Caisse Nationale des Monuments Historiques, 1966.)

56.   CHEVET OF ORLÉANS CATHEDRAL.   The first cathedral at Orléans was built in
the middle of the fourth century by St Euverte. From the beginning it was
placed under the protection of the Holy Cross, an imperious dedication, perhaps
chosen by the emperor Constantine.

Stolen in the sixth century from the town of Vienne, the body of St Mamert
soon created an important pilgrimage movement to the cathedral; later a relic
of the true cross was possibly given by Charlemagne. I have already mentioned
the role of Orléans in western France of the middle ages; the emperor Charles
the Bald, the kings Eudes, Robert the Good and Louis VI were here annointed.
At the end of the tenth century the cathedral was completely rebuilt after
destruction by fire, and the only information we have about it comes from
excavations. In 1278, the collapse of part of the nave led to another reconstruction. It is to this church of the Bishop Robert de Courtenay that the present
chevet with its nine radiating chapels, started in 1287, belongs, as we see it
illustrated here.

The nine almost identical juxtaposed polygonal absidioles, consisting each of
one unvaulted bay only – though the central one, projecting slightly, has two –
open into the ambulatory and are well lit by windows between the uprights of
their pinnacled buttresses, topped by lacy spirelets, and those of the heavier
supports which carry their internal dividing walls outwards to serve as bases
for the flying-buttresses of the apse. The resulting composition is one of
unusual beauty.

Orléans Cathedral, however, was far from finished at this stage. The right-
hand part of the choir takes us to the first third of the fourteenth century, the
transept to the last quarter of the fifteenth. The nave was to follow: two
Huguenot occupations of the town, and especially that of the troops of Condé
in 1568 were to reduce the central part of the cathedral to ruin. The rebuilding
of the nave was carried out in the seventeenth century, still 'in conformity
with the Gothic order'. As to the west front, Robert de Cotte, then Jacques
Gabriel, then Trouard under Louis XV worked on it, but it was not until
May 8, 1829 that the traditional procession of Joan of Arc came out on to the
parvis through the west door, which François Pagot had just completed.

57.   LOCHES.   The rising ground to the north provided a natural defence for the
higher part of the town *(the Haute Ville)* which was far more vulnerable from
the south. In front of the eleventh-century keep there is a network of fortifications, such as the pointed towers *(tours à bec)* with their cutwater bases
standing out in the moat, showing us many different elements of military
architecture from the thirteenth to the fifteenth century. The keep *(donjon)*
held many famous prisoners: Ludovico Sforza (il Moro) and Cardinal Balue
among them. The north side, dominating the town, is occupied by the royal

126. *Covered Market, Richelieu*

TROGLODYTE DWELLINGS:

127. *At Troo*
128. *At Les Roches-sur-le-Loir*
129. *Vines in the Region of La Vallée Coquette, Near Vouvray*

WORK IN THE DIFFERENT MONTHS. Misericord Seats in the Choir-stalls of the Trinité at Vendôme:

130. *Sowing*
131. *Grape-harvest*
132. *Sheep-shearing*
135. *Pig-killing*
133. *Wine-caves in the Rock at Rochecorbon (Marc Brédif)*
134. *Underground Stores in the Château at La Guerche-sur-Creuse*
136. *Cornfields in the Loire Valley*
137. *Inside the Dove-cote at the Château de Villesavin*
138. *The Press at the Château de Talcy*

GLASS INDUSTRY. Company of Saint-Gobin, Factory at La Chapelle-Saint-Mesmin Near Orleans

139. *Manufacture of Two-tone Duralex Plates*
140. *Manufacture of a Duralex Salad-bowl*
141. *Rubber Industry, Hutchinson's Factory at Joué-les-Tours. Assembly of Inflatable Boats*
142. *New District of Le Sanitas, Tours*
143. *The Thermal Nuclear Reactor*
144. *Basilica of Notre-Dame-de-la-Trinité, Blois. The Temptation – Detail from Scenes from the Life of Christ, by Lambert-Rucki*

130

131

133

127

128

137

138

134

132

135

140

141

lodgings, where Anne of Brittany's charming oratory is decorated with heraldic patterns of cords and ermines, and by the church of St Ours described elsewhere (cf. Nos 43 and 106).

58 to 63. CHÂTEAU DE CHÂTEAUDUN. *Castellum Dunum:* the latin and the celtic words for 'fortress' attests the ancient occupation of this spur, dominating the Loire from a height of some ninety feet. The fifteenth-century north-west angle of the château, seen here (no. 63) symbolises in the 'functional' beauty of its stark, soaring strength its defensive role. Gregory of Tours mentions Châteaudun in Merovingian times; after the Norman invasions, Thibaut the Cheat (le tricheur) felt it necessary to erect a keep there. What remains today, an enormous circular mass, with walls twelve feet thick at the base dates only from the twelfth century; its roofing preserves the carpentry that Jean de Dunois ordered on December 3, 1450 from a carpenter at Orléans. It is with Jean, the Bastard of Orléans that the history of Châteaudun really begins: this half-brother of Charles VI of Orléans received from him the territory of Dunois, with its capital in exchange for the lands of Vertus and the estates of Romorantin and Millançay in July 1439.

Apart from the keep, the remaining buildings are all later in date than 1439. Apparently Dunois and his wife, Marie d'Harcourt first started with the chapel. Work began in 1451; the bulk of the building seems to have been finished in 1454, the internal finishings some ten years later. A single space flanked by two oratories, with a nave whose asymmetric vaulting shows, as do other details of the exterior, a search for the picturesque, the Sainte-Chapelle at Châteaudun is surmounted by a tall chapel with a magnificent ceiling.

Although the interior decoration, except for the 'Judgment' on the south wall of the oratory, has disappeared, there remain twelve large statues to which have been added three others, under life-size, which form a fine collection of the fifteenth-century art of the Loire area.

58. Tradition identifies this figure wearing a cap and armour of the period of Joan of Arc as a portrait of Jean de Dunois.

59 to 62. Here are some of the larger statues: Marie the Egyptian, covered by her tresses (No. 59) an unknown saint, perhaps Ste Geneviève (No. 61); Ste Marguerite just out of the dragon, which still holds a piece of her skirt in his mouth (No. 62); a one-legged beggar (No. 60) by the feet of St Elizabeth of Hungary. These are examples of this art of great refinement, where the heavy folds of brocade recall the sculpture of Burgundy, but the charming simplicity of the faces seems to lead towards the local sculpture as we know it in the time of Louis XII.

Dunois also undertook the building of the western part of the house, to be finished by his son, to whom is due that astonishing piece of virtuosity, the staircase which, in a design then entirely new – we shall not see it reappear until at Azay-le-Rideau after 1520 – spirals across the storeys of the façade, enlivened by the ascending movement of the three buttresses with their niches and pinnacles, the landings supported by the wall of the façade itself.

The wing built by Dunois' grandson, François de Longueville was con-

structed between about 1510 and 1520, on the retaining walls that go right
down to the level of the valley. One of the master-masons of that time, Pierre
Gadier, had worked at Amboise under Charles VIII, was later in charge of the
work on the cathedral at Tours and had then been with Girolamo della Robbia
'clerk of the works' at the Château de Madrid in the Bois de Boulogne. Without giving a detailed account of the new building, I should mention the staircase, which is based on the design of the earlier one, but this time mingles
Italianate decoration with the medieval.

This is the least known and perhaps the most interesting of the 'châteaux
of the Loire', the restoration work done on it by M. Trouvelot and M. Esnault
has the rare quality of passing unnoticed, and because of the daring of its
architectural design, the novelty of some parts of it and the quality of the
statuary it deserves our attention and study.

64. LAVARDIN: RUINS OF THE CHÂTEAU. On the boundary of the Angevin lands,
overlooking the valley of the Loir, the Château of Lavardin was one of the key
positions in the feudal struggles. It was again to be used in the Religious Wars
and was dismantled on the orders of Henry IV. As to the rest, Lavardin with
its archaic Romanesque church, its old houses, the meanderings of the Loir, the
'Way of the Recluses' *(chemin des Reclusages)* which leads to Montoire is one
of the most delicious places in the valley of the Loir.

65 to 68 and 105. CHÂTEAU OF AMBOISE. This is a mighty place, rich in history.
At first a Roman fortified town it became, after the Norman invasions, a fief
conceded by the Carolingian Louis le Bègue to the Count of Anjou; then an
hereditary dynasty, which started in the eleventh century with Sulpice
d'Amboise and his son Hugues (Hugh) 1er, regroups the three fiefs, sharing
the land and taking an active part in the struggles between the houses of
Blois and Anjou. In 1431 the possessions of Louis of Amboise were confiscated
by King Charles VII: Amboise became part of the royal domain. Louis XI
founded the Order of St Michael there in 1469, and there he brought up his
son, later Charles VIII who was born and died at Amboise. (1470-1498)

At Amboise, too, in 1498, judgment was given for the dissolution of the
marriage of Louis XII and Jeanne of France, which enabled the new king to
marry Anne of Brittany the widow of his predecessor. Then François of
Angoulême and his sister Marguerite with their mother Louise of Savoy divided
their time between Amboise and Romorantin, the court of France being then
at Blois. When he became king, his wife Claude of France, the daughter of
Louis XII and Anne of Brittany, gave birth there to three children. François
1er installed Leonardo da Vinci in Le Clos-Lucé in 1516, where he lived until
his death on May 2, 1519 (*cf.* No. 146)

In 1539 François entertained the emperor Charles V at Chambord then at
Amboise. There followed the vicissitudes of the religious wars; the 'conspiracy
of Amboise' of 1560, which ended in a series of executions before the Court;
in 1563 the Edict of Amboise authorized the practice of the reformed service.
In the seventeenth century the château became a State prison and Fouquet and
Lauzun were held there. The Duc de Choiseul occupied it before the building
of Chanteloup (*cf.* No. 29). It was sold to the Duc de Penthièvre, confiscated

in 1793; given by Napoleon to Roger-Docos as a senatorial residence and thanks to this so-called conservative was largely demolished owing to lack of money for its upkeep. At the Restoration the property was returned to the Duchesse d'Orléans, daughter of the Duc de Penthièvre, and belongs today to the Comte de Paris. From 1848 to 1873, it was again confiscated and from 1848 to 1852 served as a place of internment for the Emir Abd el Kadir and his suite.

One important restoration in the time of the Duc d'Aumale, due to the architect of the Monuments historiques, Ruprich-Robert, was unfortunately lacking in finesse, but the reconstruction after the bombardment of 1940, which damaged the chapel in particular, was carried out under the direction of M. Bernard Vitry and is of a very high standard.

65. Of the immense castle that astonished the Italian ambassadors, Leonardo left us a sketch, Du Cerceau a view of the whole, and time, which destroys everything, two dwellings. In this picture we see the upper part of the Charles VIII wing and its abutment on to the enormous tower of the Minims, dominating the town and the Loire. Resting on the foundations of an impregnable fortress, it is a gothic building, constructed before the Italian journey. Tradition has it that some of the Amboise conspirators were hanged from the iron railings of the balcony outside the large windows of the upper storey, inside which is the hall, improperly called 'State' which has been completely restored.

As to the tower of the Minims (a mendicant monastic order) sited near the convent of the same name, it contains a ramp allowing horses access to the courtyard of the castle. The diameter is sixty-nine feet, and the ramp revolved round a central core, the outer walls pierced by large windows rising from the floor. The octagonal tower breaks into the line of the storeys (gallery, great hall, roof-line) of the Charles VIII wing.

66. The Hurtault tower, of a similar type, gives access to the southern part of the town across the Loire through the doorway, seen here, once furnished with a drawbridge. This tower also contains a ramp and has come down to us in its original state, with the guard-turrets added by Louis XI projecting from his surrounding wall, one can see beyond to the delicate architecture of the chapel of St Christopher.

67 and 68. This chapel again dates from the reign of Charles VIII. The lintel over the entrance door (the tympanum showing Charles VIII and Anne of Brittany is a nineteenth-century creation) pictures on the left the legend of St Christopher carrying the infant Jesus across the river, the Child growing heavier with every step, and on the right that of St Hubert, patron of huntsmen seeing the apparition of a cross between the horns of a stag attacked by his hounds.

The vaults, with liernes and tiercerons added to the main ogival ribs, are decorated with bosses delicately carved, and the springings are masked by canopies running in a lacy band along the wall. Between the windows the unpierced walls have also applied flamboyant tracery. It is elaborate but the lightness of it all gives it great refinement.

If the construction of Amboise was due to the local workshops, which by

95

their dating must influence those to follow, yet the names of the sculptors, Cornelius of Nesves and Casim of Utrecht, show that at this time, even as the Italians were arriving in the King's train, beauty outside France still came from Flanders.

69. SAINT-AGIL: ENTRANCE PAVILION OF THE CHÂTEAU. Built in 1510, it reminds one in colour of the Louis XII wing at Blois; of the Châteaux of Sologne – Le Moulin, La Morinière, Herbault – in the mixture of brick and stone and the diaper pattern in the brickwork.

The traditional defences are still here: angle towers, drawbridge, bracketed machicolations, walks round the walls; a battlemented tower overlooks the courtyard. As at Talcy, a lantern crowns the roof of the rectangular pavilion. Nevertheless, mixed up with all this military apparatus, pilasters underline the verticality of the wall-bays, a moulding runs between the ground and the first floors and, finally, two fine dormers, much in the style of Villesavin, attest the beginnings of the new taste.

70. 71. CHÂTEAU DU PLESSIS-LÈS-TOURS. The demesne of Les Montils-les-Tours, as it was originally called, had been owned by the house of Amboise since the twelfth century when Louis XI acquired it in 1463. There he built a great moated manor house of brick and stone, of which the drawings of Gaignières preserve the design. Louis died there on August 30, 1483.

Here, as at Loches, a cell is supposed to have been the prison of Cardinal Balue, but we must be careful – Balzac aside – of the legends built up by the romantics about Louis XI. Only the main building remains and it has lost its arched galleries. The stairway tower abutting the west façade is topped by a fine 'palm-tree' vault of which the delicately moulded wall ribs are gathered together on to a foliated capital of a single column.

71. LOUIS XI. The medallion on the side of his hat, the collar of the Order of St Michael which he founded at Amboise, testify to the highly superstitious piety of the King; although not contemporary, this relief, carved in wood, is of the same inconographic type as the portrait in the chapel of Behuard in Anjou. In the absence of an illustration read Philippe de Commynes, who succeeds in bringing Louis XI vividly to life.

72 to 74. 96. 113. CHÂTEAU DE BLOIS.

72. ENTRANCE TO THE LOUIS XII WING. This façade, incorporating a polychrome design of brick and stone, has remained Gothic in nearly all respects. Beneath the statue, an inaccurate piece of nineteenth-century restoration, is the porcupine of Louis XII flanked by the crowned initials of Louis and Anne de Bretagne. It is found again above the smaller door. According to the medieval Bestiary the porcupine was alleged not only to wound cruelly whoever touched it, but to deliver its 'flesches ou saiettes', its 'arrows or barbs', against its enemies at a distance, and was therefore greatly to be feared!

73. COURTYARD. It is here seen from beneath the inner gallery of the Louis XII wing; the basket-handle arches are supported alternately by pillars decorated with fleur-de-lys, and pilasters. The pilasters and all the capitals are in the new

fashion, while the picturesque gargoyle with its protruding snout in the middle of the picture shows the persistence of the French Gothic style. The Francis I wing across the courtyard, dating from a few years later, demonstrates the widespread use of Italianate decoration. The staircase remains outside the façade, but although its placing is distinctly French it is decorated in the new style; the stairway is an elegant spiral. This staircase stands at what was once the centre of the façade, but part of this was pulled down to fit in the wing built in the seventeenth century by François Mansart (cf. No. 96) for Gaston d'Orléans. The gaps can still be seen. Towards the left beside the chapel, a gallery of brick and stone supported on arches of the same design, but with simpler pillars and surmounted by stepped gables, preserves the Flemish touch. Dr Lesueur has recently shown (*Mém. de la Société des Sciences et Lettres de Loir-et-Cher*, 1963) that this is not an afterthought of Charles of Orléans at Blois but was in fact built, like the chapel, by Louis XII.

74. FAÇADE OF THE LODGES. (Living Quarters). I have already explained in the text (page 109) how this external façade was built on to the feudal wall which forms the back of the Francis I wing, facing towards the courtyard.

Although it has been suggested that this was inspired by Bramante – by such buildings as the Santo Damaso courtyard in the Vatican – it must be admitted that the master-masons of the Loire adapted the model in a singular fashion. This is not a gallery but a succession of apartments, and the storey which runs beneath the roof is a happy solution to the problem of concealing the considerable drop between the roof of the building overlooking the courtyard, and the roof of the new building. The style is thoroughly Italianate. For the translation into French of an Italian façade, our Italian friends have a proverb: '*traduttore, traditore*'; nevertheless treason can produce, as in this instance, a work of art.

75. 76 and 78.   *(See notes to No. 1.)*

77. Here is FRANKLIN, as Nini saw him when he visited M. le Ray at Chaumont.

The daughter of the gardener of M. le Ray was still alive at the end of the last century, and she spoke willingly to a then schoolboy of Chaumont, now an octogenarian, of the 'late Mr Franklin', as her father had seen him: 'he would often walk arm in arm under the trees with the late M. le Ray, even though they both had their walking sticks'.

2. 79 to 83. 87. 88. CHÂTEAU DE CHAMBORD. A few dates engraved in stone and a few remnants of building accounts have shed only uncertain light on the genesis of Chambord.

Work was begun in September 1519, four months after the death of Leonardo da Vinci at Amboise.

Francis I was known to have consulted Leonardo, most probably as soon as he arrived in 1516, for another project: a château, which was to have been built at Romorantin on either side of the river Sauldre. This project was abandoned by the king for Chambord. At the same time Francis, who had several sketches presented to him before undertaking anything, had ordered a wooden model from Dominico da Cortone. We know of a model which existed in Blois in the seventeenth century of the 'keep' without its superstructures; although in everything but the staircase the general plan of the model corresponds to the final design, the external elevation with its arrangement of arcades belongs to the Italian *Quattrocento*, and bears no relation to the château as it was built.

This is the plan of the building as it exists: the keep, a square building, is doubly symmetrical about two perpendiculars, formed by the rooms arranged in a Greek cross about the central staircase. This is contained within a circle of about thirty feet in diameter; the radiating rooms are thirty feet wide and sixty feet long, just as the pavilions which they separate have sides sixty feet long and the towers a diameter of sixty feet; as Dr Lesueur has shown the whole plan is based on a grid made up of thirty foot squares, while the surface area itself occupies one-sixth of the rectangular enclosure. Confronted with such a conception, of whom should we think? Two names spring to mind – Leonardo da Vinci? Dominico da Cortona? Was the rectangular staircase inserted by Boccador in one of the arms of the cross, discarded in favour of the two concentric spirals which are a Leonardesque conception? We can only guess. . . .

We still have the names of the master-masons: Jacques Sourdeau, then from 1521 Pierre Trinqueau who, before his death in 1538 was in charge of the most concentrated period of building; and lastly Jacques Coqueau who was in charge until 1558 when the work was stopped. The building was never really finished and while it was going on advanced but slowly. When Charles V saw at Chambord in 1539 'the sum of all that human industry can achieve' only the keep was complete; the east wing of François 1er was not ready until 1544. Later additions were to be the outside staircase and the portico on the courtyard side and to the north the 'oratory', with its spur descending to the moat, all two years later.

Indeed the apparent unity of Chambord conceals – imperfectly at close quarters – a quantity of alterations and even modifications in plan: for instance, until the eighteenth century the François 1er wing still showed traces of a projected two-storey extension to run along the whole eastern façade of the château but the lower part was never roofed; the chapel and its tower were not finished until the time of Louis XIV whose periods of residence entailed the construction on the low blocks of the south and west of attic storeys, now vanished, which were intended to accommodate the staff of the Court. These are only some examples: to them must be added the modification of the decorations decided on at the end of François' reign. The filling-in of the moat has somewhat spoilt the great façade by depriving it of the robust masonry of its outer defences.

Although the work carried out by Louis XIV is well known, it is not so well known that much was done by his uncle forty years earlier. Yet, between 1640 and 1642 Gaston d'Orléans had entirely restored the galleries and the great lantern, which were on the point of collapse; the crumbling terraces, their broken balustrades and the coffered ceilings of the keep, which were almost obliterated by the penetration of damp – he had them carefully copied from the motifs that remained. In short, he saved Chambord from ruin.

It remains for me to people the château with its ghosts: François 1er, Charles IX who, a century earlier than Louis XIV gave himself up to the joys of the chase; the Sun-King himself, who induced Molière and Lully to produce *Monsieur de Porceaugneac* here in 1669 and a year later *Le Bourgeois Gentilhomme*; then in the eighteenth century there were Stanislas Leczczinski and Maurice of Saxony, the famous Maréchal de Saxe. At the beginning of the nineteenth century, Chambord was handed over by Napoleon to Marshall Berthier who took no interest in it; in a celebrated pamphlet, Paul Louis Courier had urged that the château should be demolished. It was then that a national subscription was raised and it was offered to the Duc de Berry, son of the rightful owner; the Comte de Chambord, after the defeat of 1870, was on the point of restoring the monarchy. At last, just before the second World War, at the conclusion of a long lawsuit with the heirs, the Princes of Bourbon-Parma – who were of Austrian nationality and therefore enemies of France during the preceding war – gave up Chambord to the State.

80 to 83. 87. THE GRAND STAIRCASE. The double spiral of the staircase turns round a hollow centre as in the Hurtault and the Minim towers at Amboise (Nos 65 and 66). The photograph is taken from the first floor; the floor of the storey above is missing here and one can see through up to the coffered vault which is directly under the flat roof. On the left is a fireplace hanging in the void.

Louis de La Saussaye, the romantic historian of Chambord, and a certain number of his successors, have imagined the four radiating rooms as four naves rising straight from the ground to the vault at the top, open to the air through bays without fenestration. Dr Lesueur has shown, in an article in the *Bulletin Monumentale* (1951) the danger of this hypothesis. While admitting that the present fireplaces correspond to a second state, the two projections on the north and south façades, where the fixings still exist would not have constituted simple porches, being designed to rise at least to the first floor. It remains possible that the vaults could have been finished before the corresponding façades; the records are clumsy. But the wooden model which still existed in the seventeenth century, without doubt that of Dominico da Cortona, already foresaw the partitioning of the keep into three levels.

84 and 94. CHÂTEAU D'USSÉ. Ussé appears almost unreal in its natural setting; although the building extended over three centuries, the different styles combined nevertheless to give a general effect of exceptional elegance. The fifteenth century has left curtain walls, machicolated towers, battlements, loopholes and merlons topped by a slightly thinner storey with high gabled windows, pepper-box turrets and chimneys. It reminds one of Langeais or Le Plessis-Bourré: it is the military architecture of the reign of Louis XI. The alterations and enlargements of the Renaissance wing date from the reign of Francis I; finally, the construction of a new inside staircase in the seventeenth century entailed further alterations to the façade.

We know that the chapel, which bears the initials of Charles d'Espinay and his wife Lucrèce de Pons, was consecrated in 1538. It has a three-bay nave, and a chancel flanked by the sacristy and by one pentagonal apse. A small

145. *Château de Montsoreau*

146. *Models of Leonardo da Vinci's Inventions, Le Clos Lucé, Amboise*

147. *Joachim du Bellay – Drawing by a Pupil of Cousin, Bibliothèque Nationale*

148. *Rabelais, as Seen by Delacroix – Painting in the Musée du Vieux-Chinon*

RONSARD IN THE VALLEY OF THE LOIRE

The Manor of La Possonnière, Couture, Ronsard's Birthplace:

149. *Kitchen Window, With its Inscription*

150. *Façade on the Courtyard Side*

151. *Fireplace*

152. *Château de Talcy*

153, 154. *Château de Valençay. English Caricatures on the Prince of Talleyrand*

155. *Balzac, by Louis Boulanger, Museum of Tours*

156. *Balzac's Room in the Château de Saché*

157. *The Garden of La Béchellerie, Saint-Cyr, House of Anatole France*

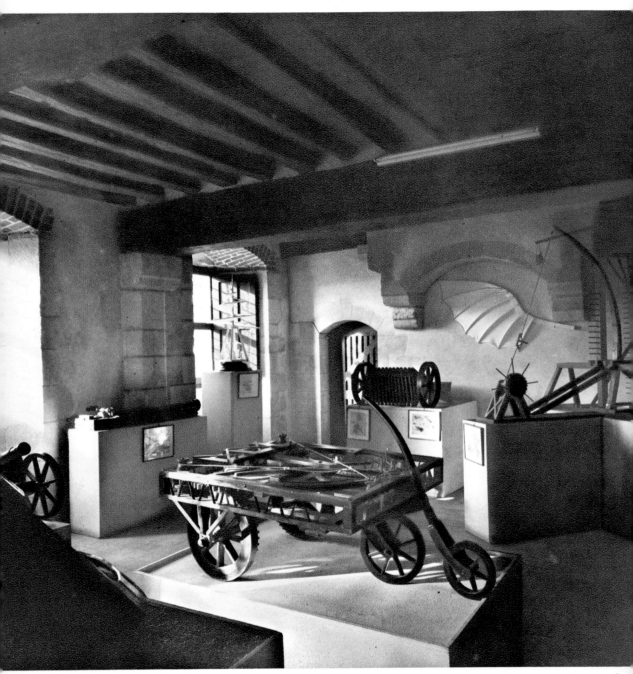

146

147

148

149

150

151

152

153

DÉDIÉ À MM.
LES CHEVALIERS DE LA GIROUETTE.

154

155

156

chapel opens off the second bay; another chapel to the north of the chancel is a seventeenth-century addition. This is still a Gothic type of architecture, but with Italian decoration of great delicacy and outstanding workmanship. The portal in the west face is extremely elegant; M. Gébelin has pointed out the inspiration of the Certosa at Pavia, which is evident in the detailing.

The choir stalls, dating from about 1540 and showing the same mixture of styles, are decorated in particular with four interesting medallions, one of which is the warrior wearing a helmet, illustrated here (No. 84).

These medallions 'à l'antique' were one of the ideas from Italy most consistently popular in the Val de Loire; from the time of Louis XII they are found often in terra cotta below the windows on a façade: as at the hôtel d'Alluye, the house of Florimond Robertet in Blois.

85. VAULT OF THE STAIRCASE, PONCÉ. This pretty house was started in about 1530; the date of 1542 is found on a console of the staircase. Although the architecture at Poncé had no innovations at the time, the staircase with its straight flights of stairs occupying the centre pavilion is famous for its coffered vaults. Two teams of craftsmen were at work here: one decorated the ceiling up to the first floor with stilted arches cut by longitudinal ribs between which the panels were decorated with lively and original motifs. After the first floor the design is different: cradle vaulting, with coffering formed by longitudinal ribs a little hesitantly traced. The carving, derived from many sources, has a rather soft quality which reminds one of later work, and is extremely varied. There are many seals; cherubs, cupids and the salamanders of Francis I are flung together (in a most amiable disorder), mingling with decorative motifs like masks, medallions, macaroons, grapes and foliage decorating the panels and also the bosses at the intersection of the ribs. The ribs rest on little brackets in the form of Corinthian capitals engaged in the lateral walls.

In addition to the terraces which form a setting for Poncé in the countryside, at the foot of the hill where the feudal castle used to stand there is the maze of hornbeam hedges, circling around an enormous central plane tree.

86. *See notes on No. 13.*

87. 88. *See note on Nos 2, 79 to 83.*

89. *See notes on No. 145.*

90. CHÂTEAU DE L'ISLETTE, CHEILLÉ. The connection between l'Islette and Azay-le-Rideau poses the problem: which influenced the other? However, it seems incontestable that l'Islette came first, for none of the features appear here which were to make Azay so charming: the staircase, the large dormer windows. At l'Islette the windows, which have been partially destroyed, had simple crocketed gables still in the fifteenth-century style – possibly in an effort to make the new building harmonize with the fifteenth-century wing which was retained – but several details of the construction make it clear that they are early Francis I.

The carving above the entrance is in accordance with this date: if the arms, 'd'azur au griffon d'or accompagné en chef d'une étoile du même', is that of Barjot de Roncée, and not of the supposed owner at the time of construction,

René de Maillé, who died in 1531, the supports, the medallion, and the decoration of pilasters and volutés must be original.

91.   HÔTEL GOUIN, TOURS.   The hôtel Gouin, rightly spared in 1940, is named after the owners from 1738 to 1910, the date at which Georges Gouin bequeathed it to the Archeological Society of Touraine. It is a fifteenth-century house put into the Italian style by René Gardette, whose coat of arms is repeated on the façade. This dates from the first quarter of the sixteenth century: short, squat columns appear rather curiously between two stages of pilasters relieved by cavetto mouldings, with an applied ring motif, and all the free surfaces are carved.

This decoration gives interest to a projecting building which was used as a lodge, in the Italian style and crowned by a steep crocketed gable in the fashion of 1450, to match the dormer windows; the same tracery adorns and spreads its embroidery over the whole surface of the renovated building.

Cover photograph, 92, 93, 108.
CHÂTEAU DE CHENONCEAU.   The history of the present château of Chenonceau is well known. Of the château rebuilt by Jean Marques in 1432 only the keep remains; a fortified mill had been established on the river Cher. Thomas Bohier, general of Finances, acquired the land of Chenonceau. Reconstruction began in 1513, but Bohier, treasurer of the wars in Italy, where he died in 1524, left the supervision of the work to his wife, Catherine Briçonnet.

It was then that the new building, replacing the mill, was erected on the Cher while the feudal tower of Jean Marques was clothed in the taste of the day. Catherine Briçonnet died, and her son Antoine Bohier deemed it wise to avoid the fate of Beaune-Semblançay and Gilles Berthelot, his uncle and his cousin, and so offered Chenonceau to Francis I in settlement of his debts. In 1547 Henry II gave it in his turn to Diane de Poitiers. It was then that a bridge was built to the plans of Philibert Delorme, connecting the castle with the left bank of the Cher.

I have mentioned elsewhere (cf. No. 1, Chaumont) how Catherine de' Medici, after the death of the King, her husband, forced his former mistress to exchange Chenonceau for Chaumont. In the meantime Diane had acquired the estate of Cheverny (cf. No. 97, Cheverny).

Queen Catherine, who gave sumptuous entertainments for her sons at Chenonceau, where she liked to stay, had grandiose plans for alterations which would have completely changed the character of this delicate building. These were only partially carried out: first the construction on the bridge of a double gallery under a steep roof which somewhat overweighted the building; then, the addition to the house itself of two storeys between the chapel and the library, and new bays pierced in the entrance front. The two additions disappeared in the nineteenth-century restoration, and the heavy caryatids which stood on either side of the new windows now adorn the park.

Lastly, the west wing of the forecourt, the only one built and now very much restored, is due to Catherine de' Medici, who enlarged and renewed the gardens planted by Diane.

102

The château was now in its final state.

I should add that Louise de Vaudémont, widow of Henry III, stayed here after the assassination of her husband; then in 1733 Chenonceau was acquired by the 'fermier général' Dupin, whose widow died there in her nineties in 1799. The Dupin family received all Paris there, and Jean-Jacques Rousseau went there as tutor to M. Dupin's son.

The Italianization of Chenonceau was discreet. It is apparent in the decoration of the gable windows, and above all in the interior staircase of the living quarters with straight flights of stairs but with the corners softened and curved. The decoration of the façade gives a 'squared' effect, to use the expression of M. Gébelin, from the double string course at the floor levels, while the pilasters on either side of the windows give the vertical emphasis.

This design, found a veritable cliché in civil buildings from the early years of the reign of Francis I, is also found at Bury, built at about the same period by Florimond Robertet. It is unfortunate that this château, known to us chiefly from the drawings of Androuet Du Cerceau, should have disappeared, for before Chambord it represented an architectural concept, in the Italian sense of the term, which contained in embryo the elements of the Classical French style.

94. *See Notes on No. 84.*

95. 110.   CHAMPIGNY-SUR-VEUDE.

95.   LA SAINTE-CHAPELLE.   Louis I of Bourbon-Montpensier undertook in 1508 the construction of a château which was completed by his son, Louis II. I have mentioned elsewhere (No. 25, Richelieu) the circumstances in which Cardinal Richelieu had the château demolished. Only the outbuildings (No. 110), now converted into a château, and the chapel escaped destruction.

This chapel was built at the beginning of the sixteenth century, the portico and the side galleries being added later during a second building period in 1558.

The pointed arches with liernes and tiercerons remain as usual, partly late Gothic. On the other hand the pilasters, colonnettes, arcades and fenestration are all in the new style. Anyone interested in comparisons should go and see the church of Montrésor.

It is the windows which have made the Sainte-Chapelle of Champigny famous.

These great windows, executed between 1560 and 1597, are each divided into three: the top portions deal with the life of Christ, the middle portions with the life of Saint Louis, and the lower portions carry portraits of the family of Bourbon-Montpensier. The creation, a great scene of the Crucifixion, and Saint Louis in his royal regalia are placed one above the other in the central window.

One should not expect from late sixteenth-century glass anything but large scenes painted on glass in the manner of a picture; but the stained glass windows of Champigny remain among the most perfect examples of their kind.

96.   CHÂTEAU DE BLOIS, LANTERN OF THE STAIRCASE OF GASTON D'ORLÉANS.   When Louis XIII's brother, who was duke of Orléans and count of Blois, was entreated

to go and breathe the air of the Loire, because it had a sedative effect and was not conducive to conspiracies, this turbulent prince and lover of the arts entrusted to François Mansart a project for rebuilding the château. We know the plan and elevation of the great architect's design. Only the building of the west face was carried out between 1635 and 1638, and it was not completed. This entailed the removal of a charming building of which a drawing has been left by Du Cerceau, and of some less interesting buildings, the west half of the Louis XII chapel and the end of the Francis I wing.

This classical building may not fit in very well with its surroundings, but we should try to imagine it in what must have been its architectural context, and framed by the gardens and terraces which, straddling the rue des Fossés, gave direct access by 'Les Allées' to the forest of Blois.

The situation has changed since then; the interior was not furnished until the nineteenth century, and work on the great staircase remained unfinished until the period between the two World Wars; but the upper portion had been finished. One looks up to an oval dome beyond the overhanging wall. The excellent decoration of this magnificent structure has a quality reminiscent of famous sculptors such as Guillain, who produced the statues of Mars and Pallas which decorate the pediment of the great door, or Michel Anguier, of whom we know only that he was working at the same period for Gaston d'Orléans. *See the notes for Nos. 72 to 74. 113.*

97 to 101. 122. 167. 168. CHEVERNY. Cheverny is above all a symbol of continuity, the continuity of the Hurault family, a bourgeois family of Blois in the thirteenth century. In 1338, Philippe Hurault acquired the manor of La Grange, and in 1340 some possessions at Saint-Denis-sur-Loire; in 1510 Jacques Hurault bought the estate of Vibraye near Le Mans. Treasurer of France, he was related by marriage to the families of Robertet, Villebresme, and Phelypeaux; his son Raoul, owner of Cour-sur-Loire, married the daughter of Semblançay, Marie de Beaune, and from Louis XII in 1510 obtained permission to fortify 'his house of le Pressoir' (wine-press), – this was the origin of the first château of Cheverny.

Difficult times followed: Semblançay was executed, Raoul Hurault died at Capua, and Marie de Beaune was forced to sell Cheverny. Nevertheless she lived long enough to see her father rehabilitated and her children repossessed of their property.

In fact Diane de Poitiers acquired Cheverny from the abbot of Pontlevoy. I have mentioned elsewhere how, after the death of Henry II, Catherine de' Medici had forced the fallen favourite of the king to exchange Chenonceau for Chaumont. Very conveniently the Queen Mother then remembered that Marie de Beaune had sold Cheverny when her children were minors, which was contrary to the law: the sale of 1528 was annulled and Diana gave back Cheverny, in exchange for monetary compensation, to Jacques and Philippe Hurault.

The former, head of the elder branch of the family, possessed Vibraye, which was made into a marquisate for his nephew and heir in 1625; Philippe Hurault, chancellor of France, guardian of the Seals and first chancellor of the Order of

Pool in Sologne

the Holy Spirit founded in 1578, married Anne de Thou, sister of the famous historian and humanist.

It was their son Henri who decided to build the present château, which was finished about 1635.

Cheverny went out of the family for a second time in 1755; Jean-Nicolas Dufont, the introducer of embassies, gained a lasting reputation as a writer of memoirs under the name of Dufort de Cheverny; but in 1825 the heir of the elder branch of Hurault, Victor, marquis of Vibraye, bought back Cheverny, which thus came once more into the hands of the family which had owned it since the end of the fourteenth century.

The architectural design of the present château, which was carried out by Jacques Bougier, a builder from Blois, appears to have been the work of P. Martellange, architect to the society of Jesus, responsible for a drawing of the old château and a project (which was not carried out) for the chapel of the Jesuit college in Blois (now the church of Saint Vincent), and a few years later for the reconstruction plans for the château of Vibraye.

A narrow central part, with the ridge of its high-pitched roof at right angles to the lie of the château, is flanked on either side by a section with two storeys under a roof with a curved slope; these in turn are flanked by massive pavilions one storey higher, with dome-like roofs surmounted by lanterns. Between the windows on the first floor, busts of Roman emperors framed in a circular motif play the role of medallions in earlier Renaissance façades, while the double string course at floor level beneath the great windows, a traditional feature in the time of Francis I, appear here again just on the eve of the reign of Louis XIV; the whole disposition of the façade is horizontal. Only the middle section projects slightly; this is because, originally, the façade was to have been a background at the far end of galleries with colonnades decorated with statues – the projected placing of these is shown on the ground by the present disposition of the parterres. The other façade has a ha-ha spanned by a stepped bridge, and is much more varied, with recessed portions and contrasting plaster work and stone quoins.

The main staircase (No. 100) from which some of the fine carving is shown here (Nos 97 and 99) is of course composed of straight flights. The beams and ceiling panels of the apartments, decorated with flowers, arabesques and emblematic figures, have a series of paintings by Jean Mosnier representing the stories of Adonis, Don Quixote and *Théagène and Charicles*, translated from the Greek in the sixteenth century, and coming into fashion in the reign of Louis XIII. A sumptuous array of paintings, furniture and tapestry completes the interior decoration; among the tapestries I should mention the series made in Paris which represents the tasks of Ulysses, based on the cartoons of Simon Vouet, and the Flemish tapestries after Téniers in the smaller drawing-room.

Its lived-in interior, its position among the tall trees of park – reflected in the river, coming to steady and animate the ornamental lake, the salle de Vénerie (No. 168) in the fine outbuildings of the château, containing the 'massacres' – the heads and antlers of all the stags taken by the hunt – and its classically proportioned orangery (No. 167) all give Cheverny the character of a large provincial seat in seventeenth-century France.

L

102 and 112. CHÂTEAU DE BRISSAC. The family of Brézé which possessed the land of Brissac sold it in 1502 to René de Cossé; his grandson Charles II, first duke of Brissac, was to undertake the reconstruction of the château in 1607. This work was taken on by architects and builders of the Maine, among whom were the brothers Jacques and Charles Corbineau, Léonard Malherbe, husband of Anne Corbineau and also remembered for his association with his brother, all working simultaneously at Brissac and at Port-Louis, and also Michel Huttin, 'architecte sculpteur', related by marriage to the concièrge of Brissac. In 1621 however the work was cut short abruptly by the death of the Duke of Brissac.

Successive owners have contributed to the main façade of the château, which in its present form shows some incoherence of design.

The two towers which 'weighted' the seventeenth-century façade were certainly intended for demolition when this was finished. Above the battlements they have a narrower storey with dormer windows lighting the roof space, reminiscent of Ussé, Langeais, Le Plessis-Bourré, reminiscent in short, of the reign of Louis XI; but the decoration of the battlements and of the chapel occupying the south-east tower cannot be earlier than Louis XII, and must postdate the acquisition of Brissac by René de Cossé.

The large entrance pavilion literally leaning on the north-west tower has a domed roof, once surmounted by a bronze Mercury, beneath which the tuscan, doric, ionic, corinthian and composite orders are superimposed with abandon. It was originally to have occupied the centre of the façade, but only one wing, the south, was built.

The north-east part of the quadrangle of the château is taken up by a gallery in the style of Louis XIII, which could not have been carried out before the project for the grand façade was abandoned : at the north-west corner this meets a projecting pavilion which was doubtless there already in some form. The unoccupied south-west corner of the quadrilateral is a court surrounded by terraces; here too, the façades belong to the second stage of the reconstruction.

I should also mention the interior decoration of the chapel, contributed to at a later date by the father of David d'Angers, and the fine assembly of furniture, tapestries, arms and objects of interest (No. 112) which give to the dwelling of the twelfth Duke an interest, compensating in some degree for losses incurred during the revolutionary period.

103. CHÂTEAU DE LANGEAIS. This photograph does not show the keep, which was built by the count of Anjou, Fouque Nerra about 994, and is the oldest surviving stone keep. Its 'gallo-romanoric' appearance, brick centering to the arches of its bays provide, as at Saint-Martin of Angers and elsewhere, an example of the archaisms which gave rise to the antique buildings surviving in Anjou and Touraine, being built right up to the Romanesque period.

The château of Louis XI, whose façades, overlooking the court, are shown here, dates from the years 1465 to 1467. Built for military reasons at the time of the League of the Public Good under the direction of Jean Bourré, the King's Counsellor, Langeais on December 6, 1491, provided the setting for the marriage of Charles VIII to Anne of Brittany, which was celebrated by Louis of Amboise, bishop of Albi. There is no Renaissance grace about this severe building, a real military lock-up on the Loire of Touraine. Langeais, which is now the property of the Institut de France, owes to Jacques Siegfried a very fine collection of medieval furniture, including some famous tapestries.

104. THE DENIAL OF SAINT PETER, by Georges de la Tour. Musée des Beaux-Arts, Tours.

105. AMBOISE: GALLERY AT THE CORNER OF THE TOUR DES MINIMES. (Cf. Nos 65 to 68, Chaumont). The long helical ramp of the minim tower abuts on to this elegant gallery with its Gothic vaulting, opening on to the gardens through a series of large three-centred arches and surmounted by a balustrade. It was built after the death of Charles VIII (1498), under Louis XII. The next build-ing on the left was contemporary except for the upper storey, which was con-structed in the reign of Francis I. There was once a gallery on the terrace to the right which overlooks the town and the Loire.

The *son et lumière* at Amboise is above all a chronicle: the polyphonic pieces selected by Norbert Dufourcq make it, in addition, a marvellous recital of old music. We wanted simply to give the spectator the impression of having turned the page of memory.

106. TOMB OF AGNÈS SOREL (LOCHES, ROYAL QUARTERS). The tomb of the mistress of Charles VII was originally in the collegiate church. Mutilated in the Revo-lution, it was restored and put in its present setting in 1808-1809. Agnès is resting peacefully with a little angel on either side of her head, her feet resting on two lambs – an allusion to her Christian name. In spite of much restoration this work of fine quality, although it has lost its architectural setting, pre-serves precious evidence of memorial tomb statuary in the fifteenth century before the coming of Italian influence. It has been compared to the tomb of Charles I and Agnès of Bourbon, (Church of Souvigny, Allier), for which a sculptor of Lyon, Jacques Morel, was responsible.

107. TOMB OF CHARLES-ORLAND, DIED 1495, AND CHARLES, DIED 1496 CHILDREN OF CHARLES VIII AND ANNE OF BRITTANY IN THE CATHEDRAL OF TOURS. Installed at Saint-Martin of Tours in 1506 and transferred to the cathedral when the Basilica was demolished, the tomb, with its elegant contours, displays the com-bined arms of France and the Dauphiné within a crown forming a medallion carried by two seated angels with spread wings; the top slab has a scotia mould-ing, the scenes from the fables (Hercules) and biblical scenes (the story of Samson) are carved between the decorations of ornamental foliage. The two recumbent figures of white marble laid on a fine slab of black marble are accompanied by four little angels: two at the heads, watching over the last sleep of the children whose heavy robes are decorated with lilies and dolphins; two more at the feet with their backs turned, bear the coats of arms.

In this work of subtle harmony the tomb itself is incontrovertibly Italian, but the touching faces of the children, if not the work of the studio of Michel Colombo, are at least attributable to some studio of Touraine in the last years of the fifteenth century; they are the work of a very great sculptor.

108. 'AU TEMPS DES DAMES DE CHENONCEAU'. ('In the Time of the Ladies of Chenon-

158. *Solognot Interior at the Museum of Romorantin*

159. *Migrating Spotted Redshank on a Marsh in Sologne*

160, 161, 162. *Faces of Sologne, Drawn by Mme Martin-Demézil*

163. *Pool Near Marcilly-en-Gault*

164. *Stags Fighting in the Park of Chambord*

165. *Aerial View of the Château du Moulin, Lassay-sur-Croisne*

166. *Aerial View of the Château de la Morinière, Mur-de-Sologne*

CHATEAU DE CHEVERNY

167. *The Orangery*

168. *Trophies in the Hunting Room*

CHATEAU DE GIEN. National Museum of Hunting and Falconry :

169. *Collection of Powder Flasks*

170. *The Château and the Loire*

171. *Black-headed Gulls on Their Spring Migration, Following the Ploughman to Feed on Worms and Field-mice*

160

161

162

166

165

167

ceau'). This spectacle of *son et lumière*, which owes so much to the enchanting composition of René Cloérec, has been holding the headlines now for fifteen years. For me, the production remains a memory of close collaboration with the engineers and musicians – one of those memories which it is pleasant to recall, together with the familiar faces of friends who then went their ways . . . *See also notes for No. 29.*

109. 121. CHÂTEAU OF LE LUDE. The setting of the château, with its gardens and terraces overlooking the Loir, is delightful; so is the *son et lumière*, arranged principally by François de Nicolay, former owner of the château, whose untimely death we deplore, and François Brou. It combines an agreeable dialogue with effects, in which the local people participate; these diverse elements are blended together with skill and artistry to produce a most enchanting illuminated ballet. Here they have been able to ally with a pleasant test, a *mis-en-scène* completed by a cast furnished by the inhabitants of the Region.

The château itself consists of four buildings separated by corner towers, forming an interior courtyard which is roughly a square, but the story of its construction is a complicated one. Le Lude came to the Daillon family in 1457. The north façade was built in the time of Louis XII by Jean Gendrot, the master-mason of René d'Anjou. The south face followed, built in the early reign of Francis I; it may even have been started before 1515.

Lastly, in 1785, another owner of Le Lude, the Marquise de La Vieuville, entrusted to Barré, construction of the east face and the arcaded portico, flanked by two pavilions taking up the west face of the château between the two large sixteenth-century corner towers. Barré had been the architect of the château de Montgeoffroy in Anjou, of the Place Royale in Brussels, and of various family houses in Paris.

The façades overlooking the inner courtyard seem to have been finished at the beginning of the seventeenth century – unless Barré copied the style of the existing parts to give unity to the whole. The interior of the château, which was heavily restored in the nineteenth century, includes a sixteenth-century painted room in the south-east tower whose precise origins have been traced by Dominique Bozo (*Gazette des Beaux-Arts*, Oct. 1965): a manuscript of the *Triomphes* of Petrarch executed for Jacques de Daillon, Lord of Le Lude, in about 1515, and Paradin's *Historical Pictures From the Bible* illustrated by Bernard Salomon, of which the first edition appeared in 1553. Apparently the painter of Le Lude used a later edition; the '1577' on an acroterium of the tower may be the approximate date of this curious work.

110. *See note for No. 95.*

111. *See note for No. 165.*

112. *See note for No. 102.*

113. BLOIS: SECRET CUPBOARDS IN CATHERINE DE' MEDICI'S ROOM IN THE CHÂTEAU. A great deal of literature in doubtful taste has made famous this fine woodwork with panels carved in Italianate style, dating them at the same time as the building: early in the reign of Francis I, and before the battle of Pavia (1525). The skirting conceals a series of pedals which operate the double doors.

The cupboards thus revealed were designed exclusively for the storage of papers. An 'oral tradition' – going back no further than the Romantic period – has it that these are 'poison cupboards' of Catherine de' Medici. But the Queen Mother (she was the first to express a wish to bear this title) of the three last of the Valois continues to inspire historical romances set in her period, and Balzac's successors in this dangerous genre, with the exception, of course, of Mérimée, come nowhere near their model. *See also the notes for Nos 72 to 74.*

114-115. CHÂTEAU OF LE PLESSIS-BOURRÉ.   Two details of the ceiling of the guard-room are shown here.

This painted ceiling, measuring approximately thirty-five feet nine inches by twenty-three feet nine inches, is quite exceptional. It consists of six panels each composed of four hexagons around a diamond shape. M. Pierre-Marie Auzas, who has studied them (Archeological congress of Angers, 1964), regards the ceiling as executed for Jean Bourré, towards the end of his life, say, before 1506. No. 114. The upper scene: a barber is practising shaving on a peasant's face.

The former is saying:

> 'Souffre, frère, frère,
> Le dur et le moul;
> Sus barbe de foul
> L'on apprend à rère!'[1]

The peasant replies:

> '... Tu me tors le coul
> Et ne me scaiz rayre'.[2]

Lower scene: This is the story of the Chicheface ('thin-face'), the beast which is ill fed, as it eats only wives who obey their husbands:

> 'Moy l'on appelle Chicheface;
> Meigre de corps et de face
> Je suis, et bien y a raison:
> Je ne mengue unque saison
> Que fames qui font le comant
> De leurs maris entièrement;
> Des ans y a pres de deux cenz
> Que celle-cy retiens aux dens.'[3]

No. 115. Upper scene (Upside down): master Aliboron.

> 'Je m'empesche de faire tout
> Tant que n'en puis venir à bout;

[1] 'Suffer brother, brother, the hard and the soft; one learns the art of shaving on the beard of a fool.'

[2] '... you are twisting my neck and don't know how to shave me.'

[3] 'People call me Chicheface; thin am I of body and face and for good reason: I only eat at any season wives who obey entirely their husbands' commands: I have been holding this one in my teeth now for well nigh 200 years.'

Pour cela m'appelle l'on
Qui me voit maistre Aliboron.'[1]

Lower scene: the breakers of eels.

'Rompre anguillez prétandons
Si comme vous voyez, aux genoux;
De ce faire souvent nous vantons,
Mais si pléantez sont sus et soubz
Qu'à chef ne povons venir de le faire :
Prenez-y donc exemple tous,
Et ne vantez rien que ne povez faire.'[2]

116. CHÂTEAU DE BEAUREGARD, THE BELL ROOM.   This is no longer the château of Cassandre Salviati's uncle, but at least it remains connected with Ronsard through the man who built it, Jean du Thier, secretary of state to Henry II, to whom Pierre de Ronsard alludes in his fourth *Ecloque*. Built about 1550, Beauregard, which Du Cerceau thought *'mignard'* – (dainty) – was a masterpiece of discreet good taste, before some tiresome alterations were made to it in the nineteenth century. It dates from the time when the scholarly and refined architecture of the Italian Renaissance had made its impression in France; one could easily attribute to a great architect the buildings preserved in Du Cerceau's drawings.

For the interior decoration, Du Thier called on famous Italian craftsmen. There remains only a fragment (now in the museum of Blois) of mural paintings by Niccolo dell'Abbate to the designs of Primatice done for the chapel which no longer exists; the woodwork was by Scibec de Carpi, who worked at the Louvre and at Fontainebleau, and from this has survived the 'bell-room', the bells being the charges on the coats of arms motifs which are repeated in the elegant carving on the ceiling and walls.

In the seventeenth century Paul Ardier, president of the Chambre des Comptes of Paris, ordered a portrait of the kind which has now almost disappeared, but which was once found in most of the larger châteaux. The portrait gallery of Beauregard is above the open gallery on the ground floor, an unaltered arrangement from the château of 1550. 363 portraits of famous people of France are there, from the reign of Philippe de Valois to the reign of Louis XIV.

While the beams and woodwork were decorated with paintings by Jean Mosnier the younger, the son of the artist who did work at the château of Cheverny, the floor was tiled – imprudently, as it turned out – with a pavement from Delft, depicting the infantry and cavalry of an army in battle in their various attitudes. This extremely interesting work, which has just been the

[1] 'I am in such a hurry to do everything, that I cannot accomplish anything, and for that reason whoever sees me calls me Master Aliboron.'
[2] 'We claim to break eels just as you see over our knees; we often boast of doing this but they bend so up and down that we can never succeed : therefore all take heed of us and boast of nothing which you cannot do.'

subject of a study by Mme de Jonghe, seems to have been based on an illustration from a treatise on military history dedicated to William of Orange. The tiles were delivered in 1627, but being difficult to install were only put in position in the first half of the seventeenth century.

117. THE KITCHEN AT FONTEVRAUD (Cf. No. 45).   On the outside, this is almost entirely a reconstruction dating from the beginning of this century, and carried out with reference to earlier surveys and the drawing of Gaignières.

The plan at ground level is an octagon with as many 'absidioles' as it has sides, each surmounted by a conic roof and crowned with a lantern; only five of these structures now remain. Four tall pointed arches give access to a square, but this is again transformed by means of squinches into the octagon of the central cone, also topped by a lantern. According to witnesses, the roof has been later re-covered with scalloped tiles. This building, which was by no means exceptional in its day, may date from the construction by Robert d'Arbrissel (before 1117).

118. FIREPLACE OF THE HÔTEL DE LA BOULE D'OR AT TOURS, NOW AT LE PLESSIS-LES-TOURS (Cf. No. 70).   The buildings which once contained this magnificent fireplace whose decoration places it at the beginning of the reign of Francis I, were attached to the house in Touraine of Thomas Bohier, the builder of Chenonceau. The motifs of arabesques, dolphins, masks and birds belong to the flower style which was popular in France at the time. This fireplace, among others, is comparable to those in the château of Blois on the first floor in the Francis I wing, and the fireplace of La Possonnière at Couture, made for the father of Ronsard.

119. KITCHENS OF THE CHÂTEAU OF MENARS (Cf. No. 27).   These are situated in the outbuildings to the west of the main courtyard. Brick has been used for the hood of the immense fireplace and the infilling of the vault; only the ribs and supports are of stone. To the left is the machine for turning the spit, with its counter-weights.

As the main courtyard did not give ideal access to the kitchens of the château in wet weather, an underground passage was made for this purpose.

120. ESAU SELLING HIS BIRTHRIGHT, BY MICHEL CORNEILLE.   This is in the Museum of Orléans. The fireplace, and Jacob's theatrical costume, place this picture towards the end of Louis XIII's reign. Michel Corneille is 'playing the Bible in modern dress'.

I would like to mention here the importance of the Museum of Orléans, as much in the domaine of sculpture as in painting. The collection of Deruet's curious paintings should also be noted; they came originally from the Château de Richelieu. Among a wealth of work by famous artists, the prodigious series of pastels by Perronneau is especially memorable.

121. *See notes for No. 109.*

122. *See notes for Nos 97 to 101.*

123 and 125. CHÂTEAU DE MONTGEOFFROY.   The estate of Montgeoffroy in Anjou

came into the possession of the Contades family in 1676. In 1733 the marshal of Contades, grandson of the first owner, commissioned the architect Barré to build a new château, a work of elegant sobriety and delicate poise.

The marshal left the choice of interior decoration to his daughter-in-law; this has come down intact to the direct descendants. The kitchen, saddle-room and reception-rooms still have the eighteenth-century fittings, furniture and even in some cases the original damasks, as well as the decorative panels of which the architectural composition and the relationship of tone and proportion, enhance the proportion of the rooms. Everything here is modest and unpretentious; it is the art of the eighteenth century in its final perfection.

124. MADAME CHEVOTET, BY PERRONNEAU. Museum of Orléans.

126. *See notes for No. 25.*

127. AT TROO.

128. AT LES ROCHES-SUR-LE-LOIR.

129. VOUVRAY : VINES NEAR LA CALLÉE COQUETTE.

130 to 132. 135. *See notes on No. 3.*

133. ROCHECORBON : WINE CELLARS IN THE ROCK. (Marc Brédif).

134. LA GUERCHE : UNDERGROUND GRANARIES AT THE CHÂTEAU. The vaulted basements of the west wing, which is washed by the River Creuse, are the curiosity of the château. Rebuilt by André de Villequier and Antoinette de Maignelais, cousin of Agnès Sorel, in the reign of Charles VII, La Guerche is of a great age, as the '*Castrum Wirchiae*' was mentioned as early as 1509.

136. CORNFIELDS IN THE VAL DE LOIRE.

137. VILLESAVIN : INTERIOR OF THE COLUMBARIUM. There are still some old pigeon houses, or '*fuies*', in the Loire Valley, round or many-sided towers with small holes all round the walls. A ladder supported by a central shaft gives access to the nests.

138. *See notes for No. 152.*

139. THE MANUFACTURER OF TWO-TONE DURALEX PLATES. Factory of Saint-Gobain, Orléans.

140. THE MANUFACTURE OF A DURALEX SALAD BOWL.

141. RUBBER INDUSTRY, HUTCHINSONS FACTORY AT JOUÉ-LÈS-TOURS. ASSEMBLY OF RUBBER BOATS.

142. TOURS : THE NEWLY-BUILT DISTRICT OF SANITAS.

143. THE GENERATING STATION AT AVOINE NEAR CHINON. In 1955 Electricité de France initiated a programme for nuclear reactors designed specifically to generate electricity with plutonium as a by-product, whereas at Marcoule it was

the principal product. The fuel used is natural uranium, the moderator is graphite and the cooling fluid carbon dioxide under pressure. The programme is above all an experimental one, the final obect being nuclear production of electrical energy which can compete in price with electricity thermally produced. The project has three main sections: EDF 1 (to the right of the photograph) where the reactor, the heat-exchangers, the turbines and the safety research have been housed in a spherical building almost 180 feet in diameter. The cylindrical building beside the river is the cooling tower (over 127 feet high). EDF 1 has a thermal capacity of 300 Megawatts, and will be able to contribute 60 Megawatts of electricity (MW) to the grid. Immediately upstream is EDF 2 with its reactor of a thermal capacity of 800 MW and its two sets of turbo-alternators of 125 MW, which will contribute to the grid about 170 WW. As can be seen, this building is entirely different from EDF 1. EDF 3 further upstream, beside the canal running parallel to the Loire, comprises a reactor with a thermal capacity of 1,250 MW which can eventually be increased to 1,570 MW, and two sets of turbo-alternators each of 250 MW; it will contribute to the grid electrical power of 375 MW, which will eventually be increased to a possible 480 MW.

144. BLOIS: THE TEMPTATION, BY LAMBERT-RUCKI. Church of Notre-Dame de la Trinité. The initiation of this building is due to the special devotion, called 'The Three Ave Marias', of the Capuchin Fathers. It was created a basilica by Pius XII in 1956. After an earlier project by Ch.-H. Besnard, building was restarted 1936 to 1939 by Paul Rouvière, then after his death was completed in the same spirit by Y.-M. Froidevaux. It is constructed of concrete on a basilican plan, designed to enhance the immensely tall stained glass windows which give on either side of the nave a luminous screen twenty-six feet high and 114 feet long. These are the work of Louis Barillet in collaboration with Jacques Le Chevallier and Hansen. The frieze beneath the windows which continues around the apse, with its semi-dome decorated by a mosaic by Barillet, is composed of reliefs modelled, carved and coloured in the wet by the sculptor Jean Lambert-Rucki. The panels of the nave feature scenes from the Stations of the Cross, and all around the apse are scenes from the Gospel evoked by 'figures of a robust and moving art', as Dr Lesueur has written.

145. CHÂTEAU OF MONTSOREAU (Cf. No. 89). Jacques Levron has told elsewhere the true story of the Lady of Montsoreau: it differs considerably from Alexandre Dumas' account; but reality could well have surpassed fiction.

   The château, built a few years before the one at Le Plessis-Bourré (1455 and 1468 respectively), shows the fortress beginning to give way to the country residence. Jean de Chambes, who had it built, was a diplomat and the King's representative in 1459 to the Vatican Republic; but the staircase tower with its early Italianate decoration, seen here, dates only from 1520.

   It is justifiable cause for regret that the building of the route nationale has cut the château off from the Loire which, until 1820, came right up to the ramparts.

146. LE CLOS-LUCÉ AT AMBOISE. MODELS OF THE INVENTIONS OF LEONARDO DA

VINCI. The château of 'le Cloux', where Leonardo spent his last years, stood at the time a little outside the town. In the nineteenth century it was the victim of numerous alterations: the addition of an east wing, and the duplication of the south face flattening the projection of the octagonal staircase tower; these, and the mediocre restoration of the carving, destroyed most of the charm of the manor house, which had been built by Etienne Leloup in about 1475, with the addition of a chapel at the turn of that century. The same could be said of the interior fittings, before the restoration undertaken by the service of the Monuments Historiques; the re-exposure of the ceiling beams, the brick bonding of the walls and the original fireplaces discovered beneath the plaster, together with some elements of a slightly later painted décor, has restored some of its dignity to the building.

The fine basement rooms are now the setting for a series of models presented to the Count of Saint-Bris, the present owner of Le Clos-Lucé, by the Société IBM – France.

It may be over-bold to detect the influence of Leonardo, or even of his pupil Melzi, in the paintings of the chapel, but these models, constructed in accordance with the notebooks of the master, display his universal genius. To remember that the sculptor, and the architect, and painter of the *Gioconda* and *The Last Supper*, was at the same time an anatomist, a noted expert in hydraulics, and an engineer who devised, among other things, an armoured tank, flying machines and submarines, is just mind-shattering.

147. JOACHIM DU BELLAY. Drawing by a pupil of Cousin. Bibliothèque Nationale, Paris.

148. RABELAIS AS SEEN BY DELACROIX. A painting from the Musée du Vieux Chinon.

149. 150. 151. LA POSSONNIÈRE AT COUTURE. This is Ronsard's home. The château was rebuilt for his father. The interior still has a magnificent fireplace decorated in the Italian style. The outbuildings next to the cellars in the tufa have lost their gallery, but have kept their Latin devices; for instance, 'sustine et abstine', which defines the good use of wine: 'sustain thyself and then abstain.'

152 and 138. TALCY. The château of Talcy is mentioned in documents from 1221, but becomes interesting to us only after 1517, the date at which Bernardo Salviati, a Florentine banker related to the Medicis, acquired it from Marie Simon, the widow of Antoine Sanguin, lord of Meudon, and sister of the bishop of Paris, Jean Simon; or, more precisely, from 1520, when on September 12, Bernardo Salviati received from Jean d'Orléans-Longueville, Lord of Beaugency and archbishop of Toulouse, permission to build a fortified residence at Talcy. Françoise Doulcet, whom he married at about that time, was the daughter of a comptroller general of the finances of the duke of Orléans; one of her sisters was the wife of René de Vimeur, a forbear of the marshall of Rochambeau; her uncle, Jean Doulcet, master of the Chambre aux Deniers, owned the château of Beauregard; but in the previous generation we find another Jean Doulcet, a

butcher of Blois to whom the Bastard of Orléans, who later became Dunois, was unable on a certain day to pay a bill, which was doubtless considerable, except by holding to ransom a money lender of Orléans whom he imprisoned in the great tower of the château of Blois. . . .

This takes us far from the Salviati family, or Cassandre, who as a girl spent her time between Blois and Talcy. I have mentioned elsewhere how 'Mme de Pray' was to marry her daughter, Cassandre de Peigné, to Guillaume Musset, in 1580.

Meanwhile Jean Salviati, brother of Cassandre, had succeeded their father as guests on the occasion of one of those conferences (which the Huguenot leaders prudently insisted be held outside the château) which were repeatedly held in the hopes of restoring peace within the kingdom.

It was in 1572 that another man of the reformed faith, Agrippa d'Aubigné, took refuge at his estate of Les Landes-Guinemer, two leagues from Talcy. We know how he fell in love with Cassandre's niece, Diane Salviati, and how he was gravely wounded and nursed at Talcy – the over-publicized episode of the intervention of Ambroise Paré is entirely apocryphal – and how the marriage plans fell through. . . .

I will also recall that the château was acquired in 1780 by Mme Gastebois, ancestor of the Stapfers who sold Talcy to the State in 1932 on condition that it retained the furniture which was, and still is, one of the château's main attractions.

This fortified house in the middle of the village beside the church, with its austere exterior, reflects the region of Beauce where it is situated, but is also reminiscent of many other Italian fortified houses in which the exterior was of little importance. It still has two wings, one with a charming gallery of flattened arches, which in spite of what has been written does not date before Salviati's time : above the gallery is a strip of wall which used to be decorated with medallions; above the windows of the upper storey, plain tall gables carry the attic windows. The square keep which includes the main porch has machicolations on both its faces and on the courtyard side next to the many-sided staircase tower, which also has defences on the doorway side; the wing at right angles gives direct access to the church. Lastly, a charming well with columns, covered by a slated dome completes the setting.

At Talcy there is also a farmyard shaded by tall trees, and the magnificent wine press (No. 138) to which I unthinkingly assigned Leonardesque origins by imprudently remarking that it 'seemed to have been taken from one of Leonard's notebooks for the good pleasure of the great giant Gargantua' : from this to building up a romance about the relationship of the two Florentines, and the wine press which resulted, there is only a step to take !

153-154 and 19. VALENÇAY : MUSÉE TALLEYRAND. Set out in the orangery, this collection of costumes, prints, letters and objects of interest wittily evokes the best wit of his time. One letter teaches the art of refusing to a mother a recommendation for her son : the astonishing merits of father too soon lost being a more powerful argument than any the Prince of Bénévent could advance. The *volte-faces* so skilfully practised by this great servant of successive régimes are represented here by two caricatures: the one of 'the five-headed man . . . dedicated to the knights of the weathercock' *('l'homme aux cinq têtes . . . dédié à MM. les Chevaliers de la Girouette')*, dating from 1815, and the one which shows the funeral procession and burial of 'Talleyrand the Sunflower' *(Talleyrand did Tournesol)*. Political hatred is not dispelled by death.

155-156. PORTRAIT OF BALZAC by his friend Louis Boulanger. This portrait preserved in the Museum of Tours reminds us that this was Balzac's birthplace, that he studied at the college of Vendôme, and returned to the capital of Touraine before the family settled in Paris; it reminds us too of his visits to the Château de Saché, where is to be found Balzac's Room, seen here, with the coffee pot which is a reminder of nights of toil spent at his work-table. Saché used to belong to M. de Margonne, a friend of his parents, and especially of Honoré's mother. Lovers of Balzac, and of the cycle of his work which reflects Touraine in particular, owe it to themselves to make this visit: it is a pilgrimage to the source.

157. LA BÉCHELLERIE at Saint-Cyr-sur-Loire. This is the Touraine home of Anatole France, who died here. As the Loire Valley still passes, rightly or wrongly, for the region where the purest French is spoken, M. France could not have made a better choice in selecting his dwelling place.

158. A SOLOGNOT (SOLOGNE) INTERIOR, MUSEUM AT THE TOWN HALL OF ROMORANTIN. Mlle Ringuenet, keeper of the museum of Romorantin, has had reconstructed here a typical interior of a *'locature'*, a farm of Sologne. Subtle lighting,—as at dawn—adds to the evocative power of the familiar objects. But all the collections are worth seeing; these also owe much to the acquisitions made by M. Bernard Edeine, author of an ethnographical thesis on the Sologne which really ought to be published.

159. BIRD OF PASSAGE, (SPOTTED REDSHANK) ON A MARSH IN SOLOGNE. Sologne is a resting place for many migratory species.

160. LE PÈRE MODESTE

161. LA MÈRE FOURREAU

162. A HAYMAKER OF TOURAINE. Drawings by Mme MARTIN-DEMÉZIL. These sketches by my mother date from the beginning of the century—but do they date at all?
    The face of the haymaker reminds me of a drawing by Fouquet; and the two local people from Soings, while they recall the old faces of my childhood, are, at the same time, part of the tradition of this region; all three subjects were born in Sologne and Touraine, and I feel in a sense, as the good country folk say, that I am *'de la même ancêtre'* — of the same stock.

163. POOL NEAR MARCILLY-EN-GAULT.

164. STAGS FIGHTING (in the park of Chambord, Avenue of Montfraut). Early in autumn, at a date which varies with the place and the weather, from approximately the middle of September until early October, is the season of romance

for the stags. At this time they are relatively easy to watch from late afternoon to early in the morning. Their call is a cry half way between a roar and a bellow. It can be heard deep in the woods as night draws on; it is a wild and beautiful sight to see the great beasts moving in the clearings.

Although the clash of antlers is often heard in thickets, stags are seldom caught fighting in the open, as they are here. This is a magnificent photograph of rare interest. Occasionally two stags are found dead, worn out by the combat, their antlers locked together.

165 and 111. CHÂTEAU OF LE MOULIN AT LASSAY-SUR-CROISNE. Two groups of buildings still stand within the moat of Le Moulin: those at the entrance, which are fortified, and the living quarters with their chapel. Philippe du Moulin, who was responsible for this building with its harmonious mixture of brick, stone and slate, began work on it about 1480; this was unfinished in 1501. The master-mason at that time was Jacques de Persigny. Meanwhile, Philippe du Moulin had gone with Charles VIII to Italy, whose life he is said to have saved at Fornovo, and had married Charlotte of Argouges, a very rich woman, the widow of a counsellor of René d'Anjou; he died at Langres in 1506. His tomb, much mutilated, is at the church of Lassay, where a great mural painting representing St Christopher has the château of Le Moulin in the background, as it was before the addition to the great east tower.

As it is now, the château is certainly incomplete; but it would be incorrect to suppose that there were once buildings on all four sides within the moat. Le Moulin has defences against a sudden attack, but not against a regular siege.

The entrance keeps the old, studded door and the ancient door furniture. One of the rooms, known as the guard room, has an octagonal central pillar, and is covered by gothic vaults. The hoods of the fireplaces of the living quarters are marred by poor carving, the work of restorers at the beginning of this century, but there is still a fine early-sixteenth-century ceiling, a minute and charming chapel, and among furniture selected with taste by the owner of Le Moulin, a statuette of St Catherine which seems to have lived here always, and which by its delicate grace and by the fact that it was originally coloured must have been the work of a sculptor in the Loire Valley before the advent of Italianism (No. 111).

I should add that the masons amused themselves by making hopscotch patterns on the outside walls, using polychrome bricks. These are known as the 'jeu du Moulin'. This pleasing conceit moreover incorporates a drawing of very early origin, which has been found by M. Edeine on the seal of a Gallo-Roman oculist; the pattern must have been used over a wide area, for the 'marelle du moulin' is found throughout western Europe.

166. MUR-DE-SOLOGNE: CHÂTEAU OF LA MORINIÈRE. '. . . I shall not say the last name . . .' (page 237).

167-168. *See notes on Nos 97 to 101.*

169 and 170. CHÂTEAU OF GIEN. This château, which belonged to Anne de Beaujeu, reconstructed at the end of the reign of Charles VIII, combines black

and red brick and stone in a great variety of decorative bonds. The château of Gien today houses a very interesting museum of hunting. It is impossible to illustrate everything, but I would like to mention too the château of La Boissière, in the north of Loiret, which houses a museum of fishing.

171. BLACK-BACKED GULLS, in their spring migration follow the ploughman to feast on worms and field mice. They do nest in Sologne (especially at the pool of Favelles, in the parish of Marcilly-en-Gault).

Notes on Bibliography

It is only possible to give a few summary indications here. I shall restrict myself to providing a few references for the reader who wishes to go more deeply into the subjects touched upon in this book, especially the history of buildings.

First of all I would like to give special mention to Roger Dion's important study of regional geography, *Le Val de Loire*, Tours, 1934, a study in which historical evolution finds its place.

I should next mention the existing historical and archeological dictionaries: the ones on Anjou by Celestin Port, re-edited by J. Levron and P. D'Herbecourt, Angers, 1965 sq., on l'Indre-et-Loire by Carré de Brusserolle, reprinted Mayenne, 1966, as well as *La Touraine archéologique* by Dr Ranjard, Tours, 1949, and the *Dictionnaire historique et archéologique du Vendômois* by R. de Saint-Venant, Blois, 1912-1917.

On a very general level the *Provinciales* of Horizons de France has issued very good works on Anjou, Poitou, Touraine and Orléanais, in which the bibliographic information will prove very useful.

The historical events and famous men of the sixteenth century need no special mention here; Pierre Rain, Pierre de Vaissière and their emulators have had and will always have successors; among the 'precursors', Louis XI and Charles of Orléans have been studied by Pierre Champion, whose *Ronsard* and works on the last of the Valois should be mentioned here, as should the books by Mme Paule Henry-Bordeaux on Louise of Savoie and Mary Stuart. Those who are interested in the eleventh and twelfth centuries will find excellent books on Anjou by Louis Halphen and Jacques Boussard, while *Thibaud le Tricheur* by Dr Lesueur (Society of Sciences and Letters of Loir-et-Cher, Mem., vol. XXXIII, 1963) views the rivalry between the two feudal houses from the side of the Counts of Blois; still on the subject of Anjou, the *Petite histoire de l'Anjou* by Jacques Levron, who formerly published at Arthaud a *Val de Loire* now out of print, is a usefully simplified version.

As for the present day – for the subjects not dealt with here consult in particular the bibliographies of the *Provinciales* collection – I would like to mention two important theses for doctorates: one by Georges Dupeux, *Aspects de l'histoire sociale et politique du département de Loir-et-Cher de 1848 à 1914*, Paris, 1962, and one by Yves Babonaux, *Villes et régions de la Loire moyenne (Touraine, Blésois, Orléanais)*, Paris, 1966. I hope soon to add the expected publication by Mouton of the ethnological thesis by Bernard Edeine on *La Sologne*.

For the history of buildings, the volumes of the Archeological Congresses of France (Blois, 1925, Orléans, 1930, Tours, 1948, Poitiers, 1951, Le Mans, 1961, Angers, 1965) contain a great many monographs on church and secular buildings.

I must also list some of the basic works: *L'art de bâtir en France des Romains à l'an 1100*, by the Abbé G. Plat, Paris, 1939; although its theories are arguable, it nevertheless has a thorough grasp of the buildings of the first Romanesque art in the region of the Loir; the works of René Crozet, *L'art roman en Berry*, Paris, 1932, and *L'art roman en Poitou*, Paris, 1948, have a considerable influence in the same field, and on the same subject the work of François Eygun, *L'art des pays de l'Ouest*, published by Arthaud in 1966, is recommended; as is the important book by André Mussat, *Le style gothique de l'Ouest de la France*, Paris, Picard, 1963, which also takes up the question of the period of origin; I will add in anticipation a volume which is in the press with the same editor, Dr F. Lesueur's *Eglises de Loir-et-Cher*.[1]

An excellent reference book on the Renaissance is the *Histoire de l'architecture classique en France* by Louis Hautecoeur, which deals with classical art from its origins to the sixteenth century (the second edition is being prepared); François Gébelin, who has published in a Larousse edition a small volume on *Le style renaissance*, is the author of an important book on *Les châteaux de la Renaissance*, Paris, 1927, and an excellent book on *Les châteaux de la Loire*, which runs to several editions. The book edited by 'Realités' in 1964, with a Preface by the Duc de Brissac, *Merveilles de la Loire*, not only yields a good crop of smaller châteaux, but has excellent iconographic documentation of the larger ones, *Blois, Chambord et les châteaux du Blésois* by Dr F. Lesueur, published by Arthaud in 1947, is unfortunately out of print, as is Paul Vitry's book *Tours et les châteaux de Touraine*, and has been for a long time.

I cannot mention here all the monographs on individual buildings; there are some excellent ones, especially in the collection of *Petits Monographies* by A. Colin (for instance, *Amboise* by Lesueur, *Chenonceau* by Terrasse, and *Cheverny* by Mme Blancher-le-Bourhis.

There is at present no detailed comprehensive study of Chambord. An article by Dr Lesueur in *L'art et la pensée de Léonard de Vinci*, Paris-Alger, 1954, p. 225 et seq., raises the point that its origins may have been connected with Léonardo, and refers one back to the article by Haydenreich in *Burlington Magazine*; in the *Bulletin monumental*, vol. CIX, 1951, an article by the same author analyses the successive stages of the building of Chambord; I myself have provided the answer to one of these questions. In a note which appeared in the *Mélanges René Crozet*, vol. II, 1967, I attributed to Gaston d'Orléans an important but hitherto unsuspected rôle in the restoration work, while an important article by Georges Penet in vol. XXXIV of *Mémoires de la Société des sciences et Lettres de Loir-et-Cher*, on *Les constructions de François Mansart à Chambord*, can be considered definitive.

Finally I would like to draw the reader's attention to the magnificent work recently published by the Caisse Nationale des Monuments Historiques; this is a book by the Inspector General R. Planchenault on the tapestries of the Apocalypse at Angers. I would also like to draw attention to two important unpublished works: one, which deals with Anjou, is Michel Melot's thesis of the Ecole des Chartes (1967), entitled *L'Abbaye de Fontevrault de la Réforme de 1458 à nos jours*; the other is Mlle Martin Garczynska's 'Diplôme des Etudes Supérieures' on the Château de Bury, which deals with a building no longer standing, but known from pictorial records. Bury, together with Gaillon, a 'Loire Château' built in Normandy and now almost totally destroyed, were the subject a few years ago of a study by Mlle Elizabeth Chrol. These buildings represent two of the first important instances of Italianate building in France. The

[1] While this important publication is awaited, E. Pilté's *Petit répertoire archéologique des édifices réligieux du diocèse actuel de Blois* . . . unfortunately out of print, should be of value.

décor of the latter, which was built by the Cardinal of Amboise, a counsellor of Louis XII, was greatly influenced by the Italian fashion, at a time when the Louis XII wing at Blois showed only very cautious innovations; the château of Bury, built for Robertet, another of Louis XII's counsellors, shows a revival of the concept of *architecture* in the French art of building.

Photographic Summary

The black-and-white illustrations in this book, as well as the ectachromes on the dust-cover and the coloured illustrations, are, except for the following, the work of Monsieur Henry Paillasson, Grenoble.

ARCHIVES PHOTOGRAPHIQUES, Paris
  Nos 22, 23, 49
MIKAEL AUDRAIN, Saint-Nazaire
  Nos 3, 28, 52, 73, 87, 104, 107, 149, 150, 151
BERNARD AURY, Paris
  Nos 32, 33, 109, 169, 170
PHOTO BARBIER-PETIT, Chantilly
  No. 164
HENRI BERTAULT, Paris
  Nos 80, 81, 82, 83, 84, 111, 120, 124
PHOTO BULLOZ, Paris
  Nos 14, 15
ÉTABLISSEMENT HUTCHINSON,
STUDIO CHABRIAIS, Joué-les-Tours
  No. 141
COMBIER, Mâcon
  No. 166
J. F. DORÉ, Blois
  Nos 75, 77, 136
HENRI DORTES, Le Perreux-sur-Marne
  Nos 20, 21, 34, 54, 78, 113, 122, 123, 130, 131, 132, 135, 138, 155, 157
PHOTOGRAPHIE GIRAUDON, Paris
  Nos 11, 12, 16, 147
MUSÉE DU VIEUX-CHINON, STUDIO
A. GUÉNAU, Chinon
  No. 148
PHOTO KARQUEL, Aulnay-sous-Bois
  No. 103
Docteur F. LESUEUR, Blois
  No. 10
LOUIS-YVES LOIRAT, Paris
  No. 96
FRANÇOIS MERLET, Montory
  Nos 159, 171 and the black and white illustration on the back of the jacket

125